TOM AIKENS ANJUM ANAND CAT ASHTON JASON ATHERTON
GERARD BAKER AMY BATES ANNIE BELL RACHEL BENSON &
MARTIN BAKER MARY BERRY & LUCY YOUNG RICHARD BERTINET
ROSIE BIRKETT RAYMOND BLANC MARK BLATCHFORD
JORDAN BOURKE & REJINA PYO JOANNA BRENNAN
ADAM BYATT RICHARD CADDICK ANTONIO CARLUCCIO
MARY CASE SAM & SAM CLARK RICHARD CORRIGAN
ANNA DEL CONTE DAN DOHERTY NIKKI DUFFY GIZZI ERSKINE
HUGH FEARNLEY-WHITTINGSTALL SABRINA GHAYOUR
OLIVER & RICHARD GLADWIN MARTIN GREEN SKYE GYNGELL
HENRY HARRIS ALICE HART ANGELA HARTNETT JASMINE &
MELISSA HEMSLEY DIANA HENRY OLIA HERCULES MARK HIX
MINA HOLLAND LUCAS HOLLWEG SIMON HOPKINSON
TIM HUGHES NADIYA HUSSAIN ANNA JONES KIM JONES
LIZZIE KAMENETZKY SYBIL KAPOOR EDD KIMBER
FLORENCE KNIGHT ATUL KOCHHAR THEODORE KYRIAKOU
NIGELLA LAWSON GARY LEE JEREMY LEE PRUE LEITH
ELISABETH LUARD UYEN LUU ELEANOR MAIDMENT
JAMES MARTIN ALLEGRA MCEVEDY ISAAC MCHALE GILL MELLER
PIPPA MIDDLETON THOMASINA MIERS ELLA MILLS
RUSSELL NORMAN TOM OLDROYD JAMIE OLIVER
YOTAM OTTOLENGHI NATHAN OUTLAW TOM PARKER BOWLES
STEVIE PARLE LORRAINE PASCALE MARCO PIERRE WHITE
JOSÉ PIZARRO ROSE PRINCE MITCH TONKS FRANCES QUINN
GORDON RAMSAY JAMES RAMSDEN THEO RANDALL
CLAUDIA RODEN SIMON ROGAN RUTH ROGERS JON ROTHERAM &
TOM HARRIS MICHEL ROUX MARK SARGEANT
HARDEEP SINGH KOHLI NIGEL SLATER DELIA SMITH RICK STEIN
JUN TANAKA KAREN TAYLOR MATT TEBBUTT MARCUS WAREING
VALENTINE WARNER SARAH WEBB ALDO ZILLI

THE REALLY QUITE GOOD BRITISH COOKBOOK

THE REALLY QUITE GOOD BRITISH COOKBOOK

EDITOR William Sitwell

PHOTOGRAPHY Lizzie Mayson
COVER ART Sir Peter Blake
FOOD EDITOR & FOOD STYLIST Rosie Ramsden
FOOD PHOTOGRAPHY ART DIRECTOR & PROPS STYLIST Tabitha Hawkins

NOURISH
EAT WELL, LIVE WELL

In association with PQ Blackwell

Casting his eye across what passed for the London food scene in the late 1930s, the French chef Marcel Boulestin was not merely struck by the feeling that, in his words, "Good meals should be the rule, not the exception" – he also noticed that the people (whom he would entertain as the country's first TV chef in *Cook's Night Out* on the BBC), looked down on the idea of talking about food. Food was an inferior topic of conversation, even more vulgar than the weather or politics. "The English habit of not talking about food strikes the foreigner, however long he may have stayed in England, as a very queer one," he wrote. "Food which is worth eating is worth discussing."

Well, how things have changed. It's now hard to meet a group of people – be they at a dinner party, a bus stop, in the office or at a football match – who aren't talking about food. Whether it's last night's episode of *The Great British Bake Off* or the new Asian place that's opened around the corner, the subject of food really is part of our common parlance today. So many of us – both men and women – are keen to express our opinions on dishes, or proud to discuss the meals that we've cooked.

And while some may think that there's an element of insular belligerence in the British character, what is happening on the high streets of towns up and down the land reveals a very different reality. For there is no other country on this planet that so warmly embraces the food of other nations. Nowhere else will you find such a convergence and confluence of cuisines – Italian, Chinese, Indian, French, Asian and many more besides – expressed through a full range of restaurants, cafés and takeaway outlets (not to mention the ingredients available in our supermarkets).

And so this book celebrates our wonderful melting pot of cuisines, as represented by the 100 cooks, bakers and chefs we have gathered – all of whom have generously shared the dishes they cook for the people they love. You'll see some of the most famous faces in Britain, mingling with those who are less well known but are clearly food stars in their own households and communities.

As well as highlighting our cultural mix – from Ukraine and the Middle East to Spain and the various regions of Britain – the dishes in this book will inspire even the most jaded of hosts. We have puddings galore, a vast array of fish and seafood, as well as great ideas for our staple meats of chicken, lamb, pork and beef. There's also plenty of game and a brilliant selection of vegetarian dishes.

While we grapple with the many issues that food throws at us – our over-consumption of beef, an obesity crisis and the hunger that besets a growing number of people in our own country (I'm so pleased that a portion of royalties from the sale of this book are going to support the vital work of The Trussell Trust, which runs food banks across Britain) – we can stand proud now, at least, as a truly great foodie nation. It's been a joy to gather contributions for this book from many of my own food heroes, plus a few foodie friends.

And as I run my eye over these pages – the delicious recipes and beautiful photographs, and the stunning cover design by the legend that is Sir Peter Blake – I'm glad to think that Boulestin would be astonished by the perpetual foodie chatter that buzzes around our island from shore to shore today. I'm sure he would also recognize (and appreciate) a traditional dash of English modesty when I say that I reckon this cookbook is, frankly, Really Quite Good.

William

CONTENTS

BREA

KFAST

JOANNA BRENNAN
PUMP STREET BAKERY

At Pump Street our approach
to food is to do the basic things
really, really well. We're a
bakery primarily, so we make
our own breads and pastries
and then we try to showcase
those things in our café. This
Brioche French Toast is a great
example of what we do.

JOANNA

*Orford,
Suffolk*

BRIOCHE FRENCH TOAST

Recipe by **JOANNA BRENNAN**, Pump Street Bakery, Orford, Suffolk

SERVINGS: 4 | **PREP TIME: 10 MINS PLUS SOAKING** | **COOK TIME: 15 MINS** | **SKILL LEVEL: 1 (EASY)**

I love this recipe because it combines a little bit of Pump Street Bakery with a little bit of Canada, which is where I'm from. The maple syrup really reminds me of home – pancakes or French toast with thick, rich maple syrup on top is the quintessential weekend morning ritual. It makes me really happy to bring that tradition to British life here in Orford.

INGREDIENTS

4 eggs
200 ml (7 fl oz) single cream
½ tsp vanilla seed paste
1 tbsp golden caster sugar
4 generous, thick slices of brioche, one day old
2 tbsp butter and 1 tbsp of vegetable oil, for the pan
2 bananas
12 rashers bacon
maple syrup, to serve

METHOD

First, make the custard. This can be done up to one day before you want to cook the French toast. Whisk the eggs vigorously, then add the cream, vanilla and sugar, and whisk again.

When you're ready to cook, place the egg mixture in a shallow dish or tub to allow space for all of the bread to lie flat and soak. Pre-heat a griddle or a couple of frying pans to a medium heat, and melt the butter and the oil.

Place all of the bread in the egg mixture. After a minute or so, turn it over and gently press all over, allowing it to soak up the egg like a sponge.

Remove the bread from the mix, pressing gently to remove excess egg and to make sure it is fully soaked. Place it on the griddle or frying pan. Cook for a few minutes on each side until a small cut in the middle shows a tender and moist (but not wet) interior, like cooked bread pudding.

In the meantime, slice the banana and fry the bacon.

Serve the French toast topped with banana and bacon, with maple syrup on the table to pour.

GRILLED BANANA BREAD
WITH TAHINI & HONEYCOMB

Recipe by **YOTAM OTTOLENGHI**, restaurateur, TV chef & columnist, London

SERVINGS: 6–8 | PREP TIME: 30 MINS | COOK TIME: 1 HOUR 20 MINS | SKILL LEVEL: 1 (EASY)

This is all about three things: an incredibly perfect banana bread, tahini, which is so smooth and nutty you could eat it by the spoon, and arriving at the table with a big cup of tea and a rumbling tummy. I pitched this to the team as my offering for Christmas breakfast. Raised eyebrows relaxed back down once the trilogy was tried. For me, tahini is the new peanut butter. It is runnier and earthier but has a similarly rich flavour and is completely impossible to resist. In many Middle Eastern cultures it is served not only as a base for hummus and other savoury sauces and dips but also as a spread served at breakfast with sweet condiments such as grape or date syrup. The banana bread can be baked in advance — a day or two, or even more — and then just sliced and grilled when you need it. Drizzle it with tahini as I do here, or leave out the tahini and make do with the butter, honeycomb and salt.

INGREDIENTS

180 g (6 oz) pecans
3 large ripe bananas, peeled and mashed (300 g/10½ oz)
275 g (9½ oz) soft light brown sugar
3 eggs, lightly beaten
140 ml (4½ fl oz) full-fat milk
70 ml (2½ fl oz) sunflower oil
275 g (9½ oz) plain flour
1 tsp bicarbonate of soda
1½ tsp baking powder

To finish
80 g (2½ oz) unsalted butter, at room temperature
60 g (2 oz) tahini paste
200 g (7 oz) honeycomb in honey
¾ tsp coarse sea salt

V

METHOD

Pre-heat the oven to 170°C/150°C fan/325°F/gas 3 and line a 900 g (2 lb) loaf tin (25 cm x 12 cm/10 in x 5 in) with baking paper.

Place the pecans on a baking tray and roast for 10 minutes before roughly chopping them and setting aside.

Place the banana, sugar and eggs in the large bowl of an electric mixer and beat until combined. With the machine running on a slow speed, add ½ teaspoon of salt, the milk and then the oil. Sift together the flour, bicarbonate of soda and baking powder and, with the machine still running, add this to the mix. Continue to mix on a medium speed for about 5 minutes, until thoroughly combined. Stir the pecans through and then pour the mixture into the loaf tin.

Place in the oven and bake for about 1 hour 10 minutes, until a skewer or knife inserted in the centre comes out clean. Leave aside for 10 minutes before removing the cake from the tin and setting aside on a wire rack until completely cool. You can now wrap the bread in tinfoil and keep for up to 5 days, or freeze for a few weeks.

Set your oven grill to high. Cut the banana bread into slices 2 cm (1 in) thick and brush with butter. Place under the grill for up to 2 minutes, until lightly toasted on one side, and remove. Drizzle over the tahini, place a chunk of honeycomb on each slice and sprinkle with coarse sea salt. Serve at once.

YOGHURT WITH APRICOTS, HONEY & PISTACHIOS

Recipe by **JASON ATHERTON**, Pollen Street Social, Mayfair, London

SERVINGS: 4 | PREP TIME: 30 MINS PLUS CHILLING | SKILL LEVEL: I (EASY)

INGREDIENTS

400 g (14 oz) Greek-style
   yoghurt
3 tbsp icing sugar, sifted
1 lemon
320 ml (11 fl oz) dry white wine
3 tbsp honey
120 g (4½ oz) caster sugar
8 apricots, halved and stoned
2 tsp orange-flower water
2 tbsp chopped pistachio nuts

To finish
2 tbsp honey
tiny mint leaves

GF, V

METHOD

Mix the yoghurt and icing sugar together in a bowl; cover and chill.

Using a swivel vegetable peeler, finely pare the zest from the lemon in wide ribbons, then squeeze the juice.

Put the white wine, lemon zest and juice, honey and sugar in a saucepan and slowly bring to the boil, stirring until the sugar is dissolved. Reduce the heat to a simmer, and add the apricots. Poach until just softened, about 5 minutes. Remove the apricots with a slotted spoon and place in a bowl.

Continue to simmer the wine syrup until reduced by a third. Take out the lemon zest and reserve. Set the syrup aside to cool. Once cooled, mix in the orange-flower water and pour over the apricots. Chill for at least 2 hours.

Meanwhile, toast the chopped pistachios in a dry frying pan over a low heat for a few minutes until fragrant. Tip into a bowl and set aside.

To serve, top spoonfuls of yoghurt with the apricot halves, a spoonful of their syrup and the reserved lemon zest. Sprinkle over the pistachios, honey and mint leaves.

CHIA CHAI BUTTERNUT BREAKFAST PUDDING

Recipe by **MELISSA & JASMINE HEMSLEY**, chefs & authors, Mayfair, London

SERVINGS: 4 | **PREP TIME: 20 MINS PLUS RESTING** | **COOK TIME: 55 MINS** | **SKILL LEVEL: I (EASY)**

This is an overnight breakfast or make-ahead dessert. We've infused omega-3-rich chia seeds with our favourite rooibos chai breakfast tea, and together they turn the usually savoury butternut squash into a sweet start to the day. It's so yummy that you'll also fancy it as a cool, creamy dessert. We love it with summer fruits, such as blackberries, grapes, figs, plums or peaches, which are just in season as butternut squash comes in. In the winter months, try apple chunks, chopped clementines or blood orange segments. If you bake the butternut squash the night before, then it's ready to go in the morning. Don't forget to chew well, in order to get the most goodness out of the tiny chia seeds. We use white chia to keep the pudding's bright orange colour, but black also works — and is cheaper and easier to find, too!

INGREDIENTS

1 large butternut squash
 (enough to make 400 g/
 14 oz cooked butternut
 squash purée)

350 ml (12½ fl oz) water

3 tbsp coconut oil

2 tsp rooibos chai tea leaves,
 or 2 rooibos chai tea bags

4 tbsp white chia seeds

1 tbsp raw honey

coconut yoghurt and goji
 berries (optional), to serve

DF, GF, V

METHOD

Pre-heat the oven to 200°C/180°C fan/gas 6 and roast the butternut squash in the oven for 40–50 minutes until cooked through and tender. Scoop out 400 g (14 oz) of the squash flesh and mash well. Any leftover squash can be frozen and used in a soup or smoothie.

Add the squash to a saucepan with the water, the coconut oil and the tea leaves or the contents of the tea bags. Bring to a medium simmer, then remove from the heat and leave to cool for a few minutes.

Stir in the chia seeds, continuously whisking at first to avoid lumps, then add the honey.

Leave to sit for at least 20 minutes to an hour for the chia to swell (unless you like it crunchy). Alternatively, transfer to a flask and by the time you get to work, you'll have a nice warm chia breakfast pudding.

Add the coconut yoghurt and goji berries, if using, and enjoy.

GILL MELLER
RIVER COTTAGE

Cooking with River Cottage for 12 years and at
The Summerhouse, where I live, has taught me a
huge amount about food, about where it comes
from, and how treating ingredients simply can give
you the best results. This recipe is one that's close
to my heart. It's a very simple dish using two of
my favourite wild foods – nettles and wild garlic
– teamed up with pollack, a fish that I cook quite
regularly. The dish takes five to ten minutes to
put together, but couldn't be more delicious.

Gill

*Rousdon,
Devon*

NETTLES ON TOAST WITH POLLACK, WILD GARLIC & POACHED EGG

Recipe by **GILL MELLER**, River Cottage, Devon

SERVINGS: 2 | PREP TIME: 10 MINS | COOK TIME: 20 MINS | SKILL LEVEL: 1 (EASY)

We should all be cooking and eating a lot more nettles. They are delicious, abundant and absolutely free. If this isn't enough, nettles are also exceptionally good for you. They make a great alternative to our more familiar cultivated greens, such as spinach or kale, and can be cooked in very similar ways. I love them simply wilted, seasoned and served with butter and good-quality olive oil. February through to late April is the time to bag them. It's the fresh, young growth you're after. Use gloved hands to pick only the tips – the first four or six leaves on each plant; this is the most tender succulent part. Here, I'm piling them on toasted sourdough and serving them with fried line-caught pollack, wild garlic and a poached egg. It makes for the perfect late-spring supper.

INGREDIENTS

250 g (9 oz) fresh young nettle tops

25 g (1 oz) butter

2 tbsp olive oil

2 x 150 g (5 oz) pollack fillet steaks

1 small bunch wild garlic

2 very fresh eggs

2 slices sourdough or good-quality country bread, toasted

METHOD

Wash the nettles in plenty of fresh water. Remove any tougher lower stalks; if it's just the crown, then that's fine. Drop the nettles into a saucepan of salted, boiling water and simmer for 2–3 minutes, until tender, then drain really well. Return the nettles to the pan, add half the butter and 1 tablespoon of the olive oil. Season well with salt and pepper, turn together and then cover and keep warm.

Set a large, non-stick frying pan over a medium to high heat. Season the fish all over with salt and pepper. Heat the remaining butter and oil in the pan and when hot, add the fish, skin-side down. Cook for 3–5 minutes, depending on its thickness, then turn the fillets over and fry for 1–2 minutes until the flakes separate when pressed lightly with a fork; this indicates the fish is cooked. Ribbon (or thickly shred) the wild garlic and add it to the pan. Spoon the wild garlic through the buttery fish juices; cover and keep warm while you cook the eggs.

Bring a medium-sized, high-sided saucepan of water to the boil. Twirl a spoon in the water to make a mini whirlpool. Crack the eggs in, turn the heat down to minimum and cook for 3–4 minutes. Remove the eggs carefully with a slotted spoon. Keep warm.

Remember: the fresher the eggs – the better they poach.

To serve, place a piece of toast on each plate. Divide the warm, buttery nettles between the plates, top with a piece of fish, followed by a poached egg, then finally spoon over the wild garlic and any buttery juices from the pan.

RACHEL BENSON & MARTIN BAKER
OLD SLENINGFORD FARM

We're really interested in food that is good and wholesome which we've grown ourselves. One of the main things we've got here at the farm is a forest garden. It's best to describe it as an edible woodland really, because everything in there is edible – from fruit trees to bushes to herbs and climbers. The weeds are allowed to grow, and then as we need to harvest each specific crop, we'll go in and tidy around the area and pick whatever we need. We let nature do its thing. *Rachel Martin*

Ripon,
North Yorkshire

STRAWBERRY JAM

Recipe by **RACHEL BENSON & MARTIN BAKER**, Old Sleningford Farm,
Ripon, North Yorkshire

MAKES: 4 LARGE JARS | **PREP TIME: 5 MINS PLUS STANDING OVERNIGHT** | **COOK TIME: 30–60 MINS**
SKILL LEVEL: I (EASY)

INGREDIENTS

1¼ kg (2¾ lb) fresh strawberries
– kept whole, or halved if very
large
1 kg (2¼ lb) sugar
1 tbsp lemon juice

DF, GF, V

METHOD

Rinse the strawberries and drain. Cover with the sugar, add the lemon juice and mix gently. Leave in a cool place overnight, mixing a couple of times to release the juice. Doing this firms up the strawberries so they don't disintegrate whilst cooking.

Place a few saucers in the freezer, ready for testing the jam.

Slowly heat to dissolve the sugar – don't bring to the boil until the sugar has dissolved or the jam will crystallize. Boil rapidly until it thickens.

Test the jam by removing it from the heat and spooning a little onto one of your chilled saucers. Leave for a minute then run your finger through the jam. If it stays parted rather than runs, it's ready – note that this jam will not be a hard set. (Firmer jams will wrinkle when you touch them – if you want this, use a jam sugar which has added pectin and more lemon juice.)

Reduce the heat so the jam is not boiling and skim the foam from the top. Ladle into hot, sterilized jars and seal immediately. Spoon onto hot sorghum toast with butter, or churn into vanilla ice cream.

RÉES

ACKS

Wandsworth,
London

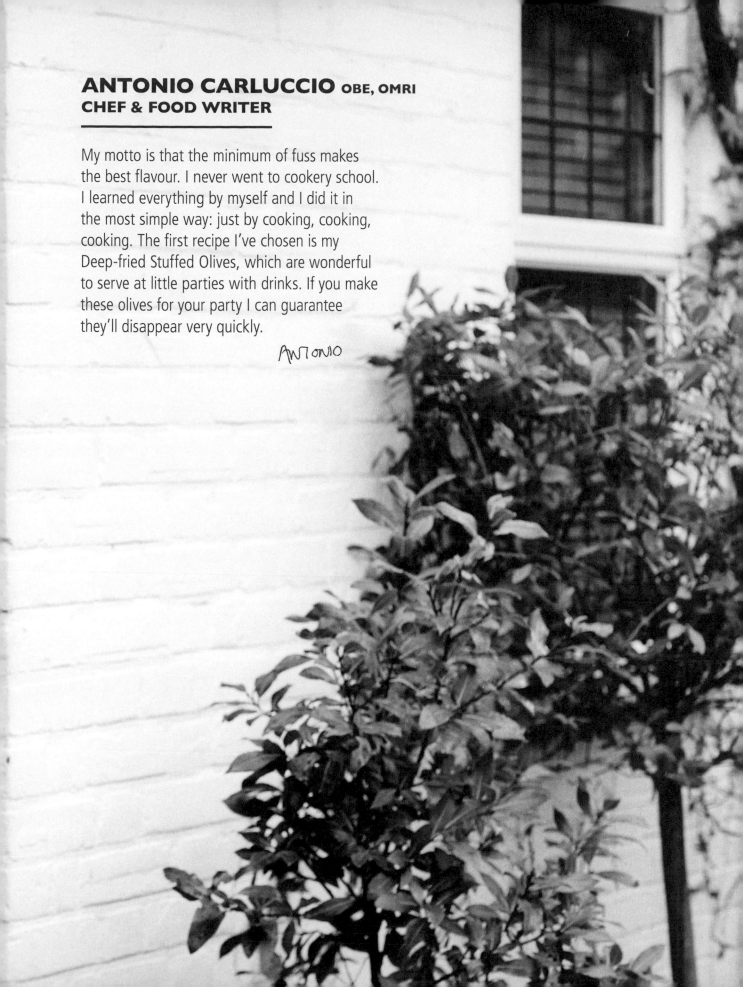

ANTONIO CARLUCCIO OBE, OMRI
CHEF & FOOD WRITER

My motto is that the minimum of fuss makes
the best flavour. I never went to cookery school.
I learned everything by myself and I did it in
the most simple way: just by cooking, cooking,
cooking. The first recipe I've chosen is my
Deep-fried Stuffed Olives, which are wonderful
to serve at little parties with drinks. If you make
these olives for your party I can guarantee
they'll disappear very quickly.

ANTONIO

DEEP-FRIED STUFFED OLIVES

Recipe by **ANTONIO CARLUCCIO OBE, OMRI**, chef & food writer, Wandsworth, London

MAKES: 50 | **PREP TIME: 30 MINS** | **COOK TIME: UP TO 1 HOUR** | **SKILL LEVEL: 2 (MODERATE)**

INGREDIENTS

For the filling

3 tbsp olive oil

50 g (1½ oz) butter

100 g (3½ oz) lean pork,
  finely minced

100 g (3½ oz) lean veal,
  finely minced

50 g (1½ oz) boneless chicken,
  minced

3 tbsp dry Marsala or sherry

1 small black truffle, diced

a few drops of truffle oil

30 g (1 oz) Parma ham, finely
  chopped

3 tbsp finely chopped parsley

½ tsp freshly grated nutmeg

finely grated zest of 1 lemon

1 egg, beaten

50 g (1½ oz) Parmesan,
  freshly grated

a little milk (if needed)

50 Ascoli olives

olive oil, for deep-frying

plain white flour, for coating

2 eggs, beaten

dried breadcrumbs,
  for coating

METHOD

To make the filling, heat the olive oil and butter in a pan. Add the minced meats and fry, stirring, for 5–6 minutes until well browned. Season with salt and pepper, add the Marsala or sherry and allow to bubble to reduce down. Remove from the heat and cool, then transfer to a food processor.

Add the truffle and truffle oil, Parma ham, parsley, nutmeg and lemon zest. Process briefly to mix, then add the egg and grated Parmesan, and whizz to combine. The mixture should be firm enough to use as a stuffing but not too dry; soften with a drop or two of milk if necessary.

Starting from the top, cut each olive in a spiral fashion to reach and release the stone inside, keeping the spiral intact. Take a little of the filling and enclose it in the olive spiral, pressing a little to regain the original shape.

Finish and cook the olives a few at a time. Heat the olive oil for deep-frying, in a suitable pan, to 180°C/350°F. Dip the olives in a little flour, then into the beaten egg, and then roll them in the breadcrumbs. Deep-fry for 2–3 minutes until brown, then drain on paper towel. Serve hot as an antipasto, with small lemon wedges if you like.

PEA & MINT CROQUETTES

Recipe by **YOTAM OTTOLENGHI**, restaurateur, TV chef & columnist, London

SERVINGS: 4 | **PREP TIME: 45 MINS PLUS FREEZING** | **COOK TIME: 40 MINS** | **SKILL LEVEL: 2 (MODERATE)**

For a while, we had a pretty wicked trio running the evening service at Ottolenghi in Islington — Tom, Sam and Myles. These croquettes are their creation and worth a little effort. They can be made well in advance and taken up to the stage where they are covered in panko breadcrumbs and frozen. You can then partially defrost and fry them as you need to. The recipe makes 16 generously-sized patties, ample for four people. To feed more, or to serve as a snack or starter, make them into smaller croquettes, weighing about 40 grams (1½ oz) each.

INGREDIENTS

For the sauce
1 tsp dried mint
120 g (4½ oz) sour cream
1 tbsp olive oil

3 tbsp olive oil
6 banana shallots, finely chopped (300 g/10½ oz)
1 tbsp white wine vinegar
700 g (1 lb 9 oz) frozen and defrosted peas
20 g (¾ oz) mint leaves, finely shredded
1 clove garlic, crushed
4 eggs
100 g (3½ oz) plain flour
150 g (5 oz) panko breadcrumbs
sunflower oil, for frying

V

METHOD

To make the sauce, place all the ingredients in a bowl with ¼ teaspoon salt and a grind of black pepper. Mix well and refrigerate until ready to use.

Place the olive oil in a medium-sized sauté pan on a medium heat. Add the shallot and sauté for 15–20 minutes, stirring often, until soft. Add the vinegar; cook for a further 2 minutes and then remove from the heat.

Place the peas in a food processor and briefly blitz. They need to break down without turning into a mushy paste. Transfer to a mixing bowl and stir in the shallot, mint, garlic, 1 egg, ½ teaspoon salt and plenty of black pepper.

Line a tray that will fit in your freezer with baking paper and shape the pea mixture into 16 patties (around 60 g/2 oz each), about 7 cm (2¾ in) across and 2 cm (1 in) thick. Freeze for a couple of hours to firm up.

Place the remaining eggs in a bowl and gently beat. Place the flour in a separate bowl and the breadcrumbs in a third. Remove the croquettes from the freezer and, one at a time, roll them in the flour, dip them in the egg, then coat them in the crumbs. You can then either return them to the freezer at this point or leave them at room temperature for about 1 hour, until partly defrosted. Whatever you do, when it comes to frying, it's important that the patties are not entirely frozen; you want them to cook through without burning the crust.

Pre-heat the oven to 220°C/200°C fan/425°F/gas 7.

Fill a medium-sized frying pan with enough sunflower oil so that it comes 2½ cm (1 in) up the sides. Place on a medium-high heat and leave for 5 minutes for the oil to get hot. Reduce the heat to medium and fry the croquettes in batches for about 4 minutes, turning once, until both sides are golden-brown.

Transfer to a baking tray and place in the oven for 5 minutes, to warm through. Serve at once, with the sauce spooned on top or placed alongside.

'NDUJA BRUSCHETTA

Recipe by **NIGEL SLATER**, food writer & TV broadcaster, Highbury, London

SERVINGS: 1 | PREP TIME: 5 MINS | COOK TIME: 5 MINS | SKILL LEVEL: 1 (EASY)

INGREDIENTS

Per sandwich

1 thick slice sourdough
   or ciabatta

olive oil

85 g (3 oz) 'nduja (a spicy,
   spreadable salami)

50 g (1½ oz) soft goat's
   curd or cheese

3 sprigs thyme, leaves
   picked

4–6 black olives, pitted

METHOD

Toast the bread lightly on both sides. Leave the grill on.

Trickle enough olive oil over one side of the toast to moisten it thoroughly. Place a slice of 'nduja on the bread, add the goat's curd or cheese, thyme leaves and a little trickle of oil, then slide under the grill for a few minutes until the 'nduja is warm. Add the olives, trickle a little more olive oil over and eat immediately.

WALNUT BAGNA CÀUDA

Recipe by **GIZZI ERSKINE**, chef & TV presenter, Bethnal Green, London

SERVINGS: 6 | **PREP TIME: 10 MINS** | **COOK TIME: 10 MINS** | **SKILL LEVEL: 1 (EASY)**

This is a recipe for which I have been searching for years. I first tried it at the famous London Italian restaurant San Lorenzo, and it has stuck with me forever. Traditionally bagna càuda is made as an oil- and butter-based dipping sauce, but my mum and I remember it being very walnutty. I researched the recipe and couldn't find a version with walnuts in it anywhere, but I did find some versions using walnut oil. I've totally made up this recipe, but it's pretty damn close to the original and, more importantly, it's delicious.

INGREDIENTS

150 ml (5 fl oz) extra-virgin olive oil

3–4 cloves garlic, finely chopped

8 anchovy fillets

100 g (3½ oz) walnuts

150 ml (5 fl oz) double cream

30 g (1 oz) butter

30 ml (1 fl oz) walnut oil

1 tsp lemon juice

crudités (such as baby fennel, artichokes, carrots and radishes)

GF

METHOD

Heat the olive oil in a saucepan, then add the garlic and fry it very slowly in the oil for about 1–2 minutes, or until the garlic has tinged a little golden. Add the anchovies and let them melt away into the oil. Next, add the walnuts and gently toast them for 1 minute. Add the double cream and butter and cook for 2 minutes, or until the mixture is piping hot, and then finish with the walnut oil and lemon juice.

Now you need to blend this to a purée in a small blender. You want it to be the texture of a thin, creamy hummus, almost like a thick, coating-consistency salad dressing. Transfer the bagna càuda to a heatproof pot with a flame underneath (the obvious choice would be a fondue pot) and plunge away at it with your crudités.

MINESTRONE SOUP
WITH ORZO PASTA & MINT PESTO

Recipe by **KAREN TAYLOR**, home economist for *The Great British Menu* and *MasterChef*, Old Basing, Hampshire

SERVINGS: 4 | **PREP TIME: 20 MINS** | **COOK TIME: 20 MINS** | **SKILL LEVEL: 1 (EASY)**

INGREDIENTS

25 g (1 oz) unsalted butter
1 onion, finely chopped
1 carrot, peeled and diced
1 stick celery, diced
1 courgette, diced
1 clove garlic, finely chopped
1¼ litres (2¼ pints) vegetable
  stock
100 g (3½ oz) orzo pasta
1 pack (100 g/3½ oz)
  asparagus tips
200 g (7 oz) peas, fresh
  or frozen

For the mint pesto
1 clove garlic, peeled
25 g (1 oz) pine nuts
25 g (1 oz) mint leaves
30 g (1 oz) pecorino cheese
50 ml (1½ fl oz) olive oil

griddled toasts, to serve

V

METHOD

Melt the butter in a large saucepan and sauté the onion, carrot, celery, courgette and garlic over a gentle heat for 10 minutes.

Pour in the stock, bring to the boil, add the orzo and cook for a further 8 minutes. Add the asparagus tips and peas and cook for 2 minutes. Season to taste.

Meanwhile, make the pesto. Place all the ingredients in a food processor and blend until smooth. Season to taste.

Ladle the soup into warm bowls and serve with the griddled toasts spread with the prepared pesto.

GOAT'S CHEESE BRUSCHETTA WITH BEETROOT RELISH

Recipe by **RACHEL BENSON & MARTIN BAKER**, Old Sleningford Farm, Ripon, North Yorkshire

SERVINGS: 4, WITH EXTRA RELISH | **PREP TIME: 20 MINS** | **COOK TIME: 45 MINS** | **SKILL LEVEL: I (EASY)**

Our forest garden produces for about nine months of the year. We don't want anything to go to waste, and so we make a lot of the extra produce into preserves — such as the beetroot relish used in this recipe.

INGREDIENTS

For the relish
700 g (1 lb 5 oz) fresh beetroot
½ tsp sugar
220 g (8 oz) onion
300 ml (10½ fl oz) cider vinegar
½ tbsp mixed spice
½ tsp dried chilli flakes
¼ tsp ground black pepper
220 g (8 oz) sugar

To serve
4 slices sourdough bread
100 g (3½ oz) goat's cheese log (such as Ribblesdale), cut into slices 1 cm (½ in) thick
a handful of rocket, to serve
olive oil, for drizzling
2 sprigs rosemary, finely chopped

V

METHOD

Boil the beetroot in a large pan of water with the sugar until starting to soften. Skin and dice finely.

Slice the onions finely and simmer in the vinegar for 10 minutes.

Add the beetroot, mixed spice, chilli and black pepper to the onions. Add the sugar and cook gently until the sugar has dissolved. Simmer for around 30 minutes until the mixture thickens. Spoon into hot, sterilized jars and seal immediately. The relish is ready to eat straight away, but will improve if left to mature for at least a month.

Heat the grill to high. Toast the bread under the grill. Place a slice of goat's cheese on top of a slice of bread and place under the grill until lightly browned. Serve with a generous amount of beetroot relish and rocket, and top off with a drizzle of olive oil and a sprinkle of rosemary.

GỎI CUỐN SAI GON

SAIGON FRESH SUMMER ROLLS

Recipe by **UYEN LUU**, author & food photographer, London Fields, London

SERVINGS: 6 | **PREP TIME: 45 MINS** | **COOK TIME: 35 MINS** | **SKILL LEVEL: 2 (MODERATE)**

This traditional recipe is from Saigon but every region has its own take on fresh summer rolls. Although they are great for special occasions, they are tasty and healthy enough to take to work for lunch — you'll be enjoying a good herb and prawn salad inside rice paper. The Vietnamese use herbs in abundance. Full of perfume, flavour and health benefits, they are used in almost every savoury dish. Coriander/cilantro, Thai sweet basil and mint are most readily available, so if in doubt, use those. Find out when your nearest Asian store has their fresh vegetable delivery and try to buy your herbs that day.

INGREDIENTS

6 rice paper sheets, about 22 cm (9 in) across

For the filling
150 g (5½ oz) pork belly

18 king prawns, shelled and de-veined

30 g (1 oz) rice vermicelli

a dash of white wine or cider vinegar

6 lettuce leaves

12 sprigs coriander, stalks on, chopped

18 garden or hot mint leaves, chopped

3 cockscomb mint sprigs

18 shiso (perilla) leaves

6 garlic chives, halved and heads removed

For the dipping sauce
1 tbsp cooking oil

1 clove garlic, chopped

2 tbsp hoisin sauce

½ tbsp white wine vinegar or cider vinegar

1 tsp sugar

½ tbsp Sriracha chilli sauce

2 tbsp roasted salted peanuts, crushed

DF, GF

METHOD

Filling: bring a saucepan of water and a few pinches of salt to the boil. Add the pork, cover with a lid and cook for 15 minutes or until the juices run clear when you prick it with a knife. Allow to cool, then cut off the skin and slice the meat very thinly.

Put the prawns and a pinch of salt in a saucepan of boiling water and poach for 2 minutes, or until opaque. Drain and allow to cool.

Put the rice vermicelli, a pinch of salt and a dash of vinegar in a bowl or pan of boiling water; cover and allow to cook to 5–10 minutes or until soft. Drain and rinse with hot water.

Once the pork, prawns and vermicelli are ready, put them and the remaining filling ingredients in their own individual bowls in front of you. Pour some warm water into a tray deep and large enough to submerge the rice paper sheets. Use a plastic board as a base on which to make the rolls.

Dip a sheet of rice paper into the water and take it out as soon as it is moist all over — do not let it sit in the water. Lay the sheet on the plastic board. Imagine the sheet is a face and place the filling where the mouth should be: line up a couple of the pork slices, 3 prawns, 1 lettuce leaf, and one-sixth of the vermicelli and herbs. Fold the 2 sides inward over the filling, as if you were making an envelope. Now fold the bottom corner over the filling. Put 3–4 pieces of garlic chives along the roll, with the tips sticking out of one end of the roll. Start to roll up the package tightly, pushing it forward and tucking in the filling in a neat cylinder as you roll it towards the far side of the sheet. Keep in an airtight container or wrap in clingfilm while you assemble the remaining rolls.

Dipping sauce: heat the oil in a saucepan over a medium heat. Fry the garlic until it browns slightly. Add the hoisin sauce, vinegar, sugar, chilli sauce and 1 tablespoon of water and bring to a gentle boil. Pour into dipping bowls and sprinkle the peanuts on top. Serve with the rolls for dipping.

RICK STEIN'S SHRIMP & DILL FRITTERS WITH OUZO

Recipe by **RICK STEIN OBE**, chef, food writer & TV presenter, Padstow, Cornwall

SERVINGS: 4–8 | PREP TIME: 20 MINS | COOK TIME: 15 MINS | SKILL LEVEL: 1 (EASY)

This comes from a tiny fishing village called Gerakas, 40 minutes' north of Monemvasia in the Peloponnese. The drive is spectacular, and Gerakas itself is the Greek fishing village by which all others must be judged. This was designed to use the tiny shrimps in the inlet on which Gerakas lies. I particularly enjoy the subtle flavours of dill and ouzo.

INGREDIENTS

175 g (6 oz) plain flour
½ tsp baking powder
½ tsp salt
300 ml (10½ fl oz) water
1 tbsp ouzo (or pastis)
300 g (10½ oz) whole raw Falmouth Bay shrimps or brown shrimps, or 175 g (6 oz) raw peeled prawns cut into slices 5 mm (¼ in) thick
2 spring onions, very finely sliced
1 tbsp chopped dill
olive oil, for shallow-frying

DF

METHOD

Into a large bowl, sift the flour and baking powder; add the salt, then make a well in the centre and add the water and ouzo or pastis. Gradually incorporate the flour into the liquid to make a thick batter. Fold in the shrimps/prawns, spring onion and dill.

Pour olive oil to a depth of about 5 mm (¼ in) into a frying pan and place over a high heat. When hot, carefully add large spoonfuls of batter into the pan and spread out a little with the back of a spoon so they develop thin, crispy edges. Cook 2–3 at a time, turn over after 2 minutes and repeat until puffed up and golden on both sides.

Remove from the pan and drain on paper towel. Serve immediately.

ASPARAGUS FLAN WITH HAZELNUT, POACHED QUAIL'S EGGS & WILD WATERCRESS

Recipe by **SIMON ROGAN**, L'Enclume, Cartmel, Cumbria

SERVINGS: 4 | PREP TIME: 45 MINS | COOK TIME: 35 MINS | SKILL LEVEL: 2 (MODERATE)

INGREDIENTS

For the asparagus flan
12 stalks asparagus
100 g (3½ oz) potatoes
100 g (3½ oz) egg white
60 g (2 oz) plain flour
60 g (2 oz) ground hazelnuts
100 g (3½ oz) melted butter

For the quail's eggs
a splash of white wine vinegar
16 quail's eggs

For the hazelnut sauce
50 g (1½ oz) crushed hazelnuts
100 ml (3½ fl oz) white wine
150 ml (5 fl oz) cream
200 ml (7 fl oz) milk
50 g (1½ oz) wild-flower honey

To serve
picked wild watercress leaves
hazelnut oil
Maldon sea salt

V

METHOD

For the asparagus flan: cook the asparagus in boiling salted water until tender; place in ice water and drain. Peel and cook the potatoes in more boiling salted water until soft; drain and mash. Whisk up the egg white until stiff peaks are formed.

Pre-heat the oven to 160°C/320°F/gas 2½.

Mix the flour, ground hazelnuts, melted butter and mashed potatoes together and add salt to taste. Fold in the egg white. Trim the asparagus spears to 10 cm (4 in) long, or to fit your moulds, and slice in half length-ways. Spoon some of the batter into four buttered 10 cm x 5 cm x 1.4 cm (4 in x 2 in x ¾ in) friand moulds, or 10 cm (4 in) round tins, so that they are three-quarters full. Place six halves of asparagus on top, brush with melted butter, season and bake in the oven for 20 minutes.

For the poached eggs: fill a high-sided pan with water, bring to the boil, add a splash of vinegar and simmer. Break the eggs into a cup, one at a time, and poach them in the water in a couple of batches for about 1 minute. Lift them out of the water with a slotted spoon and place in ice water to stop them cooking. Drain on a paper towel.

For the hazelnut sauce: roast the crushed hazelnuts in a dry non-stick pan and pour in the wine, cream, milk and honey. Bring to the boil, cook for a couple of minutes and liquidize. Season with salt and pepper and keep warm.

To serve: place some warm asparagus flan in the centre of each plate. Arrange four quail eggs on and around each piece and spoon the hot hazelnut sauce over. Dress with wild watercress leaves, hazelnut oil and sea salt.

Shepherd's Bush,
London

VALENTINE WARNER
COOK, WRITER & FOUNDER OF HEPPLE GIN

Cooking is essentially bringing the outdoors indoors, and so it's important to understand what's available around you throughout the year. You don't need a kitchen to cook, and I'd frequently describe myself as a cook without a kitchen – chopping onions on a tree stump or maybe preparing goat on a boat! *Valentine*

COURGETTE SOUP WITH CHARD BRUSCHETTA

Recipe by **VALENTINE WARNER**, cook, writer & founder of Hepple Gin, Shepherd's Bush, London

SERVINGS: 6 | PREP TIME: 30 MINS | COOK TIME: 55 MINS | SKILL LEVEL: 1 (EASY)

This recipe uses two of my favourite vegetables, chard and courgette, and because I'm keen on simplicity it's a courgette soup. Soup is a joy that I think is often forgotten, yet it's so pleasure-giving when we remember it. I only hope this recipe goes to show how delicious soup can be.

INGREDIENTS

3 tbsp olive oil

1 medium-sized onion, finely chopped

7–9 medium-sized courgettes (about 1 kg/2¼ lb), cut into 1½ cm (¾ in) slices

3 cloves garlic, peeled

a generous grating of nutmeg

a small sprig of rosemary

30 g (1 oz) Parmesan rind, if you have some handy

550 ml (1 pint) whole milk

1 tsp sea salt flakes

For the chard bruschetta

4–5 large Swiss chard leaves

extra-virgin olive oil, for splashing

a squeeze of lemon juice

6 thin slices of rustic bread or ciabatta

1 large clove garlic, peeled

To serve

Parmesan cheese

a little extra-virgin olive oil

METHOD

To make the soup, pour the olive oil into a large, heavy-based pan and in it soften the onion over a medium heat for 8 minutes or so, stirring occasionally. Add the courgettes with the garlic, nutmeg, a good grinding of black pepper, rosemary and Parmesan rind (this will give depth to the soup in the absence of stock). Mix everything together before covering with a lid and leaving to cook for a further 20–25 minutes, stirring occasionally. After this time the courgettes should be very soft while retaining a pleasant green colour. Remove the rosemary stalk, which will have dropped its leaves.

While the courgettes sweat it out, start making the bruschetta. Put a pan of salted water on to boil. Rip up the chard leaves and boil them for 5 minutes or so, until tender. Drain the chard thoroughly and chop it very finely while still hot. Put it in a bowl with a generous splash of extra-virgin olive oil, some salt and a light squeeze of lemon juice – just enough to give it a little edge. Leave the chard to one side. Pre-heat the grill to its highest setting.

To finish the soup, add the milk to the courgettes and gently simmer for 10 minutes or so, uncovered. Do not let the soup boil. Remove and discard the Parmesan rind, and purée the soup in a food processor or with a stick blender until very smooth. Return it to the pan and place over a very low heat to keep it hot. Season with the salt – probably a little more than you would normally use. Add a little more milk if you feel the soup is too thick.

To finish the bruschetta, splash the slices of bread with more olive oil and toast them on a baking tray under the grill until they take on a rich golden colour. They do not want to be shatter-dry, but instead a little chewy in the middle. When cooked, rub them with the garlic.

Ladle the soup into bowls. Load some chard onto the bruschetta, then place these onto the soup. Grate Parmesan over the bruschetta and slash the soup with one last pass of extra-virgin olive oil.

POTTED SHRIMPS ON TOAST

Recipe by **MARK HIX**, chef, restaurateur & food writer, London & Dorset

SERVINGS: 4 | **PREP TIME: 25 MINS PLUS CHILLING** | **COOK TIME: 5 MINS** | **SKILL LEVEL: 1 (EASY)**

Ask your fishmonger to order you some peeled brown shrimps, because it could take you the best part of a day to peel enough for four. They will be expensive but well worth it. If you can't find these, use cooked and peeled prawns or even crabmeat.

INGREDIENTS

175 g (6 oz) unsalted butter
juice of ½ lemon
a good pinch of freshly
  grated mace or nutmeg
a pinch of cayenne pepper
1 small bay leaf
1 tsp anchovy essence or
  paste
200 g (7 oz) peeled brown
  shrimps

To serve
good-quality brown bread
2 lemons, quartered

METHOD

Melt the butter in a pan, add the lemon juice, mace or nutmeg, cayenne pepper, bay leaf and anchovy essence or paste, and simmer gently on a very low heat for 2 minutes to allow the spices to infuse. Remove from the heat and leave the mixture to cool until it is just warm.

Add the shrimps and stir well, then season with salt and freshly ground white pepper. Put the mixture into the fridge and stir every so often (over about 20 minutes). When the butter starts to set, fill 4 ramekins with the mixture.

If you are not serving the shrimps that day, cover the ramekins with clingfilm and store them in the fridge. It is important, though, not to serve them straight from the fridge, as the butter will be too hard to spread nicely on to the toast and won't taste as good. Serve on or with toasted brown bread and lemon quarters.

BURRATA WITH LENTILS & BASIL OIL

Recipe by **RUSSELL NORMAN**, restaurateur & food writer, Soho, London

SERVINGS: 6 | PREP TIME: 20 MINS | COOK TIME: 55 MINS | SKILL LEVEL: 2 (MODERATE)

Burrata is often confused with mozzarella, but they are not the same. Burrata is made in Puglia with milk from razza Podolica cows (not buffalo) and with added cream, so it is softer and more moist than mozzarella. Burrata's creamy, sweet consistency is the perfect foil to an array of ingredients. It is a delight with bitter cime di rapa *(turnip tops), for example. This recipe combines it with lentils — a heavenly marriage. Make sure that your burrata is of the finest quality and at room temperature. Serving it fridge-cold kills the texture and the flavour.*

INGREDIENTS

For the basil oil
leaves from a bunch of basil
flaky sea salt and black pepper
extra-virgin olive oil

400 g (14 oz) Puy lentils
2 large carrots, finely chopped
3 sticks celery, finely chopped
1 small onion, finely chopped
3 cloves garlic, finely chopped
5 sprigs thyme, leaves
  removed and chopped
6 burrata balls

For the mustard dressing
(you'll only need 4 tbsp of this)
100 ml (3½ fl oz) extra-virgin
  olive oil
25 ml (1 fl oz) red wine vinegar
1 tbsp Dijon mustard
1 tsp caster sugar

GF, V

METHOD

First, make the basil oil by placing most of the basil leaves in a food processor, reserving a few of the smaller, prettier ones for decorating at the end. Add a little salt and enough olive oil to make a thin sauce. Whizz for a few seconds then set aside.

Put the lentils in a saucepan with enough cold water to cover them by about 7 cm (3 in). Don't add salt at this stage, as this will toughen the lentils. Bring to the boil and cook for about 45 minutes. Keep checking them — they need to still hold a small bite. When they are done, drain, refresh in cold water, drain again and set aside.

Now, in a large heavy-based pan, sweat the vegetables in a few good glugs of olive oil with the thyme leaves, a large pinch of salt and a grind of black pepper. When the vegetables are softened and translucent, add the cooked lentils and a splash of water to stop them sticking to the bottom of the pan.

Make the mustard dressing. Put the olive oil, red wine vinegar, Dijon mustard, a small pinch of salt, a couple of grinds of pepper and the sugar into a bowl and whisk together.

To finish the dish, add 4 tablespoons of the mustard dressing to the lentils, check the seasoning and spoon onto a large warm plate. Then tear open your burrata and place on top of the warm lentils. The heat from the lentils will melt the burrata, making it even more creamy and soft. Drizzle some basil oil over the top and scatter with the reserved basil leaves.

MICHEL ROUX OBE
THE WATERSIDE INN

I love cooking in the same way that other people might love reading or writing. For me, food is the thing. I go to the market and find something that I love, something that looks good and smells good. The dish itself will come up naturally. Small is beautiful and less is more, and this is very important – don't overcook the food. And when you've got guests, that is not the time to try to cook something new. Try it another day – the day before they come!

Bray,
Berkshire

ROQUEFORT & WALNUT SOUFFLÉS

Recipe by **MICHEL ROUX OBE**, The Waterside Inn, Bray, Berkshire

SERVINGS: 4–8 | **PREP TIME: 40 MINS** | **COOK TIME: 30 MINS** | **SKILL LEVEL: 2 (MODERATE)**

You can make these classic soufflés either in individual 10 cm (4 in) soufflé dishes or in ramekins for a smaller starter. I always allow plenty of mixture, so don't worry if you have some left over after filling the dishes – better safe than sorry!

INGREDIENTS

50 g (1½ oz) softened butter, to grease dishes

50 g (1½ oz) breadcrumbs, to coat dishes

20 g (¾ oz) butter

20 g (¾ oz) plain flour

250 ml (9 fl oz) cold milk

a pinch of cayenne

6 medium-sized egg yolks

10 medium-sized egg whites

160 g (5½ oz) chilled Roquefort (not too soft or over-ripe), cut into small pieces

12 walnuts, coarsely chopped

2 very ripe fresh figs, finely diced

V

METHOD

Generously grease the insides of eight standard 8 cm (3 in) ramekins (or four 10 cm/4 in soufflé dishes) with the softened butter. Put the breadcrumbs into one dish, rotate it to coat the inside, then tip the excess into another ramekin. Repeat to coat them all.

To make the béchamel, melt the 20 g (¾ oz) butter in a saucepan. Add the flour and cook for 2 minutes, stirring with a whisk, to make a roux. Still stirring, add the milk and bring to the boil over a medium heat. Let bubble for a minute or two, then pour the béchamel into a bowl. Season lightly with salt, freshly ground pepper and cayenne, then whisk in the egg yolks. Cover the bowl with clingfilm and let cool slightly.

Pre-heat the oven to 200°C/400°F/gas 6.

Beat the egg whites with a pinch of salt until soft peaks form. Immediately mix one-third of the egg whites into the warm soufflé mixture with a whisk; then, using a large spoon or spatula, fold in the rest with one hand while showering in the Roquefort with the other. Stop as soon as the mixture is amalgamated. Carefully fold in the walnuts and figs.

Spoon the mixture into the ramekins or soufflé dishes to come 5 mm (¼ in) above the rim. Smooth the surface with a palette knife, then use a knife tip to ease the mixture away from the sides of each ramekin or soufflé dish to help it rise.

Stand the ramekins or soufflé dishes in a deep ovenproof dish on a sheet of greaseproof paper and pour in enough almost-boiling water to come halfway up the sides. Bake the soufflés for 4 minutes (or 6 minutes for 10 cm/4 in dishes). Put the cooked soufflés on individual plates and serve at once – they won't wait!

I like to serve these with a salad of mâche (lamb's lettuce) and thick batons of apple (preferably Granny Smith), dressed with a well-seasoned vinaigrette.

COCKLE, CIDER & PARSLEY BROTH

Recipe by **MARK HIX**, chef, restaurateur & food writer, London & Dorset

SERVINGS: 6 | **PREP TIME: 20 MINS** | **COOK TIME: 45 MINS** | **SKILL LEVEL: 1 (EASY)**

In my opinion, cockles have a better flavour than clams, and are a fraction of the price. That said, you can use clams or mussels if you like. Cockles have a tendency to be a bit gritty, so make sure you wash them really thoroughly.

INGREDIENTS

1 kg (2¼ lb) live cockles
  (or clams)
150 ml (5 fl oz) cider
30 g (1 oz) butter
1 onion, finely chopped
4 cloves garlic, peeled and
  crushed
25 g (1 oz) plain flour
1 litre (1¾ pints) fish stock
2 tbsp finely chopped
  flat-leaf parsley
3–4 tbsp double cream

METHOD

To clean the cockles, leave them under slow running water for about 15 minutes, agitating them with your hands every so often to release any trapped sand. Give the cockles a final rinse and drain.

Put the cleaned cockles in a large saucepan with the cider. Cover with a tight-fitting lid and cook over a high heat for about 2–3 minutes, shaking the pan every so often, until the cockles open.

Drain the cockles in a colander over a bowl, to catch the cooking liquor, then strain the liquor through a fine-meshed sieve into another bowl and set aside.

Melt the butter in a clean saucepan and gently cook the onion and garlic for 3–4 minutes without colouring. Add the flour and stir over a low heat for 30 seconds, then gradually whisk in the strained cooking liquor and fish stock. Bring to the boil, lower the heat and simmer gently for 30 minutes. By now the liquid should have reduced by about one-third and have a good flavour.

Remove about two-thirds of the cockles from their shells. Add the parsley and cream to the broth and simmer for a couple of minutes. Taste and adjust the seasoning as necessary, then divide the shelled and shell-on cockles between warmed soup plates and pour the hot broth over them to serve.

SOBA NOODLE SOUP WITH DUCK EGG & GREENS

Recipe by **ALICE HART**, chef & food writer, Brighton, Sussex

SERVINGS: 4 | PREP TIME: 20 MINS PLUS PICKLING & SOAKING | COOK TIME: 50 MINS OR MORE
SKILL LEVEL: 1 (EASY)

This started life as a ramen-style soup, but it didn't take many tries to conclude that getting depth and richness into a vegetarian ramen would take many hours. Cue a change of tack and a light, fresh, but no less pleasing, noodle soup, with plenty of interest from pickles and vegetable goodies. Seek out a white or a pale yellow miso for this; anything darker will be too spiky — you need mellow and sweet.

INGREDIENTS

4 radishes, trimmed and sliced
  or quartered

2 tbsp rice wine vinegar

a pinch of sea salt

a pinch of sugar

1 sheet dried kombu seaweed

a handful of fresh shiitake
  mushrooms, stems separated,
  caps sliced

1 leek, washed and sliced

200 g (7 oz) soba noodles

2 duck eggs

75 g (2½ oz) bean sprouts

a large handful of seasonal
  greens, e.g. radish tops, kale,
  chard, spinach

1–2 tbsp mirin

1–2 tbsp soy sauce, or to taste

2–3 tbsp yellow or white miso,
  or to taste

2 spring onions, finely sliced

DF

METHOD

Pickle the radishes by tossing them in the vinegar, salt and sugar. Set aside in a cool place for at least 2 hours, or chill for up to 2 weeks.

If you have time, soak the seaweed and the mushroom stems in about 1½ litres (2½ pints) water for 30 minutes. Soaked or not, place the saucepan over a low heat and heat through (don't boil) for 30 minutes to infuse the broth.

Strain the broth to remove the now-soft kombu and mushroom stalks, pressing down on them to extract all the flavour, including any gelatinous liquid clinging to the seaweed. Return the broth to the pan, adding the sliced mushroom caps and leek. Bring to the boil slowly; cover and simmer for anything from 20 minutes to 4 hours, depending on how savoury and concentrated you want the broth to be and how much time you have. While the broth simmers, cook the extras.

In a separate pan, boil the soba noodles according to the packet instructions. Drain and set aside. Use the same pan to simmer the duck eggs in plenty of boiling water for 9–10 minutes. Refresh under cool water and peel when cool enough to handle.

Again, refill the pan with water and bring back up to the boil. Blanch the bean sprouts for 30 seconds. Refresh under cool water and drain.

Add the greens to the simmering broth and let wilt for a minute. Season with the mirin, soy sauce and enough miso to cloud the broth. Taste and adjust the seasoning as required. Add the noodles and warm through. Divide the soup between wide serving bowls. Top each bowl with sliced spring onions, a halved duck egg, blanched bean sprouts and a few slices of pickled radish for a bit of punch.

AJIACO

COLOMBIAN CHICKEN & POTATO SOUP

Recipe by **PRUE LEITH** CBE, restaurateur, caterer & food writer, Chastleton, Gloucestershire

SERVINGS: 8 | PREP TIME: 25 MINS | COOK TIME: 1½ HOURS | SKILL LEVEL: 1 (EASY)

I often make this soup for lunch parties, as a main course. It's basically a broth made with big lumps of chicken and big lumps of potatoes, and then you add all the garnishes – avocado, fresh cream, capers. So it's an unusual mix of flavours, but the thing that makes it really extraordinary is the guascas – a Colombian herb that you can buy in packets. The soup is delicious anyway, but the guasca gives it something extra. Everybody wants to know the recipe when they eat it.

INGREDIENTS

1 large chicken

2¼ litres (4 pints) chicken stock

2 cloves garlic, crushed

450 g (1 lb) small new or salad potatoes, peeled

3 medium-sized Maris Piper potatoes, peeled and sliced

1 small teacup (roughly 3 tbsp) dried guasca leaves

6 fresh or frozen corn on the cob, cut into 2–3 chunks

a bunch of spring onions, cleaned and cut into 2–3 cm (1 in) pieces

2 teacups (small bunch) fresh coriander leaves

To serve

½ jar (50 g/1½ oz) small capers, rinsed well and drained

185 ml (6 fl oz) double cream

3–4 ripe avocados, sliced

GF

METHOD

Put the chicken in a large pan with the stock and the garlic. Bring to the boil. Simmer for 50 minutes or until the chicken thighs feel tender when pierced and the legs will wobble. Lift out the chicken and set aside. When cool enough to handle, remove the skin and bones and cut the flesh into large chunks (use a sharp knife and cut the breast against the grain – don't shred into stringy bits). Cover the chicken with an upturned bowl while you continue with the soup.

Into the stock put both types of potato and the guasca. Cook until the Maris Pipers are breaking up, about 20 minutes. Then add the corn chunks and cook for 10 minutes. Add the spring onion and coriander leaves. Taste and add freshly ground black pepper and ground sea salt to taste.

Return the chicken to the pan and reheat gently.

Serve each person, making sure they get liquid, chicken, corn and soup. Serve the Ajiaco hot with capers, double cream and avocado slices on the side.

TIP

Guasca leaves can be bought in Colombian shops or on Amazon. If you can't get them, don't worry – but it's what makes the soup taste Colombian!

SMOKED HADDOCK SOUFFLÉ & HORSERADISH CREAM

Recipe by **MARTIN GREEN**, head chef at White's, St James, London

SERVINGS: 8 | PREP TIME: 20 MINS | COOK TIME: 50 MINS | SKILL LEVEL: 2 (MODERATE)

INGREDIENTS

you will need 8 ramekins
  (9 cm/3½ in diameter)

90 g (3 oz) unsalted butter,
  softened
30 g (1 oz) dried breadcrumbs
350 ml (12½ fl oz) milk
200 g (7 oz) undyed smoked
  haddock
100 ml (3½ fl oz) double cream
20 g (¾ oz) grated horseradish
  from a jar
45 g (1½ oz) plain flour
4 eggs, separated
10 g (2 tsp) cornflour

METHOD

Pre-heat the oven to 200°C/400°F/gas 6.

Grease the inside of the ramekins with half of the softened butter and sprinkle with the breadcrumbs so that they stick to the butter, shaking off any excess.

Bring the milk to the boil and place the haddock into it, then remove from the heat, cover the pan in tinfoil and leave to cool. Remove the haddock and flake it, making sure there are no bones, and reserve for later. Measure 300 ml (10½ fl oz) of the milk from the haddock poaching liquor into a jug.

In a small pan, boil the double cream and add the horseradish. Keep warm.

In a separate pan, melt the remaining unsalted butter on a low heat, add the flour and cook for a couple of minutes, then slowly add the reserved milk a little at a time, beating so that you don't get any lumps. When all the milk is incorporated keep stirring until the mixture thickens, then season with a little salt and pepper, remove from the pan into a suitably sized bowl, cover with clingfilm and cool slightly.

When you are ready to cook the soufflé, whisk the egg yolks into the white-sauce mixture. In a clean bowl, whisk the egg whites and cornflour to soft peaks, add a third of this to the white sauce to loosen the mixture, then add the remainder of the egg whites and fold in carefully.

Put a spoon of the mixture into each of the prepared ramekins, then divide the smoked haddock between them, spooning on the remaining soufflé mix to the top of each ramekin.

Wipe the edges of the ramekins and run a blunt knife around the top of the soufflé mix – this will help them rise. Place in the pre-heated oven and cook for 10 minutes or until golden and risen above the mould. Serve immediately, pouring a little of the horseradish cream into the top of each soufflé.

TOAD IN THE HOLE

Recipe by **VALENTINE WARNER**, cook, writer & founder of Hepple Gin, Shepherd's Bush, London

SERVINGS: 3–4 | **PREP TIME: 15 MINS PLUS RESTING** | **COOK TIME: 50 MINS** | **SKILL LEVEL: 1 (EASY)**

With no mucking around and honest as the day is long, you know where you are when the toad comes out. This excellent batter comes from a long line of tall Pattison women, a fierce tribe from Hertfordshire, and is as reliable as their friendship. The better the eggs, the more your toad batter will have a rich, golden glow.

INGREDIENTS

For the batter

115 g (4 oz) plain flour
½ tsp sea salt flakes
225 ml (8 fl oz) semi-
    skimmed milk
2 large vibrant-yolked
    free-range eggs

2 tbsp sunflower oil
6–8 good-quality, meaty
    pork sausages
tomato ketchup, to serve

METHOD

Pre-heat the oven to 200°C/180°C fan/400°F/gas 6.

To make the batter, put the flour, salt and milk into a food processor bowl and crack the eggs in. Blitz together for 15 seconds or so into a smooth batter, then pour into a jug and set aside for 30 minutes.

Pour the oil into a large, non-stick, ovenproof frying pan and sizzle the sausages over a medium heat for 6–8 minutes until nicely browned on all sides. Stir the batter well before pouring it around the hot sausages, then put the frying pan in the oven. Bake for around 35 minutes. By this time, the batter should be very well risen and golden-brown.

Remove from the oven – taking care to use an oven cloth, as the handle will be extremely hot. Eat at once, with much blobbing of tomato ketchup on top.

TIP

If you don't have a large frying pan that you can use in the oven, fry the sausages and then transfer them to a roasting tin (rather than an ovenproof dish, as the heat will conduct better through the metal and should result in a lighter batter). Tip in the sausage fat and pop in the oven for a couple of minutes to heat up before adding the batter. Whether you add the batter to the frying pan or the roasting in, the sausages and fat must be hot to help the batter to rise well.

ANJUM ANAND
WITH MAHI ANAND
FOOD WRITER & TV PRESENTER

I'm so inspired by the food in India, where almost every home cook is a great cook. When you talk to people here in Britain they often think that Indian food is butter chicken, tikka masala and pilaf rice, and you just want them to experience real Indian food because you know they're going to love it even more. I suppose that has been my core inspiration to cook.

ANJUM

London

BAKED CHARD RICOTTA WITH A HOT TOMATO, GARLIC & PEPPER CHUTNEY

Recipe by **ANJUM ANAND**, food writer & TV presenter, London

SERVINGS: 6, OR 10 AS A STARTER | PREP TIME: 15 MINS | COOK TIME: 45 MINS | SKILL LEVEL: 1 (EASY)

This lovely dish has been inspired by a vegetarian spinach and paneer kebab I tried years ago and loved but never got around to making. It has morphed in my kitchen to use ricotta instead of paneer and it is baked instead of being fried. Here we have made little bite-sized canapés that reflect the original incarnation of the dish, but you can also bake this in a cake tin and serve it in wedges. The tomato chutney is hot and garlicky and is the perfect contrast to the creaminess of the dish. If you are in a hurry and can't make the chutney, serve with a tangy, seasoned tomato salad.

INGREDIENTS

For the hot tomato, garlic & pepper chutney

8 large cloves garlic, peeled

1 red chilli, de-seeded

6 medium-sized ripe vine tomatoes, quartered

2 tbsp vegetable oil

1 red pepper, roasted or grilled (you can buy these in most supermarkets), skinned and chopped

For the baked chard ricotta

20 g (¾ oz) softened butter, for preparing the tin

3 tbsp extra-virgin olive oil

1 medium to large-sized onion, finely chopped

4 large cloves garlic, finely chopped

2 tsp chopped fresh ginger

300 g (10½ oz) chard, well washed and shredded

¾ tsp ground cumin

¾ tsp garam masala

2½ tsp chaat masala (depends on the brand and its strength)

500 g (18 oz) ricotta

2 large eggs

a good handful chopped fresh coriander

a good handful breadcrumbs

baby chard or micro herbs, to garnish

V

METHOD

For the chutney, blend together the garlic, chilli and tomatoes until smooth. Heat the oil in a medium-sized saucepan and add the blended ingredients along with some salt. Cook, stirring occasionally, until the tomatoes have released oil into the pan; around 25 minutes. It should taste harmonious. Stir in the chopped pepper and cook for another few minutes. This chutney stores for a week in the fridge.

Pre-heat the oven to 180°C/350°F/gas 4. Place a baking tray on the middle shelf. Butter a 12-hole muffin tin or a 20 cm (8 in) cake tin with a removable base.

Heat 2 tablespoons of the oil in a large non-stick sauté pan. Add the onion and cook until golden on the edges. Add the garlic and ginger and cook until done, for a minute or so. Stir in the chard, spices and seasoning, and cook until the chard has wilted and the water has evaporated. Cool.

Add the ricotta. Taste and adjust seasoning, adding a good grinding of fresh black pepper. Beat in the eggs and chopped coriander.

Pour into the muffin tin or cake tin, sprinkle over the breadcrumbs, drizzle with the remaining oil and cook until golden and set (20–25 minutes in the muffin tin or 35–40 minutes in the cake tin). Serve with the chutney and garnish with baby chard or micro herbs if you like.

SAUSAGE MEAT & APPLE TURNOVER

Recipe by **SARAH WEBB**, home cook, Weston, Northamptonshire

SERVINGS: 8–10 | **PREP TIME: 30 MINS PLUS COOLING** | **COOK TIME: 40 MINS** | **SKILL LEVEL: 1 (EASY)**

INGREDIENTS

10 large, good-quality pork sausages

1 medium-sized onion

2 cooking apples

a little oil and butter, for frying

1 tsp thyme, chopped fresh or dried

500 g (1 lb 2 oz) puff pastry

1 egg, beaten

mustard, to serve

METHOD

Remove the skins from the sausages and put the meat onto a plate. Chop the onion finely. Peel, core and dice the apples.

In a large, deep frying pan, heat a little oil and butter. Sauté the onion until soft; add the skinned sausages and break them up, stirring them to brown the meat lightly. Add a little water to prevent sticking and loosen the meat slightly. Add the diced apples and lightly season with salt, pepper and the thyme. Mix together well, then remove from the heat and set aside to cool.

Pre-heat the oven to 190°C/375°F/gas 5.

Roll the puff pastry into a rectangle approximately 30 cm x 40 cm (12 in x 16 in), then lay it on a baking tray.

Spoon the sausage meat and apple mixture down one-half of the pastry's length. Brush the beaten egg around the edges of the pastry, then carefully lift one side and fold it over to join the other. Gently press the edges down and trim off any excess pastry if necessary. Using a fork, press the edges or pinch them into a neat pattern. The fold should either be hidden underneath the roll or be sealed firmly at the side. Use a sharp knife to cut light slits diagonally down the length of the turnover, then brush all over with the remaining beaten egg.

Bake in the pre-heated oven for 30–40 minutes or until it becomes a deep golden-brown all over and the pastry is cooked through. Serve with mustard.

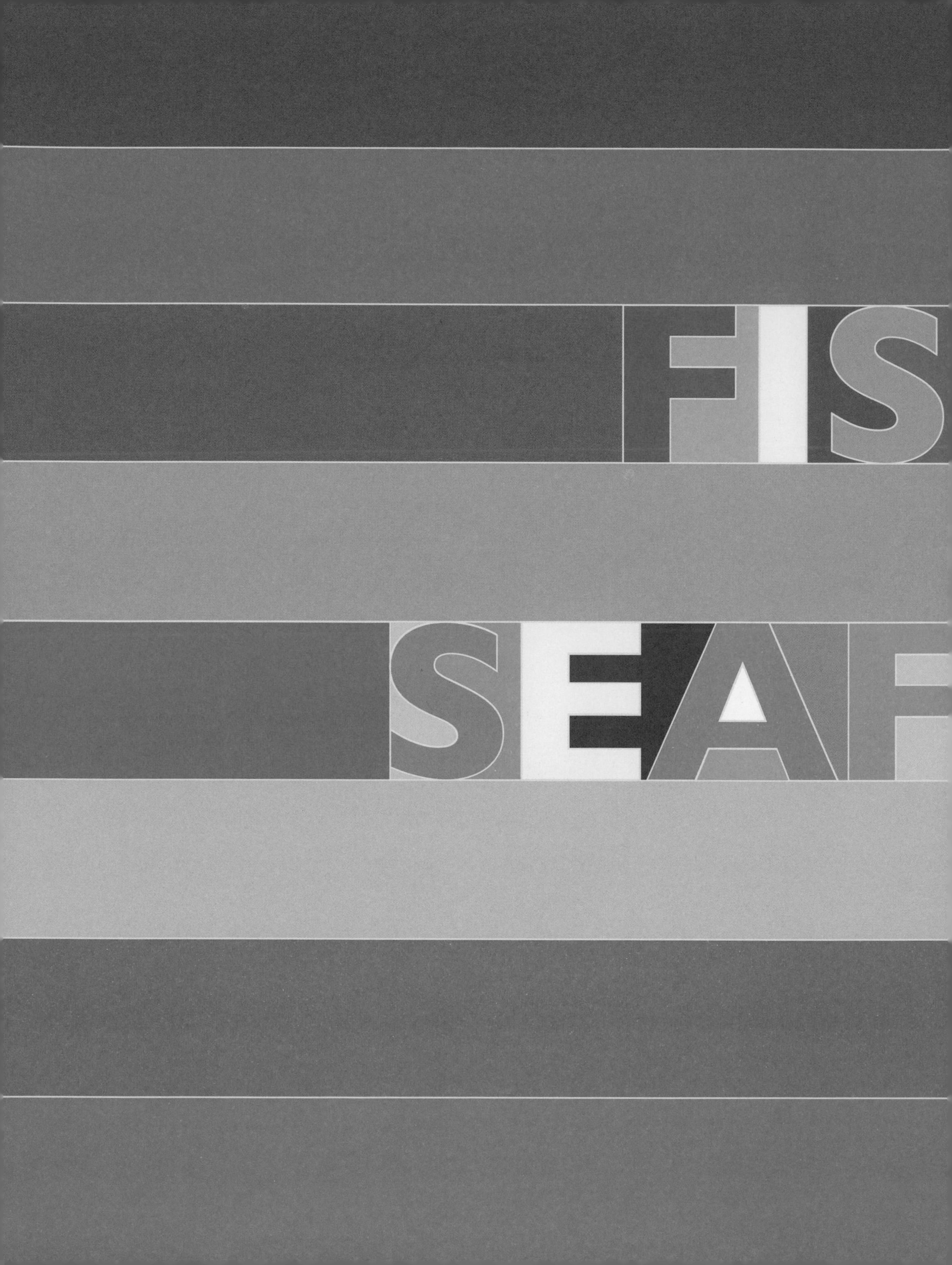
FIS
SEAF

H & OOD

NATHAN OUTLAW
RESTAURANT NATHAN OUTLAW

My approach to cooking is seasonal, and obviously seafood is my main thing. In this mackerel dish, the capers bring a lovely saltiness, while the cucumber has a nice crunch and freshness. And the lemon and shallot dressing draws the whole thing together. It's a great dish to eat by the seaside, or at home in the garden with family and friends.

Nathan

*Port Isaac
Cornwall*

MACKEREL CURED IN CUCUMBER & OYSTER JUICE WITH CUCUMBER, DILL & CAPER SALAD

Recipe by **NATHAN OUTLAW**, Restaurant Nathan Outlaw, Port Isaac, Cornwall

---

SERVINGS: 4 | PREP TIME: 35 MINS PLUS PICKLING & CURING | COOK TIME: 15 MINS
SKILL LEVEL: 1 (EASY)

This recipe was invented by accident. Someone had forgotten to cover the oyster juice in the fridge and as the door shut it toppled over onto my beautifully prepared mackerel fillets. I came into work to find the mess... and my mackerel swimming in oyster juice! I may have uttered a few expletives at the time, but soon discovered that the fish was, in fact, not ruined but delicious. Instantly I set about creating this dish. Whoever it was in my kitchen who slammed that fridge door never owned up so I can't credit them, but this recipe is dedicated to them anyway!

INGREDIENTS

For the white wine shallots (makes enough for 10 servings)
4 large banana shallots, peeled
150 ml (5 fl oz) white wine
75 ml (2½ fl oz) white wine vinegar
75 g (2½ oz) caster sugar
Cornish sea salt

4 mackerel, filleted, skinned and pin-boned

For the cure
1 cucumber, roughly chopped
200 g (7 oz) sea salt
100 g (3½ g) caster sugar
10 g (⅓ oz) dill
6 oysters, shucked, juice strained and reserved

For the salad
1 cucumber
3 tsp small capers in brine, drained
2 tsp white wine shallots (see column 1)
2 tsp chopped dill, plus extra sprigs to garnish
4 tsp lemon juice
8 tsp cold-pressed rapeseed oil
Cornish sea salt and freshly ground black pepper

GF, DF

METHOD

First, make the white wine shallots. Finely chop the shallots and place in a clean container. Put the wine, wine vinegar and sugar into a saucepan and bring to a simmer over a medium heat. Add a pinch of salt.

Pour the hot pickling liquor over the shallots, make sure they are submerged, and leave to cool. Seal and leave for at least 12 hours before using. Stored in a sterilized jar in the fridge, these pickled shallots will keep for 3 months.

For the cure, put the cucumber, salt, sugar and dill in a food processor with the oysters and their juice and blitz for 1 minute.

Lay the mackerel fillets on a tray (that will hold them and the cure) and pour the cure over them, distributing it evenly and making sure the fillets are covered all over. Cover with clingfilm and place in the fridge to cure for 2 hours.

Wash off the cure well with cold water and pat the fish dry with paper towel. Wrap the fish tightly in clingfilm and place in the fridge for an hour or so. (At this stage, you can freeze the fish for up to a month.)

In the meantime, prepare the salad. Peel the cucumber, then pare long ribbons from the sides, using a vegetable peeler, until you reach the seeds, then stop. Put the cucumber ribbons into a bowl with the capers, white wine shallots and chopped dill.

Pre-heat your grill to medium. Unwrap the cured mackerel fillets and grill them, skin-side up, for 2 minutes, then remove and break into flakes. Gently toss the mackerel with the cucumber salad. Dress with the lemon juice and rapeseed oil, and season with salt and pepper to taste. Finish with a scattering of dill sprigs.

Serve either as a sharing dish in the centre of the table or on individual plates.

SALTED COD WITH WINTER CABBAGE, BACON & BEER SAUCE

Recipe by **JASON ATHERTON**, Pollen Street Social, Mayfair, London

SERVINGS: 4 | PREP TIME: 30 MINS PLUS SALTING & CHILLING | COOK TIME: 40 MINS
SKILL LEVEL: 2 (MEDIUM)

INGREDIENTS

4 skinned cod fillets
  (about 120 g/4½ oz each)

15 g (½ oz) sea salt

½ pointed hispi (sweetheart)
  cabbage

about 4 tbsp olive oil, plus extra
  to drizzle

2 shallots, peeled and sliced

3 sprigs thyme, leaves picked

2 cloves garlic, peeled and finely
  chopped

250 ml (9 fl oz) bitter (English beer)

600 ml (1¼ pints) chicken stock

100 ml (3½ fl oz) double cream

1 tsp lemon juice

175 g (6 oz) thick-cut bacon,
  cut into 5 cm (2 in) long batons

40 g (1½ oz) butter

2 tbsp dark brown sugar

120 g (4½ oz) baby onions, peeled

6 bay leaves, split in half
  lengthways, to garnish

GF

METHOD

Rinse the cod fillets, pat dry with paper towel and check for small bones, removing any with kitchen tweezers. Lay on a tray and sprinkle with the salt, coating both sides evenly. Wrap in clingfilm and refrigerate for 4–6 hours. Rinse the cod in cold water to remove the salt and pat dry with paper towel. Cover and chill.

Trim the cabbage, cutting out the core, then slice into strips 6 cm (about 2½ in) wide. Blanch in a pan of boiling salted water for 2–3 minutes until just tender. Immediately drain and immerse in a bowl of ice water. Drain and set aside.

To make the beer sauce, heat a drizzle of olive oil in a large saucepan over a medium heat and sauté the shallots for a few minutes to soften. Add the thyme leaves and garlic and cook for another 3–4 minutes. Pour in the beer and let bubble to reduce down to almost nothing, 4–5 minutes. Pour in 500 ml (18 fl oz) of the chicken stock, increase the heat to medium-high and reduce by half, about 8 minutes. Add the cream and simmer gently for about 5 minutes to reduce and thicken, then stir in the lemon juice.

While the sauce is reducing, cook the bacon and onions. Place a wide pan over a medium heat and add a drizzle of olive oil. When hot, fry the bacon until just crisp and golden, then remove and drain on paper towel.

Add the butter, sugar, remaining chicken stock and baby onions to the oil left in the pan and cook, turning frequently, until the onions are tender and caramelized, 5–6 minutes. Return the bacon to the pan and toss well. Keep warm.

When the sauce is ready, add the blanched cabbage and turn to coat and warm through. Set aside; keep warm.

Heat a non-stick frying pan over a medium-high heat and add 3 tablespoons of olive oil. When hot, fry the bay leaves until just crisp, about 1 minute. Remove and drain on paper towel.

Now add the cod fillets to the frying pan and fry for about 4 minutes each side, depending on thickness, until cooked through and golden around the edges.

Divide the cabbage leaves between warm plates. Lay a cod fillet on top and scatter the bacon and shallots on and around the fish. Spoon over some of the beer sauce, drizzle the plate with olive oil and garnish with the crisp bay leaves. Serve the rest of the sauce in a jug alongside.

HOT BUTTERED CRAB

Recipe by **TOM PARKER BOWLES**, food writer & critic, London

SERVINGS: 2 | **PREP TIME: 10 MINS PLUS CRAB PICKING** | **COOK TIME: 5 MINS** | **SKILL LEVEL: 1 (EASY)**

INGREDIENTS

2 x 1 kg (2¼ lb) boiled crabs, picked – yielding about 400 g (14 oz) white meat and 250 g (9 oz) dark meat – and shells cleaned

a very fine grating of nutmeg

1 tbsp olive oil

2 tbsp sherry vinegar

Tabasco sauce, to taste

75 g (3 oz) fresh breadcrumbs

50 g (1½ oz) butter, melted

METHOD

This is best made with a freshly picked crab, using both brown and white meat.

Pre-heat the grill to hot. Put the crabmeat in a bowl and mix with the nutmeg, olive oil, sherry vinegar, a big dash of Tabasco and salt and pepper. Add about three-quarters of the breadcrumbs and all the butter. Mix well.

Spoon the mixture into the cleaned crab shells (or into two shallow ovenproof dishes) and cover with the remaining breadcrumbs; then place under the grill for 5 minutes, or until golden and piping hot.

LOBSTER ON TOAST WITH CRUSHED BROAD BEANS, PEA SHOOTS & LEMON DRESSING

Recipe by **TIM HUGHES**, Caprice Holdings, London

SERVINGS: 4 | **PREP TIME: 40 MINS** | **COOK TIME: 20 MINS** | **SKILL LEVEL: 2 (MODERATE)**

INGREDIENTS

To cook the lobster

3 litres (5¼ pints) water

200 g (7 oz) sea salt

2 x 500 g (1 lb 2 oz) lobsters

1 medium (size & strength) fresh red chilli, finely diced

100 g (3½ oz) broad beans, cooked, shelled and crushed

30 g (1 oz) mayonnaise

40 g (1⅓ oz) pea shoot leaves, carefully washed and dried (you can use rocket if you can't find pea shoots)

4 slices brioche or focaccia

For the dressing

2 tbsp good-quality white wine vinegar

6 tbsp olive oil

4 tbsp extra-virgin rapeseed oil (available at most good-quality supermarkets)

juice of ½ lemon

DF

METHOD

Bring the water to the boil and add salt; place the lobsters into the boiling water and cook for 12 minutes; take out of the water and leave to cool. Once cool, remove the claws from the lobsters, then crack the shells and put the meat to one side. Remove each tail by twisting it away from the head, then, with a heavy knife, cut the tail in half lengthways.

Cut the lobster meat into approximately 5 cm (2 in) pieces, place in a bowl with the diced chilli and crushed broad beans, and mix with the mayonnaise.

Whisk together the dressing ingredients in a separate bowl.

To serve, place the lobster mixture onto toasted brioche or focaccia, and finish with pea shoot leaves tossed in the lemon dressing.

SEA TROUT, COCKLES & SOUSED VEGETABLES

Recipe by **MATT TEBBUTT**, TV presenter & consultant chef to Schpoons & Forx, Bournemouth, Dorset

SERVINGS: 4 | PREP TIME: 15 MINS | COOK TIME: 50 MINS | SKILL LEVEL: 1 (EASY)

INGREDIENTS

For the poaching liquor
4 sticks celery
2 large onions, peeled
4 carrots
2 bay leaves
1 tsp black peppercorns
1 tsp coriander seeds
400 ml (14 fl oz) white wine
200 ml (7 fl oz) white wine vinegar
100 ml (3½ fl oz) water

4 sea trout or wild salmon fillets
400 g (14 oz) cockles, scrubbed and rinsed
100 g (3½ oz) wild sorrel
50 ml (1½ fl oz) extra-virgin olive oil

DF, GF

METHOD

First, make the poaching liquor. Cut all the vegetables, on an angle, quite thinly but all to the same thickness. Throw in a saucepan with all the remaining ingredients. Bring to the boil and simmer for 30 minutes. Remove from the heat.

Slip the fish pieces into the poaching liquor and cook very gently, without boiling, for 6–7 minutes until just cooked. Remove the fish and keep warm.

Put some of the cooking liquor in a small saucepan, bring to the boil and throw the cockles in. Cover with a lid and shake the pan from time to time. The cockles should take 2–3 minutes to open. Remove them from the heat and discard any that have not opened. Shell some of them, keeping others in the shell as a garnish.

To serve, place some soused vegetables on a warm plate, put a piece of fish on top and scatter some shelled cockles around the plate. Garnish with the wild sorrel, a splash of extra-virgin olive oil and the in-shell cockles.

BURNT GARLIC, LEMON & CHILLI SQUID

Recipe by **NADIYA HUSSAIN**, baker, cook & food writer, Milton Keynes, Buckinghamshire

SERVINGS: 5 | **PREP TIME: 30 MINS** | **COOK TIME: 5 MINS** | **SKILL LEVEL: 1 (EASY)**

INGREDIENTS

4 whole squid with tentacles (or 25 baby squid), cleaned

4 cloves garlic

3 tbsp olive oil

1 lemon, cut into 8 slices

2 tbsp chopped coriander

2 spring onions, finely chopped

1 whole fresh red chilli, finely chopped

½ tsp pink peppercorns, crushed

oil, for cooking

DF, GF

METHOD

Cut the squid into pieces of roughly similar size, and score with a knife, making sure not to cut all the way through the flesh.

Place the garlic cloves into a heatproof bowl, or a metal bowl. Blow-torch the pieces of garlic with the skins on until they are completely black. Chop the burnt garlic into small pieces, making sure not to discard any of the charred black bits; all this adds to the flavour (you can also cook them under a very hot grill).

To the garlic add the lemon slices, squeezing some juice out of each one. Then add the coriander, spring onion, chilli, salt to taste and pink peppercorns. Give it all a good stir.

Place a frying pan on a medium heat and add oil, and when the oil is hot add the squid. Give it a good stir and after a few seconds add the spicy mix in. Cook for about 4 minutes. You know it's done when it curls up and looks less translucent.

Do not overcook, or the squid will become rubbery.

Clavering,
Essex

JAMIE OLIVER MBE
CHEF & CAMPAIGNER

These days it's so important to buy delicious but less famous fish like gurnard, coley and pouting, which are just as wonderful as cod but much more plentiful. If you are going to use cod or haddock, the best advice I can give you is to make sure it's MSC approved.

HAPPY FISH PIE

Recipe by **JAMIE OLIVER MBE**, chef & campaigner, Clavering, Essex

SERVINGS: 6–8 | **PREP TIME: 20 MINS** | **COOK TIME: 30 MINS** | **SKILL LEVEL: 1 (EASY)**

Fish pie is one of the cornerstones of great British comfort food, not really surprising when you consider that even when you're furthest inland in Britain you're still no more than 70 miles from the sea. I've called this version from my book Jamie's Great Britain *'happy fish pie' because it's simple, delicious, and makes use of more underused varieties of fish. Enjoy.*

INGREDIENTS

2 large leeks

2 large carrots

2 sticks celery

2 rashers higher-welfare smoked streaky bacon

2 sprigs fresh rosemary

2 knobs unsalted butter

2 fresh bay leaves

sea salt and white pepper

1 kg (2¼ lb) Maris Piper potatoes

olive oil

1 whole nutmeg, for grating

300 ml (10½ oz) single cream

2 tsp English mustard

2 handfuls grated mild cheddar cheese

1 lemon

1 kg (2¼ lb) fish fillets from sustainable sources, skin off and pin-boned (gurnard, coley, pouting, trout would be a lovely mixture – ask your fishmonger)

GF

METHOD

Strip away the tough outer leaves from the leeks, then halve, wash well and finely slice the rest. Roughly chop the carrots, celery and bacon, and pick and finely chop the rosemary.

Place a casserole pan (roughly 20 cm x 30 cm/8 in x 12 in) over a medium heat, then add a knob of butter and the bacon. Once golden, add all the herbs and prepped veg, then season with sea salt and white pepper. Pop the lid on, turn the heat down to low and cook for around 15 minutes, or until sweet and tender, stirring occasionally.

Preheat the oven to 220°C/425°F/gas 7. Meanwhile, peel and chop the potatoes into 2 cm chunks, then cook in boiling salted water for 12–15 minutes, or until tender. Drain, steam dry, then mash with a drizzle of oil and a generous knob of butter (I don't like to mash too much, because it can make the potato gluey rather than light and insanely crisp). Season with sea salt, white pepper and a nice grating of nutmeg.

When the leeks are sweet, add the cream and mustard, simmer for a few seconds, then turn the heat off and sprinkle in half the grated cheddar. Stir and season to taste, add a good few gratings of lemon zest, squeeze in the juice and stir again. Slice the fish into 2 cm chunks, dot evenly around the sauce, then jiggle the dish gently so the fish gets slightly submerged. Sprinkle the rest of the cheddar on top. Put forkfuls of mash all over until the surface of the pie is evenly covered, then use a fork to pat, poof and rough it up, leaving a few little gaps for the sauce to bubble through. Bake at the top of the oven for 30 minutes, or until golden, crisp, bubbling and delicious. Serve with fresh lovely things like peas, beans or spinach.

TIP

Here the pie is baked straight away, but if you want to make it in advance, allow everything to cool before assembling, then bake for about 45 minutes at 180°C/350°F/gas 4.

BROWN SHRIMP, KOHLRABI & APPLE

Recipe by **FLORENCE KNIGHT**, chef, food writer & columnist, Soho, London

MAKES: 4 SMALL PLATES | PREP TIME: 15 MINS | SKILL LEVEL: 1 (EASY)

This is my take on the classic prawn cocktail. I love kohlrabi and, if you haven't discovered it already, I think you might too. It can look a little alien with its greeny-purple tinge, bulbous and gnarly shape and large leafy stems poking out the top. Often thought of as a winter vegetable, it's actually best in the summer when it's the size of a small fist, with the crunch of an apple and a refreshing mild watery taste. It adds a clean flavour and texture here, which balances out the strong ketchup. I like to make this with crunchy sweet Pink Lady apples, but feel free to use other varieties.

INGREDIENTS

1 tsp caraway seeds
1 unwaxed lemon
1 small kohlrabi
1 eating apple
a pinch of salt
1 tsp ketchup
1 tbsp crème fraîche
100 g (3½ oz) peeled
  brown shrimp
extra-virgin olive oil

GF

METHOD

Toast the seeds in a hot pan for a minute or two until they smell fragrant. Set aside to cool. Zest the lemon, then halve and squeeze out the juice.

Peel the kohlrabi and slice it very, very thinly into discs on a mandolin or carefully by hand. Slice the whole, unpeeled, cored apple, cutting it horizontally through the middle to give you very thin hoops. Place the kohlrabi and apple in a bowl with the lemon juice and salt; this will stop them from browning as well as helping to soften and break down the kohlrabi.

In a small bowl, mix the ketchup, crème fraîche, shrimps and caraway seeds, then gently fold through the kohlrabi and apple slices.

Add salt and pepper to taste and dress with the lemon zest and a splash of olive oil before serving.

PULPO GALLEGO

OCTOPUS, POTATOES & PAPRIKA

Recipe by **SAM & SAM CLARK**, Moro and Morito restaurants, North London

SERVINGS: 4 | **PREP TIME: 45 MINS** | **COOK TIME: 1½ HOURS** | **SKILL LEVEL: 2 (MODERATE)**

Probably the most famous tapa from Galicia. Excellent olive oil and crunchy rock salt are essential for this dish.

INGREDIENTS

1¼ kg (2¾ lb) fresh or
   defrosted frozen octopus,
   preferably double-sucker
1 onion, halved
3 bay leaves, preferably fresh
8 tbsp extra-virgin olive oil
800 g (1½ lb) potatoes,
   peeled
¼ tsp smoked sweet Spanish
   paprika
¼ tsp smoked hot Spanish
   paprika
rock salt

DF, GF

METHOD

If the octopus hasn't already been prepared by your fishmonger, you will need to clean it. To prepare the octopus yourself, first slice its head, or 'hood', open and remove the gelatinous sac of guts from inside. Now remove the hard, black, beaky mouth, located at the centre where the 8 tentacles meet. Place the octopus in a large saucepan and add the onion, bay leaves and 2 tablespoons of the olive oil, and enough water to cover by about 5 cm (2 in). Gently simmer the octopus for 45 minutes to 1 hour or until tender. To check whether it's ready, insert a small skewer through the thickest part of a tentacle. When the skewer goes through the centre without finding rubbery resistance, it's done. Remove the octopus from the pan, reserving the cooking water. Slice the tentacles into discs 1½ cm (¾ in) thick, place in a bowl and keep warm.

Add the potatoes to the octopus cooking water and simmer for around 20–30 minutes or until just tender. Remove from the pot, drain and leave to dry for 5 minutes. Slice the potatoes into discs 1½ cm (¾ in) thick, place in the centre of a warm plate and surround with the warm octopus. Drizzle the remaining olive oil over everything. Finally, sprinkle the paprika and some rock salt evenly on top. Serve while still warm.

RUSSELL NORMAN
RESTAURATEUR & FOOD WRITER

I love the rule of three ingredients – quite often I'll look
at a recipe and see what I can take away rather than
what I can add. The Clams with Borlotti Beans & Wild
Garlic is a perfect example: that trinity of good ingredients
working well together. I was walking through a forest in
East Kent recently and the entire wood was filled with
wild garlic. It was such an amazing fragrance and I was
reminded of this recipe.

Russell

*Soho,
London*

CLAMS, BORLOTTI BEANS & WILD GARLIC

Recipe by **RUSSELL NORMAN**, restaurateur & food writer, Soho, London

SERVINGS: 4 | PREP TIME: 20 MINS PLUS OVERNIGHT SOAKING | COOK TIME: 1¼ HOURS
SKILL LEVEL: 1 (EASY)

Wild garlic has a short season in Britain, usually mid-March to late May, but it is wonderful. It is exceptionally fragrant and begs to be used when you can find it. (The tiny white flowers, if you can get them, make a good final garnish.) If your timing is slightly off, don't worry. You can pick up garlic chives at Chinese supermarkets and these work very well. Borlotti beans are beautiful. The pink, purple and white pattern of the pods has been compared to Missoni fabric. And the beans are similarly stippled. How disappointing, then, that the colours fade away during the cooking process and they end up a uniform mid-brown. It's a good job they are so tasty — otherwise this drab metamorphosis would be unforgivable.

INGREDIENTS

200 g (7 oz) dried borlotti beans, soaked in cold water overnight

1 onion, halved

2 carrots, cut into large chunks

2 sticks celery, cut into large chunks

4 sprigs rosemary

1 bulb garlic, cut in half horizontally

extra-virgin olive oil

flaky sea salt and black pepper

500 g (1lb 2 oz) small clams, washed

1 clove garlic, finely chopped

a knob of butter

50 ml (1½ fl oz) dry sherry

100 g (3½ oz) wild garlic, washed and cut into 3 cm (1¼ in) strips

GF

METHOD

Drain the soaked borlotti beans and put them in a large saucepan. Add the onion, carrot, celery, rosemary, garlic bulb and 75 ml (2½ fl oz) olive oil. Add enough water to cover generously. Place over a high heat to bring to the boil, then reduce to medium for a rolling boil and cover. After about an hour, once the beans are cooked, discard the vegetables and herbs, transfer the beans to a clean container and season well with flaky sea salt and black pepper. Reserve the cooking liquid.

Heat a good glug of olive oil in a lidded saucepan, and when it's hot throw in the clams. Cover and keep the pan over a high heat, shaking the clams around a few times. They will start to open within a few minutes. Once they do, and you have discarded any that did not open, add the beans, about 100 ml (3½ fl oz) of the bean cooking liquid, the chopped garlic clove, the butter and the sherry. Bring to the boil and simmer for a minute or two. Add the wild garlic strips and stir well.

Transfer the bean and clam mixture to warmed bowls. Drizzle with a little olive oil.

JOHN DORY WITH CURRY SAUCE, CABBAGE & SHALLOTS

Recipe by **NATHAN OUTLAW**, Restaurant Nathan Outlaw, Port Isaac, Cornwall

SERVINGS: 4 | **PREP TIME: 45 MINS PLUS CHILLING & OVERNIGHT INFUSING** | **COOK TIME: 35 MINS**
SKILL LEVEL: 2 (MODERATE)

Using a mayonnaise-based sauce is a good way to get flavours into a dish without overpowering the taste of the fish. John Dory has a lovely delicate flavour, which is enhanced here by a subtle, fresh-tasting curry sauce. Buttery cabbage and shallots contrast the moist texture of the fish beautifully.

INGREDIENTS

For the curry oil (makes about 400 ml/14 fl oz)
4 tsp mild curry powder
400 ml (14 fl oz) light rapeseed oil

For the cabbage
1 savoy or hispi (sweetheart) cabbage
75 g (2½ oz) unsalted butter
2 large banana shallots, peeled and thinly sliced
2 John Dory, about 600 g (1 lb 5 oz) each, gutted, filleted, skinned and pin-boned

For the curry sauce
2 medium-sized egg yolks
1 tsp mild curry powder
3 tsp white wine vinegar
200 ml (7 fl oz) sunflower oil
75 ml (2½ fl oz) apple juice

GF

METHOD

First, make the curry oil. Sprinkle the curry powder into a dry frying pan and toast over a medium heat for 1–2 minutes until it releases its aroma; don't let it burn. Pour the oil into the pan and remove from the heat. Give it a good stir and then pour it into a jug. Leave to infuse and settle for 24 hours, then decant the curry oil into another container. It will keep for three months in a dark cupboard.

Bring a large saucepan of lightly salted water to the boil. Remove and set aside 6–12 large outer leaves from the cabbage (you may need fewer for the sausage shape, depending on the size of your cabbage); halve, core and shred the rest.

Add the whole cabbage leaves to the boiling water and blanch for 2 minutes. Remove and drain thoroughly, then plunge into ice water to refresh; drain and set aside.

Heat the butter in a pan over a medium heat. When hot, add the shallot and shredded cabbage and cook for 3 minutes to soften, then tip onto a tray, spread out and leave to cool.

Lay a sheet of clingfilm on your work surface. Lay the cabbage leaves out on the clingfilm, overlapping them slightly to form a sheet. Spread the shredded cabbage and shallot evenly on top, then roll up to form a sausage and wrap tightly in the clingfilm, twisting the ends to secure. Pierce the clingfilm with the tip of a knife to release any excess water, then chill the sausage for 2 hours.

To make the curry sauce, beat the egg yolks, curry powder, ½ teaspoon salt and the wine vinegar together in a bowl, then slowly whisk in the oil, drop by drop to begin with, then in a steady stream to make a smooth, thick mayonnaise. Stir in the apple juice until evenly combined, then taste and adjust the seasoning if necessary.

Heat your oven to 180°C. Heat your grill to its highest setting and oil a grill tray. Season the fish with salt and place, skin-side up, on the grill tray.

Slice the cabbage roll carefully into four even lengths and remove the clingfilm. Place the cabbage rolls on a lined baking tray and warm through in the oven for 5 minutes or so.

Meanwhile, place the fish under the grill for 6 minutes or until just cooked. Gently warm the sauce in a pan until it just starts to steam, then take it off the heat and give it a good whisk.

When the fish is ready, spoon the sauce into warm, deep plates. Add a cabbage roll and a fish fillet to each and finish with a drizzle of curry oil.

Mayfair,
London

RICHARD CORRIGAN
CHEF & RESTAURATEUR

My background as a farmer's son gives me a unique understanding of the land, the soil, the seasons and what's going to grow well where you reside. That's what's really important to me. My approach to food in my restaurants is to keep it seasonal, simple, delicious; nothing more than that. No tricks, not too many chefs' hands – just gorgeous, seasonal ingredients served with a little bit of panache.

WHOLE SEA TROUT WITH 'COASTAL GREENS'

Recipe by **RICHARD CORRIGAN**, chef & restaurateur, Mayfair, London

SERVINGS: 4 | PREP TIME: 20 MINS | COOK TIME: 45 MINS | SKILL LEVEL: 2 (MODERATE)

Wild sea trout is such a beautiful seafood. It has a short season — April to July is the perfect time for eating it, just when the wild samphire comes into its own as well. These are unique, very fine-flavoured ingredients, enjoyed for that moment in time; I think that's what makes this dish so special.

INGREDIENTS

For the butter sauce
1 shallot, finely diced
50 ml (1½ fl oz) white wine
50 ml (1½ fl oz) white wine vinegar
200 g (7 oz) butter, diced
lemon juice, to taste

1 whole sea trout, gutted, scaled, fins removed, head on or off whichever you prefer (ask your fishmonger to do this)
a little vegetable oil, for frying
about 500 g (18 oz) mixed coastal greens, such as samphire, sea purslane, sea beet and/or sea splurry
50 g (1½ oz) butter, cubed
a squeeze of lemon juice

GF

METHOD

First, make the butter sauce. Put the shallot into a heavy-based pan with the white wine and vinegar. Allow the mixture to bubble up, until the liquid has reduced to a glaze. Turn the heat down low and vigorously whisk in the butter, piece by piece. Season with salt and add lemon juice to taste. Pass through a sieve into a clean bowl and keep warm.

Pre-heat the oven to 220°C/425°F/gas 7. Season the fish. Use the biggest roasting tray that will fit into your oven. Pour in a little vegetable oil, put the tray on the hob and when hot, put in the fish. Colour it on both sides, then transfer the tray to the oven and cook for 20–25 minutes. To check whether the fish is ready, insert the tip of a small knife as far as the bone, withdraw it and check that it is hot.

Have a pan of boiling salted water ready, and just before you take the fish out of the oven, lower the coastal greens in. Cook for 1 minute, then drain in a colander, put in a warmed bowl and toss with the butter, black pepper, salt and a squeeze of lemon juice.

Transfer the fish to a big carving board or plate, cut into pieces and serve with the greens, a bowl of new potatoes, if you like, and the sauce separately.

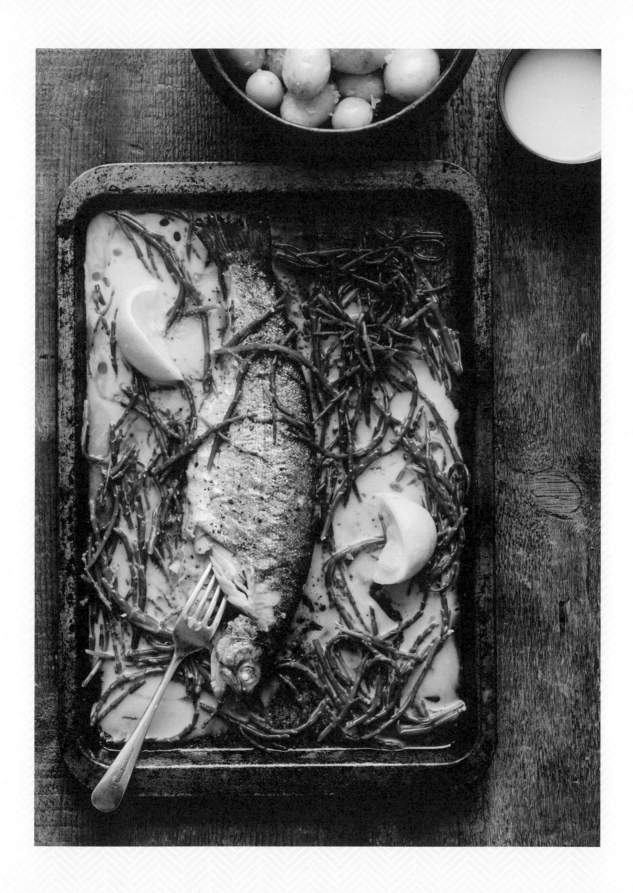

MUSSELS IN PERNOD WITH GARLIC FRITES

Recipe by **MARK SARGEANT**, chef, food writer & restaurateur, Folkestone, Kent

SERVINGS: 4 | **PREP TIME: 45 MINS** | **COOK TIME: 30 MINS** | **SKILL LEVEL: I (EASY)**

Ah, moules et frites — a dish with the ability to make you feel you're on holiday wherever you are and whatever mood you're in. For this recipe I have swapped the wine for Pernod, a drink I always have for elevenses when holidaying in France. You need nice large mussels for this. They should be sweet and juicy as well as giving lots of juice to soak up with crusty bread. The fries are tossed in butter, garlic and parsley once crisp — another trick I picked up from Boodle's gentlemen's club.

INGREDIENTS

25 g (1 oz) unsalted butter

2 leeks, trimmed and thinly sliced

1 bulb fennel, trimmed and thinly sliced

1 clove garlic, peeled and crushed

2 kg (4½ lb) fresh mussels, cleaned

80 ml (2½ fl oz) Pernod

85 ml (2¾ fl oz) double cream

sea salt and freshly ground black pepper

For the garlic frites

vegetable oil, for frying

4 Maris Piper potatoes, peeled and cut into matchsticks

50 g (1½ oz) salted butter

2 cloves garlic, peeled and crushed

2 tbsp chopped fresh flat-leaf parsley leaves

GF

METHOD

Melt the butter in a saucepan large enough to hold the mussels. Add the leek, fennel and garlic and fry gently for about 5 minutes, until the vegetables are softened. Add the mussels to the pan, cover tightly and cook over a medium heat for 4–5 minutes, until the shells open, shaking the pan occasionally. Stir in the Pernod and 125 ml (4 fl oz) water, then bring back to the boil. Discard any unopened mussels. Carefully pour the cooking liquid into a small pan and set the covered pan of mussels aside. Stir the cream into the cooking liquid and heat gently without boiling. Season to taste with sea salt and freshly ground black pepper.

Meanwhile, heat the oil to 140°C (275°F) and fry the potatoes in the usual fashion until they are soft, then drain and turn the heat up to 180°C (350°F). Place a large frying pan on the heat and melt the butter, then add the garlic and fry for a few minutes. Dip the chips back in the oil to crisp up, then drain well before tossing them into the garlic butter. Throw the chopped parsley in and toss well again, so the chips are covered in the lovely buttery mixture. Remove to a suitable dish to serve with the mussels and enjoy.

HAKE FILLET
WITH GOLDEN BEET & RADISH SALAD

Recipe by **SIMON ROGAN**, L'Enclume, Cartmel, Cumbria

SERVINGS: 4 | PREP TIME: 25 MINS | COOK TIME: 45 MINS | SKILL LEVEL: I (EASY)

INGREDIENTS

4 hake escallops, weighing
  100 g (3½ oz) each
300 g (10½ oz) golden
  beetroot
1 tbsp cider vinegar
2 tbsp rapeseed oil
1 bunch radishes, trimmed
  and sliced
2 tbsp plain, unsweetened
  yoghurt
3 tbsp mayonnaise
10 g (2 tbsp) chopped parsley
5 g (1 tbsp) chopped mint
5 g (1 tbsp) chopped chives
watercress leaves and
  rapeseed oil, to serve

GF

METHOD

Rinse the fish under cold water and dry on paper towels. Cook the beetroots in their skins in boiling salted water until you can pierce them easily with a knife. Refresh in ice water, peel, cut into 2 cm (¾ in) dice and put into a salad bowl. Mix the beetroot with the cider vinegar and 1 tablespoon of rapeseed oil and then toss the sliced radishes in. Fold in the yoghurt, mayonnaise and all the herbs, and season with salt and pepper.

Season the fish with salt and pepper on both sides and fry in a large heated frying pan with the other tablespoon of rapeseed oil. Cook for 2–3 minutes on one side, flip it over and cook for another 30 seconds on the other. Place a heap of your salad in the middle of a plate and place the hake on top. Finish by scattering some fresh watercress and a drizzle of rapeseed oil over the top.

ALDO ZILLI
CHEF & TV PRESENTER

I created this cod recipe when I was losing weight for the television show *Celebrity Fit Club*, about 15 years ago. The other contestants couldn't get enough of it, and we ate it nearly every day. It's got a very small amount of calories, so it's a great, healthy dish and my customers love it.

Aldo

Covent Garden, London

BAKED COD
WITH OLIVE CRUST & LENTILS

Recipe by **ALDO ZILLI**, chef & TV presenter, London

SERVINGS: 4 | PREP TIME: 15 MINS | COOK TIME: 40 MINS | SKILL LEVEL: 1 (EASY)

Cod is the traditional choice for fish and chips, but this is a lighter way to cook it. So, no more deep-frying! Mackerel makes a tasty and cheaper alternative.

INGREDIENTS

100 ml (3½ fl oz) extra-
virgin olive oil
1 carrot, diced
1 celery stalk, diced
1 onion, diced
500 g (1 lb 1 oz) Puy lentils
2 bay leaves
1½ litres (3 pints) vegetable
stock
1 tbsp breadcrumbs
1 tsp fresh rosemary leaves
1 tsp fresh thyme leaves
100 g (3½ oz) black olives
4 cod fillets (about 180 g/
6 oz each)

DF

METHOD

Heat half the oil in a large pan and add the diced vegetables. Cook until soft, about 3–4 minutes, stirring to ensure they don't stick. Add the lentils and bay leaves, stir a couple of times, then add the stock and cook gently until it has been absorbed by the lentils (about 30 minutes). Keep warm.

Pre-heat the oven to 180°C/160°C fan/350°F/gas 4.

In a food processor, blend the remaining oil with the breadcrumbs, herbs and black olives until you have a smooth mix.

Place the cod in a roasting tray and divide the olive mixture between the fillets, pressing it down with your fingers over the top and making sure you have an even distribution of the mix. Bake in the oven for 7–8 minutes. Serve the fish on top of the lentils.

BLACK PUDDING
& SMOKED HADDOCK HASH

Recipe by **HENRY HARRIS**, chef & importer of fine brandies and digestifs, London & Warwickshire

SERVINGS: 4 | **PREP TIME: 15 MINS** | **COOK TIME: 15 MINS** | **SKILL LEVEL: 1 (EASY)**

INGREDIENTS

500 ml (18 fl oz) milk

1 bay leaf

500 g (18 oz) smoked haddock, trimmed and skin removed

50 g (1½ oz) clarified butter

2 small red onions, finely chopped

300 g (10½ oz) cooked new potatoes, thickly sliced

2 black puddings, peeled and cut into 1 cm (½ in) slices

4 hard-boiled eggs, peeled and quartered

3 tbsp red wine vinegar

2 tbsp Worcestershire sauce

½ bunch of parsley, chopped

1 tbsp grain mustard

1 tbsp Dijon mustard

a few generous spoonfuls of hollandaise sauce, to serve

GF

METHOD

Bring the milk and bay leaf to the boil in a saucepan. Slide in the haddock. Bring back to the boil, remove from the heat and set aside, uncovered.

Melt the butter in a skillet and sauté the onions briskly for 2–3 minutes; you want them to colour lightly but still retain some crunch. Add the potatoes and black pudding, stirring so they are well heated through and lightly coloured. Add the eggs, vinegar and Worcestershire sauce and cook for a further minute. Add the parsley and, using a fish slice, lay the haddock on top. Toss the pan, or fold the haddock in with a large spoon. Heat through and check the seasoning, though it is unlikely to need any.

Stir the mustard into the hollandaise sauce and thin down with a little hot water. Spoon the hash onto four plates and drizzle the hollandaise over the top.

POU

MEAT

LTRY,

& GAME

MELISSA & JASMINE HEMSLEY
CHEFS & AUTHORS

This recipe is the new way to spaghetti Bolognese!
As a nutritious alternative to pasta, we use courgetti
– long strands of raw courgette cut using a spiralizer
or julienne peeler. If you don't have one of these, try a
vegetable peeler for very wide ribbons, pappardelle-style.

Melissa + Jasmine

*Mayfair,
London*

COURGETTI & BEEF RAGÙ

Recipe by **MELISSA & JASMINE HEMSLEY**, chefs & authors, Mayfair, London

SERVINGS: 4 | **PREP TIME: 45 MINS** | **COOK TIME: 2¾ HOURS** | **SKILL LEVEL: 1 (EASY)**

For our beef ragù, we like to add as many vegetables as possible to make the meaty sauce go further, even using courgettes again and carrots for added sweetness. It's also a good place to hide a nutritious chicken liver — finely dice and cook the liver with the sauce for a rich flavour.

INGREDIENTS

2 tbsp ghee or butter

2 onions, finely chopped

4 cloves garlic, diced

2 dried bay leaves

¼ tsp mixed spice (or try a tiny pinch of nutmeg)

2 tsp dried oregano

400 g (14 oz) minced beef (chuck or braising steak and don't go for lean meat)

a large glass of red wine, about 250 ml (9 fl oz)

14 large tomatoes, roughly chopped, or 2 x 400 g (14 oz) cans of chopped tomatoes or 800 g (1 lb 12 oz) passata

2 tsp tomato purée

200 ml (7 fl oz) bone broth or water (you won't need as much if using canned tomatoes)

2 large carrots, finely grated

a large handful of fresh parsley, finely chopped

4 large courgettes

a knob of butter

To serve

extra-virgin olive oil

2 handfuls of grated Parmesan

GF

METHOD

Heat the ghee or butter in a large saucepan, and gently fry the onion over a low heat until softened but not browned (about 10 minutes). Add the garlic, bay leaves, mixed spice, oregano (and any other herbs that you choose) and fry for a further 2 minutes.

Increase the heat and add the beef to the pan, using a wooden spatula to break it up as you cook.

After 5 minutes, pour in the red wine and stir to deglaze the pan, then add the tomatoes, tomato purée and bone broth or water.

Bring to the boil, cover with a lid, leaving the lid just slightly off, then reduce to a gentle simmer, stirring occasionally, for 2½ hours until rich and thickened. It is even better after 3–4 hours — keep an eye on it and add more liquid if needed.

Add the grated carrots 15 minutes before the end of cooking. Turn up the heat to a medium simmer and season with sea salt, a good grind of pepper and the fresh parsley.

Meanwhile, use a spiralizer or julienne peeler to make the courgetti. Or use a regular vegetable peeler to slice the courgettes lengthways into very wide ribbons, which you can then slice in half. You might also want to cut the long strands in half to make them easier to eat.

Soften the courgetti in a pan with a little butter, stirring over a low heat for 3 minutes. Alternatively, save washing up another pan by just running some of the hot sauce through your spirals — the heat and salt in the sauce will soften them.

Drizzle each bowl of courgetti and ragù with extra-virgin olive oil and serve with Parmesan for everyone to help themselves.

KEFTEDES

RICK STEIN'S VEAL, MINT & OREGANO MEATBALLS IN A RICH TOMATO SAUCE

Recipe by **RICK STEIN OBE**, chef, food writer & TV presenter, Padstow, Cornwall

SERVINGS: 4–8 | **PREP TIME: 30 MINS** | **COOK TIME: 45 MINS** | **SKILL LEVEL: I (EASY)**

Don't we all love meatballs? This recipe comes from a tavern that was part of a farmhouse near Pylos, by the bay of Navarino, run by Nakos, Saini and Saini's wife, Georgia, who did the cooking for the tavern. While the kitchen was being set up for filming, I wandered through the farm and was accosted by an angry dog who barked ferociously then came roaring up to me wagging his tail. A bit like Chalky but bigger and fiercer, though not really fierce. Beyond the kennel was a vegetable garden filled with ripe aubergines, tomatoes, courgettes and okra. I could feel a piece-to-camera coming on, in which I say I am a little bit jaundiced by the view through the windows of an elegant restaurant into a carefully manicured vegetable garden. This scruffy but delightful garden, full of ripeness, guarded by a dog whose bark was worse than its bite, is what country restaurants should be like.

INGREDIENTS

500 g (1 lb 2 oz) minced veal
  (or beef)

150 g (5 oz) coarse breadcrumbs

1 egg, beaten

a handful of mint leaves, chopped

1 tsp dried oregano

1 onion, grated

10 g (2) cloves garlic, crushed or
  grated

50 ml (1½ fl oz) olive oil, plus extra
  for frying

30 ml (1 fl oz) white wine

1 tsp salt

12 grinds black pepper

plain flour, for coating

For the tomato sauce

60 ml (2 fl oz) olive oil

6 tomatoes, roughly chopped

1 tsp salt

12 grinds black pepper

1 stick cinnamon

METHOD

In a large bowl, mix together the meat, breadcrumbs, egg, mint, oregano, onion, garlic, olive oil, white wine, salt and pepper. With your hands, roll into golfball-sized meatballs and flatten slightly. Dust lightly in flour and fry in olive oil over a medium heat for 3–4 minutes per side, turning frequently to cook evenly.

In a separate pan over a medium heat, warm the olive oil for the tomato sauce, then add the tomatoes, salt, pepper and cinnamon, and cook gently for 20 minutes to make a pulpy sauce. Add the meatballs to the sauce, re-heat for 5 minutes and serve.

SPATCHCOCK POUSSINS WITH SWEET CHILLI & YOGHURT MARINADE

Recipe by **ALLEGRA McEVEDY** MBE, chef, writer & broadcaster, London

SERVINGS: 2 | **PREP TIME: 25 MINS PLUS CHILLING** | **COOK TIME: 30 MINS** | **SKILL LEVEL: I (EASY)**

Roughly speaking, poussins are handy portion-sized young chickens, and although they're cute just roasted whole, flattening them out ('spatchcocking') allows more of the skin to get crispy... and we all know how heavenly crispy chicken skin is. With the addition of this no-brainer marinade, it goes simply stratospheric.

INGREDIENTS

3 tbsp Greek or natural yoghurt
3 tbsp sweet chilli sauce
2 poussins, spatchcocked
 (ask your butcher to do this)

To serve
long-grain rice
a small bunch of coriander,
 chopped
2 limes, halved
green salad
Tabasco sauce (optional)

GF

METHOD

In a large bowl, stir together the yoghurt and sweet chilli sauce with some salt and pepper. Drop in the birds and use your hands to give them a thorough coating all over.

Cover the bowl with clingfilm and put it in the fridge for 15 minutes to 1 hour.

Pre-heat the oven to 210°C/190°C fan/gas 6½ and get your rice going.

Lay the birds, skin-side up, on an oiled baking or roasting tray. Use the palm of your hand to press down on them so they are as flat as possible. Give them another light season with salt and pepper and roast for 25–30 minutes, until they are deliciously golden and the juices run clear when you insert a knife into the base of the thigh joint.

When the rice is cooked, stir through most of the coriander along with a squeeze of lime juice. Serve with the green salad, halved limes, a scattering of the remaining coriander on top and Tabasco alongside.

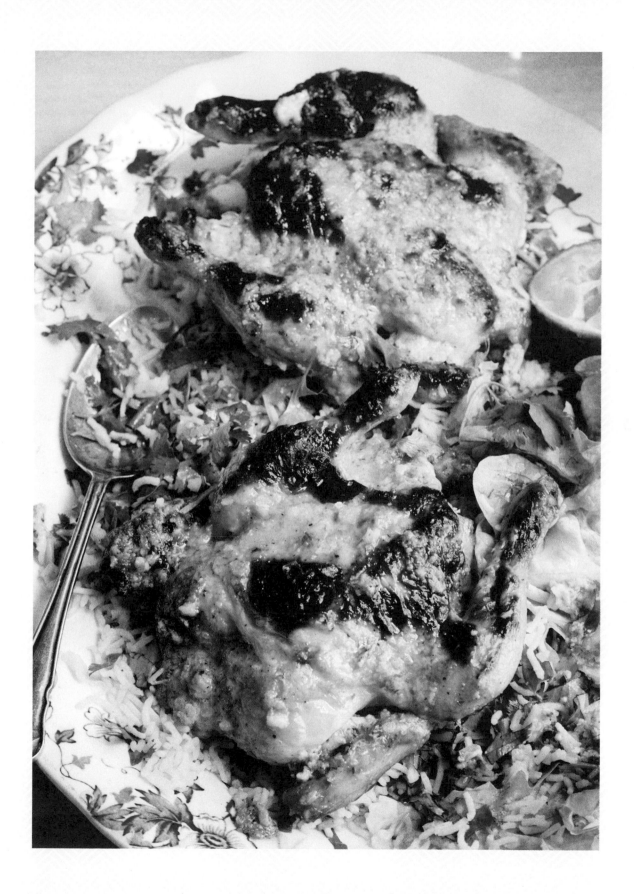

TAGLIATA DI MANZO

THINLY SLICED RARE PAN-FRIED BEEF WITH BALSAMIC-DRESSED SALAD

Recipe by **THEO RANDALL**, Theo Randall at the InterContinental, Mayfair, London

SERVINGS: 4 | PREP TIME: 5 MINS | COOK TIME: 5 MINS | SKILL LEVEL: I (EASY)

This is a great way to serve a seared piece of fillet. The crusting of the thyme and sea salt on the outside gives it a lovely flavour and texture. Being such a simple dish, it is all about good-quality ingredients — the tomatoes should be sweet and the Parmesan fresh. If you have some good balsamic vinegar, use it on this because it will work really well with the other ingredients.

INGREDIENTS

1 x 500 g (1 lb 2 oz) piece of beef fillet (tail)
4 tbsp extra-virgin olive oil
1 tsp chopped thyme
150 g (5 oz) datterini or cherry tomatoes, cut into quarters
100 g (3½ oz) wild rocket
juice of ½ lemon
1 tsp aged balsamic vinegar
75 g (2½ oz) Parmesan shavings

GF

METHOD

Rub the fillet with 1 tablespoon of olive oil, then sprinkle the thyme over and season with salt and pepper.

Heat a heavy-based frying pan. Add the fillet and cook for 3–4 minutes, turning frequently to ensure an even searing that gives the meat a browned crust. Remove from the pan and leave to rest for 3 minutes.

Meanwhile, combine the tomatoes and rocket in a large bowl. Add the remaining olive oil and the lemon juice. Season to taste. Toss together gently, then spread the tomatoes and rocket on a large plate.

Slice the beef thinly and arrange on top of the tomatoes and rocket. Drizzle the balsamic vinegar over the beef and add a grinding of black pepper. Finish with the Parmesan shavings.

ROAST PARTRIDGES WITH CABBAGE & JERUSALEM ARTICHOKES

Recipe by **JEREMY LEE**, Quo Vadis, Soho, London

SERVINGS: 6 | **PREP TIME: 30 MINS PLUS RESTING** | **COOK TIME: 45 MINS** | **SKILL LEVEL: 1 (EASY)**

INGREDIENTS

75 g (2½ oz) unsalted butter, plus 150 g (5 oz) softened butter to liberally spread over each bird

2 small onions

1 medium-sized carrot

2 sticks celery

150 g (5 oz) piece very good-quality smoked streaky bacon

2 sprigs thyme

2 bay leaves

1 large head Savoy cabbage

150 g (5 oz) Jerusalem artichokes

6 partridges (grey leg if you can find them)

sea salt and a fully charged pepper mill

GF

METHOD

Pre-heat the oven to 200°C/400°F/gas 6.

Take a wide-bottomed, heavy braising pot and sit it upon a gentle heat. Melt the butter therein.

Peel the onions and chop small; likewise the carrot and then the celery. Tip these into the butter and let cook gently for 20 minutes or so, until softened. Cut away and reserve the rind and any bony nodules within the bacon. Slice the bacon, not too thinly, and then cut into small strips. Add these to the pot and stir within the vegetables. Lay out the piece of bacon rind and wrap the herbs and nodules of bacon in it and tie very well. Add it to the pot. Place a lid upon the pot and let cook for a further 20 minutes or so. Stir from time to time.

Snap off and discard any limp outer leaves from the cabbage. Cut away any excess root and throw this away too. Cut the cabbage, through the root, into six pieces; this to keep the cabbage intact whilst cooking. Gently slide the cabbage pieces into the vegetables, pushing here and there to have the cabbage settle, sitting side by side. Add a cup of water to the pot and cover, letting sit and steam gently over a gentle heat.

Peel the Jerusalem artichokes and cut into slices about 1 cm (½ in) thick. Rinse these well. Lift up the lid of the pot and push the slices down into the vegetables, between the pieces of cabbage. Add a little more water if the vegetables seem to be drying up. Place the lid back on top and let cook for a further half an hour or so, lifting the lid from time to time to see that all is well and the pan is not drying up at all. Once done and the artichokes are softened, and indeed the cabbage also, set aside, keeping warm.

Liberally butter each partridge and sit upon a roasting tray. Grind pepper over the birds and also some sea salt.

Place in the oven and cook for 15 minutes. Remove the birds from the oven and sit them on the cabbage and pour over any juices accumulated upon the tray. Place the lid back upon the pot and let sit, keeping warm for a further half hour or so.

POACHED CHICKEN
WITH SAFFRON SAUCE & CUCUMBER

Recipe by **SIMON HOPKINSON**, chef, food writer & TV presenter, Brook Green, London

SERVINGS: 2 | **PREP TIME: 45 MINS** | **COOK TIME: 1 HOUR 50 MINS** | **SKILL LEVEL: 2 (MODERATE)**

INGREDIENTS

For the chicken

1 x 1½ kg (3 lb 6 oz) chicken, preferably corn-fed

1 onion, stuck with 3 cloves

2 sticks celery, chopped

1 carrot, thickly sliced

1 leek, cleaned, trimmed and thickly sliced

2 large tomatoes, roughly chopped

2–3 sprigs thyme

a small bunch of parsley, roughly chopped

250 ml (9 fl oz) dry white wine

For cooking the cucumbers and making the sauce

300 ml (11 fl oz) of the chicken broth

4–6 small cucumbers, depending on size, or 1 medium-sized cucumber, halved and each half cut into quarters lengthways

2 tsp pastis (optional, but for me essential)

25 g (1 oz) butter

2 rounded tsp flour

1 tsp saffron threads

100 ml (3½ fl oz) double cream

a small squeeze of lemon juice (optional)

METHOD

Put the chicken into a roomy pot, breast-side up, and make sure there is enough room around the bird to also accommodate the flavouring vegetables and herbs. Add these, then pour in the wine and sprinkle a little salt over. Pour in enough water so that it does not entirely cover the chicken; try to leave the breasts about a quarter exposed, because the leg and thigh joints (immersed in liquid) take much longer to cook than the breasts will, effectively, steam.

Place over a moderate heat and allow to come up to a simmer. When a fair amount of unsightly grey scum has accumulated on the surface, start to skim this off with a large spoon until almost none remains; a little more will be generated throughout the cooking time, but remove when and if necessary. Now let the chicken cook very gently for 45–50 minutes, covered. Keep a keen eye on the proceedings, as you only want the broth to blip gently, not boil. After the time has elapsed, switch off the heat and leave to rest in the broth, still covered, for a further 15 minutes.

Lift out the bird, remove any bits of stray vegetable matter and place the bird on a dish. Strain the broth into a bowl using a fine sieve and discard the exhausted vegetables. Wipe out the original cooking pot and return the chicken to it. Return the cooking broth to the chicken in its pot and keep warm, covered.

To cook the cucumber, first measure off about 300 ml (11 fl oz) of the broth surrounding the chicken. Put the cucumber into a medium-sized saucepan that will accommodate it snugly. Pour over the broth, add the pastis (if using) and simmer the cucumber until tender when poked with a skewer; it should be soft, but not on the verge of collapse. Remove the pieces with a slotted spoon and put them in the remaining broth surrounding the chicken, to keep warm. Keep the cucumber cooking liquid to hand.

To make the saffron sauce, melt the butter in another small saucepan and stir in the flour to make a roux. Cook for a minute or two, then start to whisk in the cucumber cooking liquid until smooth and beginning to thicken. Allow to simmer very gently, stirring regularly, for about 10 minutes, before sprinkling in the saffron. Stir it in (don't use a whisk, as all the saffron stamens will become entangled in it); switch off the heat and cover the pan, allowing the saffron to infuse in the sauce for about 5 minutes. Now add the cream and a little salt and pepper, and let it come back to a simmer. Add a squeeze of lemon juice, for a sharper edge to the sauce.

To serve, take the chicken from the pot and carve off the breasts. Remove the skin from each breast and cut the chicken in slanting slices. Lay on two hot plates, arrange the cucumber alongside and spoon plenty of the saffron sauce over. Some small, peeled new potatoes would be very nice here, too, if you wished.

JAMES RAMSDEN
WITH THOM RAMSDEN
FOOD WRITER & RESTAURATEUR

If I had to describe my cooking style, I'd call it modern British home cooking. I like doing something a little bit different — I think it's fun to play around with ingredients, while paying respect to the wonderful produce we have in this country. This recipe is a bit of a twist on the classic lamb and anchovy theme. And while I'm not sure a toddler should be eating lamb and clams yet, Thom's quite an adventurous little guy so he will usually sit at the table banging his fist until he gets to try some.

Homerton,
London

STUFFED SHOULDER OF LAMB
WITH COCKLES OR CLAMS

Recipe by **JAMES RAMSDEN**, food writer & restaurateur, Homerton, London

SERVINGS: 6–8 | **PREP TIME: 45 MINS PLUS RESTING** | **COOK TIME: 3½ HOURS** | **SKILL LEVEL: 2 (MODERATE)**

The union of lamb and seafood — particularly bivalves, though notably also anchovies — is one of the most perfect in all of cooking. Lamb's natural sweetness against the salty, ozone tang of a wobbly mollusc makes as much sense as potatoes and cream, or ham and mustard. Ask your butcher to butterfly the lamb shoulder for you, or buy a ready-boned shoulder from the supermarket. You'll need some kitchen string to tie it up once you've stuffed it; there are useful videos online if you'd like visual guidance on tying up boned joints of meat, but don't worry if it doesn't look particularly professional — as long as it holds its shape it's fine. It's something that's worth doing well in advance. And while the lamb's in the oven, you've got 2 or 3 hours to organize the rest of your menu. I serve it with a courgette gratin, flageolet bean salad, or lentils with feta, rocket, chilli and croutons.

INGREDIENTS

olive oil
250 g (9 oz) unsmoked streaky
  bacon, chopped
2 onions, finely chopped
4 cloves garlic, crushed to a paste

1 tsp chopped thyme leaves
400 g (14 oz) chard, leaves stripped
  from stalks and chopped (discard
  the stalks)
1 shoulder of lamb, boned and
  butterflied

500 g (1 lb 2 oz) cockles or clams
100 ml (3½ fl oz or 7 tbsp) dry white wine
a small handful of parsley, finely chopped

DF, GF

METHOD

Heat a little oil in a large-ish saucepan; add the bacon and fry until crisp. Add the onion and a good pinch of salt and pepper; cover and cook over a low heat for 10 minutes, until softened. Add the garlic and thyme; stir for a minute, then add the chard. Cover and cook for 8 minutes until fully wilted, then take off the heat and leave to cool.

When the stuffing is completely cooled, lay the lamb shoulder out flat, skin-side down. Season the lamb with salt and pepper, then spread with the stuffing and roll up, tying tightly with string. Refrigerate until needed — or proceed, skipping the next step.

Remove the lamb from the fridge: it must be at room temperature before cooking.

Pre-heat the oven to 220°C/425°F/gas 7. Rub the outside of the lamb with salt, pepper and olive oil, and put in a roasting pan. Cook for 30 minutes, then turn the oven down to 160°C/325°F/gas 3 and roast for a further 2½ hours. Remove from the oven and rest in a warm place.

Pick through the cockles or clams and discard any that have broken shells or that remain open after a gentle tap. Put them in a bowl and cover with cold water. Leave for 20 minutes, then lift out the cockles (don't tip them into a colander, as this will only chuck the grit back over them).

Put a large pan over a medium heat and add a splash of oil. After 30 seconds, throw in the cockles and wine. Cover and leave for 5 minutes, shaking occasionally, until the clams have opened. Toss in the parsley and stir.

Cut the lamb into thick chunks and serve with the cockles and a good spoonful of the cockle cooking liquor.

TIPS

The stuffing can be oomphed up with the likes of chopped anchovies, black olives and chilli. If you can't find chard, use spinach or spring greens. This recipe would also work well with a rolled leg of lamb. And, of course, you can omit the cockles/clams if you can't find any.

Fry a spoonful of ras el hanout (a North African spice mix found in most supermarkets these days) in a little oil, and then add slices of the leftover lamb and a small glass of wine. Cover and cook for 20 minutes until soft and warm. Serve with couscous and a dollop of yoghurt.

BRITISH CHICKEN 'MUSAKHAN'

Recipe by **CAT ASHTON**, Paradise by Way of Kensal Green, Queen's Park, London

SERVINGS: 4 | **PREP TIME: 25 MINS PLUS MARINATING** | **COOK TIME: 40 MINS** | **SKILL LEVEL: 2 (MODERATE)**

INGREDIENTS

For the chicken

2 cloves garlic, crushed with
  ½ tsp salt
½ tsp ground cardamom
½ tsp dried chilli flakes
½ tsp dried oregano
½ tsp freshly ground black
  pepper
2 tbsp olive oil, plus extra for
  drizzling
4 boneless chicken thighs

For the spinach

3 tbsp olive oil
2 onions, finely chopped
2 cloves garlic, thinly sliced
2 tsp ground cinnamon
1 tsp ground allspice
1 tsp sumac
3 bags large spinach leaves
  (blanched, squeezed and
  chopped well)
200 g (7 oz) cooked chickpeas
150 ml (5 fl oz) chicken stock

4 large wholemeal flat-breads
  (tortillas or pitta breads)

For the whipped feta

200 g (7 oz) feta, diced
200 g (7 oz) yoghurt
1 small clove garlic, minced
1 tsp Dijon mustard
squirt of olive oil

METHOD

To prepare the chicken, mix together the garlic, spices and olive oil and then rub all over the chicken. Leave in the fridge to marinate for a few hours.

For the spinach, heat the oil in a large pan and sauté the onion and garlic until soft (about 5–7 minutes), then stir in the spices. Add the spinach and chickpeas and turn up the heat to high. Stir through the stock, and cook for a few minutes until tender and the stock has been incorporated. Season with salt and pepper to taste and set aside to cool.

Pre-heat the oven to 200°C/400°F/gas 6 and line a baking tray with baking paper.

Lay the flat-bread on your work surface and place a big spoon of the spinach mix in the centre, placing the marinated chicken on top. Season with salt and pepper and fold the flat-bread, wrapping up the chicken into a little parcel with string.

Place on the baking tray, drizzle with olive oil, sprinkle over some sea salt and bake for 25–30 minutes, until the chicken is cooked through and the musakhan parcels are golden.

For the whipped feta, place all ingredients in a blender and blend until smooth. Pour the feta sauce into four shallow bowls, placing the musakhan on top. Drizzle with olive oil and sprinkle with a little extra salt, sumac and chilli flakes.

'LAMBCHETTA' A LA GREQUE

GREEK-STYLE STUFFED & ROLLED ROASTED LAMB

Recipe by **THEODORE KYRIAKOU**, The Greek Larder, Kings Cross, London

SERVINGS: 6 | **PREP TIME: 40 MINS PLUS CHILLING OVERNIGHT & RESTING** | **COOK TIME: 1 HOUR 20 MINS**
SKILL LEVEL: 2 (MODERATE)

Lamb is a classic at Easter, particularly leg of lamb. Ask your butcher to bone and butterfly it for you so to be a dream to stuff and carve it.

INGREDIENTS

For the stuffing

2 tbsp fennel seeds, toasted
  and ground
1 bunch flat-leaf parsley, chopped
1 tbsp fresh oregano leaves,
  finely chopped
2 cloves garlic, finely chopped
200 g (7 oz) rocket, finely chopped
50 g (1½ oz) dried sour cherries,
  finely chopped

200 g (7 oz) cooked chestnuts,
  finely chopped
1 tsp ground cinnamon
zest of 1 lemon
zest of 1 orange
60 ml (2 fl oz) olive oil

For the lambchetta

2½ kg (5½ lb) leg of lamb,
  boned and butterflied

fine sea salt, for seasoning
butcher's string
vegetables to scatter around the
  lamb (2 carrots, peeled and cut
  in half lengthways; 2 banana
  shallots, peeled and sliced in half;
  and 4 celery sticks)
100 ml (3½ fl oz) boiling water

DF, GF

METHOD

Prepare the lambchetta a day in advance of serving. Pat the lamb dry. Combine all the stuffing ingredients in a large bowl and mix well to combine. Lay the lamb out, skin-side down, on a flat surface. Patch any holes with slices of meat from the edge. Evenly spread the stuffing over the meat, reserving about 1 tablespoon. Beginning with the long end, roll up the lamb as tightly as you can, enclosing the stuffing. Snugly tie crosswise at 3 cm (1¼ in) intervals and around the length, with butcher's string.

Salt the skin with fine sea salt. Coat the ends of the rolled joint with the remaining stuffing, then place on a wire rack over a roasting tin and refrigerate overnight, uncovered.

Remove the rolled joint from the fridge and let it stand at room temperature for an hour. Pre-heat the oven to 170°C/325°F/gas 3.

Cover the ends of the rolled joint with tinfoil, scatter the vegetables around the lamb and pour 100 ml (3½ fl oz) of boiling water in the roasting tin under the joint. The vegetables surrounding the lamb not only absorb some of the lamb juices but also turn them very nutritious and flavoursome. Roast the lambchetta for 80 minutes, or until an instant-read thermometer inserted into the centre of the thickest part registers 62°C (144°F) should you prefer eating lamb medium.

Remove from the oven, allow to rest for at least 30 minutes, then serve with the roasted vegetables, drizzled with the roasting juices.

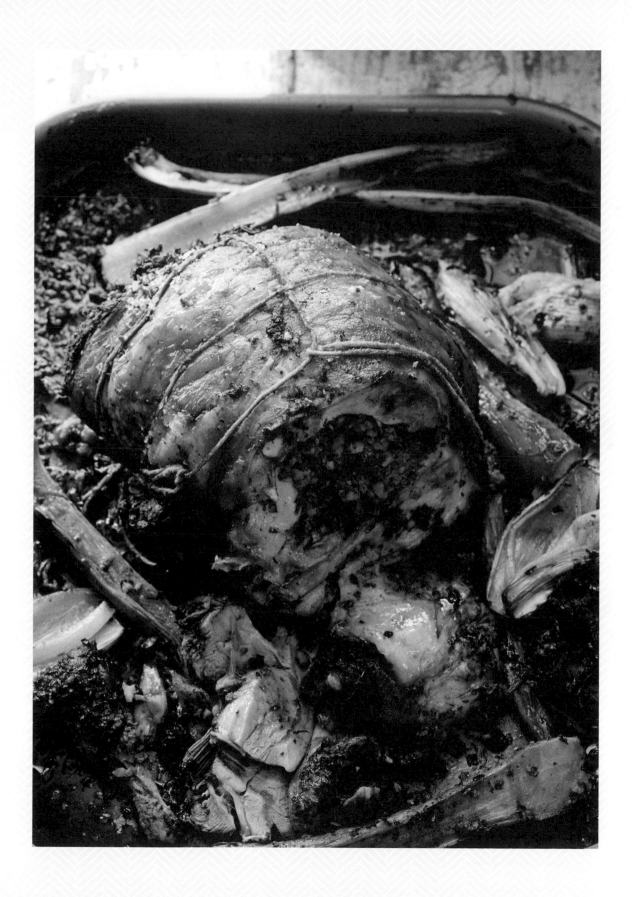

ROASTED SHAVED BEEF FLANK, HORSERADISH CARAMEL, RAINBOW CARROT SALSA

Recipe by **RICHARD & OLIVER GLADWIN**, Rabbit, Chelsea, London

SERVINGS: 6 | **PREP TIME: I HOUR** | **COOK TIME: 45 MINS** | **SKILL LEVEL: 2 (MODERATE)**

INGREDIENTS

600 g (1 lb 5 oz) flank of beef
  (onglet or hanger)

For the coriander and thyme salt

1 tbsp coriander seeds, toasted and blitzed

1 tbsp of picked thyme leaves (save the
  stalks to add to the caramel)

1 tbsp Maldon sea salt

For the beef dripping emulsion

3 egg yolks

20 g (¾ oz) Dijon mustard

15 ml (1 tbsp) sherry vinegar

10 ml (2 tsp) honey

100 ml (3½ fl oz) oil

150 ml (5 fl oz) beef dripping
  (see method)

50 ml (1½ fl oz) water

For the horseradish caramel

100 g (3½ oz) caster sugar

35 g (1¼ oz) butter

1 clove garlic, crushed

100 g (3½ oz) peeled, grated
  horseradish

100 ml (3½ oz) veal stock

10 ml (2 tsp) brandy

For the rainbow carrot salsa

100 g (3½ oz) purple carrot

100 g (3½ oz) orange carrot

100 g (3½ oz) white carrot

100 ml (3½ fl oz) rapeseed oil
  (or green parsley oil)

15 ml (1 tbsp) apple cider vinegar

50 g (1¾ oz) washed rapeseeds
  (these are not easy to come by so
  if you can't find them, use toasted
  black mustard seeds or poppy
  seeds)

25 g (1 oz) finely chopped parsley

a handful of tarragon leaves, picked

GF

METHOD

Set up a charcoal grill well in advance so that the coals are glowing red-hot for searing the beef. (You could also use a very hot grill pan on the stove.)

Pre-heat the oven to 180°C/160°C fan/350°F/gas 4. Trim the beef flank, keeping all the trimmings. Roast the trimmings in the oven for 25 minutes and reserve the drippings for the emulsion. If the flank is too lean, buy drippings from your butcher.

Meanwhile, make the coriander and thyme salt by mixing together the coriander, thyme leaves and salt.

Season the flank steak, also known as onglet or hanger steak, well with the coriander and thyme salt and a kiss of oil. Sear really well on the very hot charcoal grill. Chill as soon as it's off the heat by putting it in the fridge uncovered. This will stop the cooking process.

Make the beef dripping emulsion by whizzing together the egg yolks, mustard, vinegar and honey in the small bowl of a food processor, then gradually adding the oil to make a thick mayo. Then add the dripping and water and whizz until thick and smooth. Season to taste and put into a squeeze bottle or a piping bag.

Make the horseradish caramel by melting the sugar in a dry pan and cooking it to golden bronze. Remove from the heat and quickly add the butter, then the garlic, thyme stalks and horseradish and stir through. Next add the veal stock, and put the caramel back on a low heat to cook for 5 minutes to help infuse. Finally, add the brandy and strain the caramel through a fine sieve.

Make the carrot salsa by finely slicing the carrots into rounds on a mandolin or with a very sharp knife. Add the oil, vinegar and rapeseeds and finish with the parsley.

To serve, shave or very finely slice the beef against the grain of the muscle with the sharpest knife in your kitchen. Cutting against the grain achieves tenderness. Arrange the beef shavings to cover the surface of the plate, drizzle with the caramel and randomly spoon on the carrot salsa. Finish with dollops of dripping emulsion.

Garnish with tarragon leaves to give a bit of height to the plate.

UYEN LUU
AUTHOR & FOOD PHOTOGRAPHER

When I cook I like to use what's on hand in my fridge and what's available seasonally to create a meal that's healthy as well as delicious. I aim for the perfect balance of sweet, sour and salty, as well as beautiful textures and colour. I really love using lots of herbs, and serving herbs as a salad instead of just a garnish – they make everything taste fresh and crunchy and alive.

Uyen

London Fields, London

CÀ RI GÀ

CHICKEN CURRY

Recipe by **UYEN LUU**, author & food photographer, London Fields, London

SERVINGS: 2 | **PREP TIME: 40 MINS** | **COOK TIME: 35 MINS** | **SKILL LEVEL: 1 (EASY)**

Vietnamese curry is fragrant, light and milky, eaten with baguette to kick-start your day. It is more like a stew with chicken, carrots and potato and lots of lemongrass and coconut curry to dip your bread into. You can add more heat and other vegetables to your liking. When I was little, my mother so cleverly saved money and time by cooking a delicious and nutritious meal in one pot. When we couldn't get baguette, she would make white bread toast and butter for us to dip in – it's still one of my most favourite things today.

INGREDIENTS

1 tbsp cooking oil

1 red onion, roughly chopped

1 thumb's worth of fresh ginger, peeled and finely chopped

1 stalk lemongrass, finely diced

2 large chicken legs, cut into bite-sized pieces, or 6 whole drumsticks, skin on

3 tsp curry powder

2 cloves garlic, finely chopped

165 ml (5½ fl oz) coconut milk

300 ml (10½ fl oz) chicken stock

2 medium-sized potatoes, cubed

1 carrot, roughly sliced

4 tbsp fish sauce

1 tsp sugar

ground black pepper (optional)

½ aubergine, cubed

a handful of okra, cut into bite-sized pieces (optional)

6 Asian shallots, peeled

a handful of mange tout (snow peas) (optional)

warm baguette and butter, or steamed rice, to serve

Garnishes (all chopped)

Thai sweet basil

spring onion

bird's-eye chillies

DF, GF

METHOD

Heat the oil in a medium-sized saucepan over a low heat. Gently fry the red onion, ginger and lemongrass. Once the onion has softened, add the chicken legs and fry, turning often, until they're evenly browned.

Add the curry powder, stirring well until the chicken legs are well coated. Add the garlic, coconut milk, chicken stock, potato and carrot, and stir. Cover with a lid and simmer for about 10 minutes.

Season the curry with the fish sauce, sugar and a pinch of black pepper (if wished), then add the aubergine, okra (if using), shallots and mange tout (if using). Cook for a further 8–10 minutes, or until the chicken is cooked through.

Garnish with Thai sweet basil, spring onion and chilli. Serve with a fresh, warm baguette and butter, or a bowl of steamed rice.

VEAL HOLSTEIN

Recipe by **TOM PARKER BOWLES**, food writer & critic, London

SERVINGS: 4 | **PREP TIME: 20 MINS** | **COOK TIME: 10 MINS** | **SKILL LEVEL: 1 (EASY)**

When I see this breadcrumb-clad beauty on the menu, little else matters. I couldn't care less if it's retro, or in or out of fashion. It's a northern European classic, simply schnitzel with added punch — topped with a fried egg, capers and anchovies. The Wolseley in London does a wonderful version, but I wish they wouldn't add the gravy. As for the veal, try to go for British rose veal. It doesn't have quite the same bland tenderness as the Continental milk-fed veal (in fact, it's almost a different product entirely), but as the calves are allowed space to move around and have a more natural, mixed diet, you can eat with conscience clear.

INGREDIENTS

25 g (1 oz) plain flour

a large pinch of mustard powder

6 large eggs

100 g (3½ oz) fresh breadcrumbs

4 veal escalopes (about 150 g/ 5 oz each), bashed between two pieces of clingfilm with a rolling pin until almost paper-thin

150 g (5 oz) unsalted butter

1 tbsp sunflower oil

2 heaped tbsp non-pareil capers, drained

2 tbsp finely chopped fresh parsley

juice of ½ lemon

8 anchovy fillets (the best you can find), drained

METHOD

Season the flour with the mustard powder, salt and pepper, and put it on a plate. Break two of the eggs into a shallow bowl and beat lightly. Put the breadcrumbs in another shallow bowl. Lightly season the veal, dip it in the seasoned flour, then the beaten egg, then the breadcrumbs.

Melt one-third of the butter with the oil in a large, heavy-bottomed frying pan over a medium heat and cook the escalopes, two at a time, until golden — about 1½–2 minutes on each side. Remove and keep warm.

Wipe out the pan with a wad of paper towel; add half the remaining butter and fry the remaining eggs. Top each escalope with a runny-yolked fried egg.

Melt the remaining butter in the pan, add the capers and warm for a few seconds; then remove from the heat and add the parsley and a good squeeze of lemon.

Criss-cross each egg with two anchovy fillets, spoon over the capers and parsley, and serve with French fries or sautéed potatoes.

Covent Garden, London

THE IVY'S MOROCCAN SPICED RUMP OF LAMB WITH HUMMUS, HARISSA & SMOKED AUBERGINE

Recipe by **GARY LEE**, executive chef at The Ivy, Covent Garden, London

SERVINGS: 2 | PREP TIME: 40 MINS PLUS SOAKING | COOK TIME: I HOUR 45 MINS
SKILL LEVEL: 2 (MODERATE)

INGREDIENTS

2 rumps of lamb,
    approx. 200 g (7 oz) each,
    fully trimmed

2 tsp harissa

For the hummus

100 g (3½ oz) raw
    chickpeas, soaked
    overnight in cold water

2 cloves garlic, crushed
    with 1 tsp salt

juice of 1 lemon

60 ml (4 tbsp) tahini paste,
    stirred well

For the dukkah

8 tbsp sesame seeds

4 tbsp coriander seeds

2 tbsp cumin seeds

40 g (1¼ oz) hazelnuts

1 tsp salt

½ tsp freshly ground pepper

*For the smoked aubergine
(baba ghanoush)*

800 g (1 lb 12 oz) aubergine

1 clove garlic, peeled and
    crushed

¾ tsp salt

2½ tbsp light tahini or
    ½ tbsp sesame oil

3–4 tbsp lemon juice

¼ tsp cayenne pepper

1–2 tbsp extra-virgin
    olive oil

DF, GF

METHOD

To make the hummus, take the chickpeas that have been soaking overnight, and while they are still in water, rub them with your fingers to loosen their skins. These will float to the surface and can then be discarded. Place the chickpeas in fresh water and cook for 40–60 minutes on the hob until they are tender. Strain them, being careful to retain the cooking liquid. Place the drained chickpeas in a food processor with the crushed garlic, lemon juice, tahini and 2 tablespoons of the cooking liquid. Blend until the mixture is smooth, adding more cooking liquid if required, and season with salt and pepper. Leave to one side.

To make the dukkah, roast all the ingredients, except for the salt and pepper, separately on a baking sheet. If the hazelnuts have skins on them, these can be removed after roasting by rubbing the nuts in a cloth. Pound the roasted seeds in a mortar and pestle or gently blend them in a food processor, being careful not to over-blend them so that they form an oily paste. Combine the seeds, nuts and salt and pepper, and keep in an airtight container until ready to use.

To make the smoked aubergine, pre-heat the grill. Slit the skin of each aubergine once or twice. Place them on a baking sheet and place under the pre-heated grill 10 cm (4 in) from the element. Grill for 20–30 minutes or until the skin is blackened, blistered and burnt, and the pulp is soft. Turn them once. Remove from the grill and allow to cool slightly. Scrape the pulp from the skin and place it in a blender. Purée for a few seconds and then add the garlic, salt, tahini or sesame oil, lemon juice, cayenne pepper and olive oil. Blend well.

Pre-heat the oven to 200°C/180°C fan/390°F. Season the rumps of lamb and seal in a pre-heated frying pan for at least 4–5 minutes to ensure that all the flavours are locked in, and then place in the hot oven for 3–4 minutes. Once cooked, remove the lamb from the oven and allow it to rest for 5 minutes, loosely covered in tinfoil, saving the cooking sauces to one side.

When ready to serve, place a small amount of harissa onto each plate and a large spoonful of hummus adjacent to it; finish with a drizzle of olive oil. Slice the warm lamb rumps and arrange on the plates. Sprinkle the lamb with the dukkah and finish with a little jus from the meat. Serve with the smoked aubergine.

GARLICKY WHITE RABBIT

Recipe by **OLIA HERCULES**, chef, food writer & food stylist, Turnpike Lane, London

SERVINGS: 4 | **PREP TIME: 20 MINS PLUS RESTING** | **COOK TIME: 55 MINS** | **SKILL LEVEL: 1 (EASY)**

This 1980s number was our family's favourite for many years — that is until Uncle Vadik, who had certain fancy connections, bought my mum her first Western cookbook in the mid-1990s (International Family Favorites by Ron Kalenuik, which we still use!). Mr Kalenuik's superb French rabbit au vin (with pork belly and mushrooms) had almost irrevocably replaced this old favourite. But we have now decided to bring the 1980s white rabbit back. Don't be alarmed by the amount of garlic — it will mellow and become sweet.

INGREDIENTS

80 g (3 oz) butter
1 rabbit, about 1¼ kg (2½ lb), jointed
16 small cloves garlic, thinly sliced
250 ml (9 fl oz) soured cream or crème fraîche
300 ml (½ pint) chicken stock or water
2 tbsp sunflower oil
fusilli pasta or rice, to serve

METHOD

Place the butter in the bottom of a heavy-based pan. Keeping 2 thinly sliced garlic cloves behind for a crispy garnish later, add the rabbit pieces and lace with the remaining garlic slices on top.

Mix the soured cream or crème fraîche and stock or water together and season generously with salt. Pour over the rabbit and bring to the boil, then lower the heat and simmer gently for 1½ hours or until the rabbit meat falls off the bone.

Heat the sunflower oil in a frying pan and fry the reserved garlic slices until light golden. Be careful not to burn them. Remove and drain on paper towel.

We love pulling the meat, mixing it with the sauce and serving it with fusilli or rice. Don't forget to sprinkle the crispy garlic on top.

PAN-FRIED PIMENTÓN CHICKEN WITH MASHED POTATO

Recipe by **JOSÉ PIZARRO**, restaurateur, Bermondsey, London

SERVINGS: 4 | **PREP TIME: 15 MINS** | **COOK TIME: 50 MINS** | **SKILL LEVEL: 1 (EASY)**

I prefer to use pimentón de la Vera picante *for this dish, but please use it with caution! Mashed potato made with olive oil is just gorgeous with this.*

INGREDIENTS

For the chicken

3 tbsp extra-virgin olive oil

4 cloves garlic, unskinned

1 bay leaf

sea salt and freshly ground black pepper

8 boneless, unskinned chicken thighs, cut in half

1 tsp *pimentón de la Vera picante* (hot smoked paprika)

6 tbsp Fino sherry

For the mashed potatoes

4 large red potatoes

4 cloves garlic, peeled

1 bay leaf

6 tbsp extra-virgin olive oil

sea salt and freshly ground black pepper

DF, GF

METHOD

First, you want to infuse the oil that the chicken is going to be cooked in with the flavours of the garlic and bay leaf. So, heat the oil over a very gentle heat and add the garlic cloves and the bay leaf. It should take about 20 minutes to colour the garlic, very slightly: it's a warm-bath, not a frying-pan experience. Once cooked, remove the garlic and bay leaf. Set the garlic cloves to one side (you'll need them later).

Turn the heat up to high. Season the chicken, add it to the pan and fry for 4 minutes before turning the pieces over – you want them nice and crispy golden on the outside. Cook for another 4 minutes. Add the pimentón and the Fino sherry; give everything a good stir and leave to bubble gently for 5 minutes.

For the mash, peel the potatoes and cut them into large chunks. Boil with the garlic cloves, bay leaf, 2 tablespoons of the olive oil and a pinch of salt. Once cooked, skim off the olive oil and reserve. Drain the potatoes and remove the garlic and bay leaf. Mash the potatoes with all the olive oil (the reserved and the remaining olive oil), and keep going until you have made a smooth purée. Season to taste.

Spoon the mashed potatoes into the middle of a platter, place the chicken on top, and pour the juices over. Serve with the fried garlic cloves.

NIGELLA LAWSON
FOOD WRITER & TV PRESENTER

This recipe is from *How to Eat*, with some rejigging (just because it's not in my nature to leave things completely alone), and I don't apologize for reproducing – or rather recasting – it because I simply cannot urge you strongly enough to try this.

NIGELLA

London

HAM IN COCA-COLA

Recipe by **NIGELLA LAWSON**, food writer & TV presenter, London

SERVINGS: 8 | **PREP TIME: 30 MINS** | **COOK TIME: 3½ HOURS** | **SKILL LEVEL: 1 (EASY)**

The first time I made this, it was, to be frank, really just out of amused interest. I'd heard, and read, about this culinary tradition from the Deep South, but I wasn't expecting it, in all honesty, to be good. The truth is it's magnificent, and makes converts of anyone who eats it. But, if you think about it, it's not surprising it should work: the sweet, spiky drink just infuses it with a spirit of barbecue. I have to force myself to cook ham any other way now; though often I don't bother with the glaze but just leave it for longer in the bubbling Coke instead. But just one thing before we start: don't even consider using Diet Coke; it's full-fat or nothing.

INGREDIENTS

2 kg (4½ lb) mild-cure gammon

1 onion, peeled and cut in half

2 litres (3½ pints) Coca-Cola

For the glaze
a handful of cloves

1 heaped tbsp black treacle

2 tsp English mustard powder

2 tbsp Demerara sugar

DF, GF

METHOD

I find now that mild-cure gammon doesn't need soaking, but if you know that you're dealing with a salty piece, then put it in a pan covered with cold water, bring to the boil, then tip into a colander in the sink and start from there; otherwise, put the gammon in a pan, skin-side down if it fits like that, add the onion, then pour over the Coke. Bring to the boil, reduce to a good simmer, put the lid on, though not tightly, and cook for just under 2½ hours. If your joint is larger or smaller, work out the timing by reckoning on an hour per kilogram (2½ lb), remembering that it's going to get a quick blast in the oven later. But do take into account that if the gammon's been in the fridge right up to the moment you cook it, you will have to give it a good 15 minutes or so extra so that the interior is properly cooked.

Meanwhile, pre-heat the oven to 240°C/450°F/gas 9.

When the ham's had its time (and ham it is, now it's cooked, though it's true that Americans call it ham from its uncooked state), take it out of the pan and let cool a little for ease of handling. (Indeed, you can let it cool completely then finish off the cooking at some later stage if you want to). Then remove the skin, leaving a thin layer of fat. Score the fat with a sharp knife to make fairly large diamond shapes, and stud each diamond with a clove. Then carefully spread the treacle over the bark-budded skin, taking care not to dislodge the cloves. Gently pat the mustard and sugar onto the sticky fat. Cook in a tinfoil-lined roasting dish for approximately 10 minutes or until the glaze is burnished and bubbly.

Should you want to do the braising stage in advance and then let the ham cool, clove and glaze it and give it 30–40 minutes, from room temperature, at 180°C/350°F/gas 4, turning up the heat towards the end if you think it needs it.

This is seriously fabulous with anything, but eggily golden sweetcorn pudding is perfect: ham and eggs Southern style.

TEMPURA DUCK HEARTS, RED WINE LENTILS, LOVAGE, BLACK CARROT, BACON JAM

Recipe by **RICHARD & OLIVER GLADWIN**, Rabbit, Chelsea, London

SERVINGS: 6 | PREP TIME: 1 HOUR | COOK TIME: 1¾ HOURS | SKILL LEVEL: 2 (MODERATE)

INGREDIENTS

For the bacon jam
40 g (1⅓ oz) butter
2 large onions, diced
4 cloves garlic, diced
300 g (10½ oz) smoked bacon lardons
300 g (10½ oz) skinless pork belly, diced
200 ml (7 fl oz) cider vinegar
200 g (7 oz) Demerara sugar
a handful of picked thyme leaves

For the red wine lentils
300 g (10½ oz) Puy lentils
200 ml (7 fl oz) red wine
150 ml (5 fl oz) veal stock
100 ml (3½ fl oz) water
30 g (1 oz) whole allspice
a bunch of lovage, chopped

For the tempura batter
200 g (7 oz) rice flour
200 g (7 oz) gram flour
500 ml (18 fl oz) sparkling water
12 g (2 tsp) bicarbonate of soda
15 g (½ oz) ground coriander
15 g (½ oz) ground star anise
20 ml (¾ fl oz) cider vinegar
20 g (¾ oz) sugar

To finish
18 duck hearts
cooking oil, for frying
1 large black carrot, very finely
    sliced

METHOD

Make the bacon jam by melting the butter in a heavy-bottomed pan on a low heat. Once melted, turn the heat up and add the onions to fry for 3 minutes, then add the garlic. When golden and caramelized, add the bacon and pork belly and turn the heat down to low. Cook slowly for 20 minutes, pouring off a little of the liquid if there's too much.

Add the vinegar and sugar to the bacon and pork belly and cook for a further 30 minutes, until sticky; it should hold together on a spoon. If the jam looks split, add a little water and rumble it in a food processor to stabilize it and to create a jammy set. Finish with the thyme and leave to cool at room temperature.

For the red wine lentils, start by rinsing the lentils well in water. They should be cooked to al dente in the red wine, veal stock, water and spices. Bring the pot to the boil, then simmer for 15 minutes. Be careful not to overcook. The lentils should be coated with a rich, sticky sauce. Leave warm and ready to plate, finishing by stirring through fresh chopped lovage just before serving.

For the tempura, combine all the ingredients, whisking the water into the flour. The batter should be smooth and thick enough to coat the back of a spoon.

The final preparation should be to trim the duck hearts, roll them in flour and tap off the excess.

Heat a pan filled with 5 cm (2 in) of cooking oil to 165–170°C (329–338°F). Dip the duck hearts in the batter and fry them for 2 minutes each side until golden-brown. The duck hearts should be served cooked but pink.

To serve, the idea is to build the dish in layers of colour, flavour and texture. Spoon the warm lentils down the centre of the length of the plate. Put dollops of the bacon jam in and around the lentils, then cut the hearts in half lengthways and lay them over the top. Finish by topping with the finely sliced black carrot.

AYLESBURY DUCK, ROASTED CABBAGE & ANCHOVY

Recipe by **JON ROTHERAM & TOM HARRIS**, The Marksman, Bethnal Green, London

SERVINGS: 4 | **PREP TIME: 30 MINS** | **COOK TIME: 2½ HOURS** | **SKILL LEVEL: 2 (MODERATE)**

INGREDIENTS

2 tbsp duck fat

1 Aylesbury duck
 (about 2 kg/4½ lb)

10 anchovy fillets

6 cloves garlic

2 bay leaves

10 baby onions

8–10 whole baby turnips,
 cleaned

3 tbsp wine or cider vinegar

200 ml (7 fl oz) dry white
 wine

1½ litres (2 pints 12 fl oz)
 chicken stock

2 white or hispi
 (sweetheart) cabbages

4 sprigs thyme

a shot of sherry

buttered new potatoes
 or mash, to serve

GF

METHOD

Pre-heat the oven to 150°C/300°F/gas 2.

Heat the duck fat in a heavy-based pot large enough to hold all the ingredients. Over a high heat, brown the duck on all sides and set aside.

In the same pot, fry the anchovies, whole garlic cloves and bay leaves over a medium heat until slightly browned. Set aside.

Add the onions and turnips to the pot and fry until browned. Set aside.

Return the duck to the pot, breast-side down. Add the vinegar, dry white wine and chicken stock, and season to taste. Return the vegetables and garlic mix to the pot and give it a gentle shake to let the mixture settle. Bring to a good simmer, then place the pot in the oven, covered. Leave for 1 hour, then remove the lid and gently continue cooking for another 1½ hours, or until the meat is tender enough to pull off the bone.

At the same time the pot is in the oven, roast the cabbages whole for 1 hour. Once tender, remove and discard the outer leaves, and cut into quarters. Add to the pot once the duck is ready so that the cabbage soaks up all the juices.

You can remove the duck and vegetables and put them to one side before reducing the stock to make it thicker. Add the shot of sherry at this stage and check the seasoning.

Serve with a bowl of buttered new potatoes, or mashed potatoes.

GRILLED SKIRT STEAK
WITH ANCHOVY CAULIFLOWER CHEESE

Recipe by **STEVIE PARLE**, Dock Kitchen, Ladbroke Grove, London

SERVINGS: 4 | **PREP TIME: 25 MINS** | **COOK TIME: 35 MINS** | **SKILL LEVEL: 1 (EASY)**

Skirt steak is an excellent, cheap cut. It must be well hung or it will be tough. Skirt has a coarse grain and must be cooked rare; well done it is inedibly chewy. I cooked this when Jay Rayner reviewed Dock Kitchen in the early days; he said that the addition of anchovy to the cauliflower cheese was the prosaic made gloriously elegiac. I was lucky to have added the anchovies. Without, the excellent review may have read rather differently. This is super-simple as I just enrich crème fraîche rather than making béchamel.

INGREDIENTS

1 cauliflower

250 ml (9 fl oz) crème fraîche

3 egg yolks

100 g (3½ oz) pecorino
  (or another hard, tangy
  cheese), grated

8 salted anchovy fillets

4 beef skirt steaks
  (total weight 1 kg/2¼ lb)

lemon juice (optional)

extra-virgin olive oil
  (optional)

GF

METHOD

Pre-heat the oven to 200°C/400°F/gas 6. Pre-heat a griddle pan, or light your barbecue.

Boil a pan of well-salted water. Break the cauliflower into florets and boil until just soft (about 5 minutes). Drain and put the cauliflower into a medium-sized baking tray that can accommodate it all in one tight layer.

Mix the crème fraîche with the egg yolks and cheese, and dollop this on top of the cauliflower. Lay the anchovies over the top and bake in the oven until well browned.

Season the steaks well with salt and pepper and grill on the very hot griddle pan or barbecue for a couple of minutes on each side. It should be nicely charred but still bright red within. Let them rest for a couple of minutes.

I often also squeeze a lemon over and pour on a little oil.

LAMB CHOPS
& DIRTY SWEET POTATOES

Recipe by **MARK BLATCHFORD**, chef & restaurateur, Clerkenwell, London

SERVINGS: 4 | PREP TIME: 10 MINS | COOK TIME: 30 MINS PLUS HEATING THE COALS
SKILL LEVEL: 1 (EASY)

INGREDIENTS

4 medium-sized sweet
  potatoes, washed
8 lamb loin chops
25 ml (1 fl oz) olive oil
a squeeze of lemon juice
1 sprig mint

DF, GF

METHOD

Build a little charcoal fire. Let the fire burn down and the coals ash up. Throw in your sweet potatoes and let 'em burn. You are not literally burning them but that's what they will look like. Keep turning them now and again. The outside of the potato will burn but it will be steaming the orange flesh inside.

When the potatoes are really black and soft, remove them from the coals and allow them to cool slightly.

Season the lamb chops with salt and pepper. Cook them over a high direct heat for about 5 minutes on each side, ensuring that you crisp up the fat. You will need to pay close attention to this part of the process. When you are happy your lamb is cooked, remove it from the grill and let the meat rest for at least 10 minutes. This is really important as the fibres of the meat need to relax and the juices disperse evenly.

Toss the meat in the olive oil and season with salt, pepper, lemon juice and ripped mint leaves.

TOM AIKENS
TOM'S KITCHEN

In terms of the food that I love to cook and prepare, it's all about seasonality and great produce, and also farm-to-plate culture. I think I can say that I was one of the first chefs to pioneer the farm-to-plate culture way back in 2006, when we first opened Tom's Kitchen here in Chelsea. I had worked on a farm a few years earlier – with Carole Bamford at Daylesford – and that's where I really got to understand the whole philosophy of good food. *Tom*

Chelsea, London

BRAISED LAMB SHANKS WITH PEARL BARLEY & HONEY-ROAST GARLIC

Recipe by **TOM AIKENS**, Tom's Kitchen, Chelsea, London

SERVINGS: 4 | PREP TIME: 15 MINS | COOK TIME: 2½ HOURS | SKILL LEVEL: 2 (MODERATE)

I love this dish because it's very simplistic. Everything is cooked in one pot, so you get the lovely flavour of the lamb combining with the aromatic vegetables and the braised pearl barley. This is very much a sharing dish for family and friends.

INGREDIENTS

4 lamb shanks

coarse sea salt and freshly ground black pepper

150 ml (5 fl oz) vegetable oil

6 large carrots, peeled

5 banana shallots, peeled

4 onions, peeled

25 g (1 oz) butter

8 cloves garlic, peeled and split in half

2–3 sprigs fresh thyme

20 g (1 oz) tomato paste

20 g (¾ oz) plain flour

1 litre (1¾ pints) white chicken stock

6 plum tomatoes, quartered

60 g (3 oz) pearl barley

For the honey-roast garlic

100 ml (3½ fl oz) olive oil

20 g (¾ oz) unsalted butter

3 whole bulbs garlic, split in half

1 small sprig fresh thyme

40 g (1½ oz) clear honey

METHOD

Pre-heat the oven to 170°C/325°F/gas 3.

Season the lamb shanks with salt and pepper. Place a large casserole dish on a medium heat, add the vegetable oil and then the lamb. Colour the lamb all over in the pan until golden-brown, which will take approximately 8–10 minutes, then remove from the casserole dish onto a tray.

During this time, cut the carrots, shallots and onions into 2½ cm (1 in) pieces, keeping them separate. Add the butter to the oil in the casserole dish, and when it melts, add the carrot. Start to colour this up, then after 5 minutes add the split garlic cloves and thyme. Keep colouring these, then after a few more minutes add the shallot, onion, 1 teaspoon of sea salt and 4–6 turns of freshly ground black pepper.

After another 5–8 minutes, when the vegetables are all coloured, turn the heat down and add the tomato paste. Cook for a further 2 minutes, then add the flour and cook again for 2 more minutes. Add the stock and tomatoes, turn the heat up and bring this to a slow simmer, then skim off the scum. Add the pearl barley and the lamb back to the casserole dish. Cover with a lid and cook in the pre-heated oven for 2½ hours.

While this is cooking, you can make your honey-roast garlic. Place a small sauté pan on a very low heat. Add the olive oil and butter and, when the butter has just melted, add the garlic, cut-side down, with the thyme. Add a little salt and then cook very slowly until the garlic starts to colour. After approximately 15 minutes, add the honey, then continue cooking until the garlic is soft (about another 15–20 minutes).

Once the lamb is cooked, serve a shank on each plate with some of the pearl barley and vegetables, and a half garlic bulb.

BEEF BRISKET WITH NEW POTATO PICCALILLI SALAD

Recipe by **GORDON RAMSAY OBE**, chef & TV presenter, Chelsea, London

SERVINGS: 6 | PREP TIME: 40 MINS | COOK TIME: 3½–4½ HOURS | SKILL LEVEL: 1 (EASY)

Brisket is a cut of beef from the cow's lower chest and is traditionally used to make salt beef and pastrami. However, I'm not brining it here, but instead poaching it in aromatics, sautéed off first to boost their flavour. Just like salt beef, this is great served with piccalilli.

INGREDIENTS

2 kg (4½ lb) beef, boned, rolled and tied

olive oil, for frying

1 carrot, peeled and roughly chopped

2 sticks celery, trimmed and roughly chopped

1 bulb garlic, cut in half horizontally

1 tsp black peppercorns

1 tsp cloves

1 tsp freshly grated nutmeg

For the new potato salad

500 g (1 lb 2 oz) new potatoes of a similar size

1 small cauliflower, cut into florets

275 g (10 oz) green beans, topped and tailed

1 carrot, peeled and grated

1 small shallot, peeled and finely sliced

3 spring onions, trimmed and finely chopped

a pinch of ground turmeric

1–2 tsp English mustard powder, to taste

1 tbsp wholegrain mustard

1–2 tsp honey, to taste

3 tbsp white wine vinegar

100 ml (3½ fl oz) olive oil

DF, GF

METHOD

Pre-heat the oven to 140°C/275°F/gas 1.

Season the brisket all over with salt and pepper. Heat a large flameproof casserole dish or high-sided roasting tray on the hob. Add a glug of oil and brown the meat in the hot dish for about 5 minutes until coloured on all sides. Turn the heat down to medium, add the carrot, celery, garlic and spices, and stir them through the oil at the bottom of the pan.

Pour in enough water to almost cover the brisket. Bring to the boil, then cover tightly. Transfer the dish to the pre-heated oven and leave to cook for 3–4 hours, turning the meat halfway through, until it is really tender. Remove the meat from the cooking liquor and allow it to rest for 20 minutes.

Meanwhile, make the salad. Boil the new potatoes in salted water for about 15 minutes, until tender and cooked through. Blanch the cauliflower and green beans by dropping them into boiling salted water for 2 minutes until their rawness has been removed but they are still crunchy. Refresh immediately in cold water.

Mix together the carrot, shallot, spring onion and turmeric, and add the potatoes, cauliflower and green beans. To make the dressing, stir the mustard powder into the wholegrain mustard, making sure there are no lumps. Add the honey and vinegar; mix well, then slowly pour the oil in, stirring as you do so to thicken. Dress the salad and season with salt and pepper to taste.

Slice the rested brisket and serve with the salad.

ANNIE BELL'S PHEASANT WITH CALVADOS & APPLE

Recipe by **ANNIE BELL**, food writer, London

SERVINGS: 2–3 | **PREP TIME: 1 HOUR** | **COOK TIME: 45 MINS** | **SKILL LEVEL: 1 (EASY)**

If I had to name my favourite way of cooking pheasant, then this would be it. The marriage of game with caramelized apples and earthy Calvados resonates with autumn.

INGREDIENTS

30 g (1 oz) unsalted butter
1 tbsp groundnut or vegetable oil
1 pheasant, trussed (see tip below)

75 ml (2½ fl oz) Calvados (or brandy)
200 ml (7 fl oz) dry cider
150 g (5 oz) crème fraîche

2 eating apples, peeled, quartered, cored and sliced lengthways

GF

METHOD

Colour the pheasant: heat 15 g (½ oz) butter and the oil in a large non-stick frying pan over a medium-high heat. Season the pheasant and colour it thoroughly on all sides in the hot fat. Transfer the golden pheasant, breast-side up, to a medium-sized cast-iron casserole dish.

Flambé the Calvados (see tip below): gently warm the Calvados in a ladle over the gas or hob (you may need to do this half at a time), then light and pour it a little at a time over the pheasant, adding more as the flames die down. It's very important to do this in a controlled fashion and not to panic.

Pot-roast the pheasant: add the cider – don't worry if the Calvados is still alight – and bring to the boil. Then cover the pan with a lid and cook on the smallest ring over a low heat for 30 minutes.

Rest the pheasant and finish the sauce: remove the cooked pheasant to a warm plate and set aside to rest for 10 minutes. Meanwhile, return the pan to a medium heat, add the crème fraîche and let it bubble away vigorously until the sauce appears to thicken slightly and seems richer.

Fry the apples and dish up: heat the remaining 15 g (½ oz) butter in a separate non-stick frying pan over a medium-high heat and fry the apples until well coloured and just starting to burn around the edges, approximately 5 minutes. Meanwhile, carve the pheasant breasts and remove any tender meat from the legs. Serve the pheasant with the sauce spooned over, scattered with the apple slices.

TIPS

Why a trussed bird? Whilst I prefer to untruss a chicken, pheasants do benefit from having their legs tied to their body during cooking; otherwise they splay all over the place.

Flambéing gets rid of the raw alcohol while retaining the character of the liquid. I usually rope my husband in to help me because I am a bit timid when it comes to playing with fire. If you're totally fazed by the idea, simply add 2–3 tablespoons of Calvados to the pan with the cider, forgoing the flames.

KIM JONES
COOK AT MARCHMONT ESTATE

I like to use the produce that's available on the estate as often as I can, simply because it's available and it's ethical and organic. We always use the lunch hut for the game shoots, and everybody loves it here because it's so rustic and friendly. We've just got a stone floor so there's no faffing about with carpets and putting your slippers on; you can just walk in wearing your wellies. There's a huge fire inside and a big table, so it's everybody in together and it's very sociable. The family love it here as well because it's like bonfire night all the time.

Berwickshire,
Scotland

LOIN OF VENISON
WITH REDCURRANT REDUCTION

Recipe by **KIM JONES**, cook at Marchmont Estate, Berwickshire, Scotland

**SERVINGS: 4–6, DEPENDING ON SIZE OF LOINS | PREP TIME: 10 MINS PLUS CHILLING
COOK TIME: 15 MINS | SKILL LEVEL: 1 (EASY)**

Don't be scared of cooking venison; anybody can do it. In this recipe you roll the fillets in crushed black peppercorns to form a crust – don't worry about putting too much on; the more the merrier. I always serve this with Dauphinoise potatoes, grated cooked beetroot heated up in melted butter, carrot and sweet potato purée and petit pois (small green peas). I was taught to cook this dish by the chef who had been cooking for the family for 25 years: a wonderful lady called Judith Hettrick.

INGREDIENTS

2 venison loins
approx. 4 tbsp ground black
  pepper
a large glug of olive oil
a large knob of butter
200 ml (7 fl oz) venison or
  beef stock
100 ml (3½ oz) red wine
approx. 1 tbsp redcurrant jelly
25 g (1 oz) cold butter, cubed

GF

METHOD

Roll each loin tightly in clingfilm, twisting at each end to form a sausage shape, and refrigerate for at least 2 hours. Spread a chopping board with plenty of black pepper, then unwrap loins and roll in pepper, coating all over.

Heat oil and butter in a non-stick frying pan over a high heat. Fry loins, turning frequently, for approximately 5–7 minutes, depending on thickness of meat. It is important to serve this rare, so be brave and do not overcook! Remove from the pan and allow to rest in tinfoil.

Deglaze the pan with stock and wine, and reduce a little. Add redcurrant jelly and reduce until it becomes a little syrupy, then add the cold cubed butter and stir to incorporate.

Slice loins on the diagonal (approximately 1½ cm (¾ in) wide) and serve 2 or 3 slices with the reduction spooned over.

STICKY BOURBON RIBS

Recipe by **LIZZIE KAMENETZKY**, food stylist & writer, Kent

SERVINGS: 4 | **PREP TIME: 15 MINS PLUS MARINATING OVERNIGHT** | **COOK TIME: 4 HOURS**
SKILL LEVEL: 1 (EASY)

Tangy, sweet and sticky, these ribs hit the spot every time. The key is to cook them low and slow with plenty of marinade, only lifting the cover to let them get sticky towards the very end.

INGREDIENTS

1 x 400 g (14 oz) can tomatoes
4 cloves garlic, crushed
100 g (3½ oz) soft light brown sugar
75 ml (2½ fl oz) maple syrup
150 ml (5 fl oz) barbecue sauce
150 ml (5 fl oz) tomato sauce
100 ml (3½ fl oz) bourbon
50 ml (1½ fl oz) cider vinegar
2 tbsp black treacle
3 tbsp soy sauce
2 tbsp Worcestershire sauce
2 kg (4½ lb) baby back or spare ribs

DF

METHOD

Whizz the tomatoes with the remaining ingredients, except the ribs, until smooth. Pour over the ribs in a non-metallic container. Cover and marinate overnight in the fridge.

Pre-heat the oven to 150°C/300°F/gas 2.

Transfer the ribs to a roasting pan, reserving any spare marinade. Cover with tinfoil and roast for 3–3½ hours, basting occasionally, until tender. Pour off any marinade into a pan and add any reserved marinade. Place over a medium heat and bubble until thick and glossy.

Increase the oven to 200°C/400°F/gas 6. Pour the thickened glaze over the meat and return the ribs to the oven for 20–25 minutes until sticky.

GIZZI ERSKINE
CHEF & TV PRESENTER

What I love most about cooking is the creative side. I like being able to build something from nothing, and I love the fact that I'm feeding people. I'm quite maternal, so I love scooping people up and looking after them, and what better way to do that than feeding them? When I was a kid I used to get a lot of praise for being a big eater, and anyone who knows me knows I can eat; I could do it as an Olympic sport!

Bethnal Green,
London

SPANISH CHICKEN STEW WITH CHORIZO, SHERRY & GARBANZO BEANS

Recipe by **GIZZI ERSKINE**, chef & TV presenter, Bethnal Green, London

SERVINGS: 4–6 | **PREP TIME: 30 MINS PLUS SOAKING** | **COOK TIME: 2 HOURS** | **SKILL LEVEL: 1 (EASY)**

INGREDIENTS

200 g (7 oz) dried garbanzo beans (chickpeas), soaked for 12 hours

2 tbsp olive oil

1 large free-range chicken, skinned and jointed into 10 pieces (you can ask your butcher to do this)

3 whole uncooked chorizo sausages, about 240 g (9 oz) in total

1 bulb garlic, cut in half horizontally

2 onions, finely chopped

350 ml (12 fl oz) dry sherry

1 tsp sherry vinegar

1 litre (1¾ pints) fresh white chicken stock

a generous pinch of saffron threads

2 bay leaves

1 sprig rosemary

a few sprigs of thyme, leaves picked

a small bunch of flat-leaf parsley, chopped

zest of ½ lemon, grated

DF, GF

METHOD

Rinse the garbanzo beans thoroughly; place in a large saucepan and cover generously with cold water. Cover with a lid and bring to the boil for 25 minutes, or until the outsides feel cooked but the centres still feel a little chalky. They will cook more in the stew.

Pre-heat the oven to 200°C/400°F/gas 6. I like to cook my stew in stages and fry everything separately in a frying pan before building the stew in a casserole dish with a lid; but if you're worried about too much washing up, then you can, by all means, brown everything off straight away in the casserole. Heat the oil in a frying pan. Season the chicken pieces with salt, then add them to the frying pan in batches, skin-side down, and brown them thoroughly. It's really worth persevering with getting a good caramel colour on the outside of the chicken as this is where all the meaty flavour comes from, and it will render down all the fat from the skin as well. Once the chicken pieces are browned, remove them from the frying pan with some tongs and set aside on a plate.

Brown the chorizo all over in the same frying pan, then remove and set aside. I like to cook the chorizo whole in the stew and then slice it afterwards. Next, lay the garlic bulb halves in the frying pan, cut-side down, for a minute, until golden, then remove and set aside.

Now you need to pour away the excess fat from the frying pan (there will be a fair amount) until you are left with about 2 tablespoons of oil. Add the onion and fry it slowly for about 10–12 minutes, until it has softened and has started to tinge golden; then transfer to the casserole dish. Pour the sherry, vinegar and stock over; add the saffron, bay leaves, rosemary, thyme and half the parsley and bring to the boil. Add the chicken, chorizo, garlic and beans to the casserole. The chicken needs to be 90 per cent immersed in liquid so, if necessary, top up with more stock to ensure this. Pop the lid on the casserole dish and place in the oven for 15 minutes. Turn the oven down to 180°C/350°F/gas 4 and cook for a further 45 minutes.

Now, this is where it gets complicated. This isn't what most people do when cooking stews, but it's what they *should* do. Remove the casserole from the oven and carefully remove the chicken breast pieces and set aside, leaving the chorizo and chicken thigh and leg meat in the dish. There will still be a fair amount of liquid in the casserole and the beans will not be cooked fully yet, so pop the casserole on the hob, with the lid off, and cook over a lowish heat for another 15–20 minutes to reduce the sauce, making it taste nice and strong, and until the beans are cooked fully (when they are completely tender but still holding their shape). Don't worry about the chicken thigh and leg meat as this is hard to overcook. Once you're happy with the flavour and thickness of the stew and the beans are cooked through, return the chicken breast pieces to the casserole. Remove from the heat, stir in the remaining parsley and the lemon zest and season to taste. Pop the lid on and leave the stew to rest for 10 minutes. This will make the chicken tender and the beans cooked in a uniform way.

Remove the chorizo from the casserole dish and slice each sausage into about 10 pieces. Pop the slices back in the dish and stir through. Spoon a couple of pieces of chicken, some chorizo, beans and sauce onto each plate and serve with a fresh green salad.

POT-ROAST CHICKEN WITH CHICORY

Recipe by **LUCAS HOLLWEG**, food writer & columnist, Camberwell, London

SERVINGS: 4 | **PREP TIME: 25 MINS** | **COOK TIME: 1½ HOURS** | **SKILL LEVEL: 1 (EASY)**

This is a great thing to do with a chicken, the wine, cream and juices making a more-ish sauce in the pot. It's particularly good with mash. By the way, when I say chicory, I mean what much of the world calls Belgian endive: the tight flame-shaped bundles of yellow-tipped white leaves. The naming of vegetables can be a bit perverse sometimes.

INGREDIENTS

1 free-range chicken, about 1½ kg (3 lb 5 oz)

½ lemon

2 tbsp vegetable oil

25 g (1 oz) butter

4 plump heads chicory, halved lengthways, with the hard cores at the base removed

4 tsp sugar

3 plump cloves garlic, peeled and halved

100 ml (3½ fl oz) dry white wine

4 sprigs fresh thyme

6 rashers smoked streaky bacon

100 ml (3½ fl oz) double cream

a handful of chopped parsley, to serve

GF

METHOD

Pre-heat the oven to 180°C/350°F/gas 4. Season the bird inside and out. Squeeze the half lemon and keep the juice to one side. Put the squeezed shell inside the bird.

Heat the oil in an ovenproof casserole dish (you want one with a lid and which will just hold the bird when it is placed on top of the chicory). Add the chicken and cook over a medium heat until brown all over. Remove and put to one side.

Tip out the oil, then throw in the butter and let it melt. When it starts to froth, add half the chicory, cut-side down, and cook over a moderate heat for 2 minutes until it starts to wilt and caramelize. Turn over and give it 2 minutes more, then remove and put to one side. Repeat with the rest of the chicory, then return it all to the pan and throw in the sugar and garlic.

Put the bird on top and add the wine, reserved lemon juice and thyme. Turn up the heat and bubble for 5 minutes, then drape the bacon over the breast. Season, cover and place in the oven for 45 minutes. Remove the lid and return to the oven for a further 30 minutes. Then pour the cream around the outside of the bird and cook for 5 minutes more.

You can carve at the table, or joint the bird first. To joint it, lift the bird onto a board, pull the legs away and, with a sharp knife, slice through the joint connecting them to the body. Remove the bacon and keep to one side. Cut down on either side of the breast bone to remove a breast and wing, cutting through the joint that attaches the wing to the carcass. Scatter with parsley and serve.

HIGADO DE TERNERA ENCEBOLLADO AL BRANDY

CALVES' LIVER WITH ONIONS & BRANDY

Recipe by **CLAUDIA RODEN**, food writer, North London

SERVINGS: 4 | **PREP TIME: 20 MINS** | **COOK TIME: 35 MINS** | **SKILL LEVEL: I (EASY)**

Offal was always the food of the poor, and levels of consumption went down as Spain grew rich. But since immigrants from Latin America have arrived in large numbers, over a decade or so the offal stands that had almost disappeared from city markets are doing a roaring trade once again. Calves' liver, though, has always been considered a delicacy. It is important not to overcook it.

INGREDIENTS

2 large onions, cut in half and sliced

3–4 tbsp olive oil

500 g (1 lb 2 oz) calves' liver, thinly sliced and cut into 2 cm (¾ in) strips

4 tbsp brandy

DF, GF

METHOD

In a large frying pan, sauté the onion in the oil over a low heat, covered, until it is soft, stirring occasionally. It can take up to 25 minutes because of the large amount of onion. Then cook, uncovered, over a medium heat, stirring often, until golden.

Add the calves' liver to the pan and sauté briefly for 1 minute, adding salt and pepper to taste and turning the strips over quickly to brown them lightly on both sides. Pour the brandy all over them and then cook over a high heat for 1 minute to reduce the sauce – the time depends on the thickness of the liver. It should still be pink inside.

VARIATION

For an Andalusian version, use chicken livers instead of calves' liver, and sauté very briefly, stirring and turning them constantly to brown them all over. Use Oloroso sherry instead of the brandy.

RACK OF SPRING LAMB WITH HERBS & GRATIN POTATOES

Recipe by **AMY BATES**, writer & columnist, Moreby, Yorkshire

SERVINGS: 8 | **PREP TIME: 25 MINS** | **COOK TIME: 25 MINS** | **SKILL LEVEL: I (EASY)**

INGREDIENTS

3 shallots, peeled

3–4 ransoms/wild garlic, washed and trimmed (or 2–3 cloves garlic, peeled)

2 tbsp chopped fresh rosemary

2 tbsp chopped fresh parsley

3 tbsp butter

6 tbsp fresh breadcrumbs

4 racks of spring lamb, French-trimmed allowing for 3 ribs per person, skin removed and fat removed (ask your butcher to do this)

DF

METHOD

Heat the oven to 200°C/400°F/gas 6. Put a shallow roasting tin into the oven to heat up.

Chuck the shallots, ransoms/wild garlic, herbs, butter, and salt and pepper into the bowl of a food processor. Whizz until it is all thoroughly chopped and combined. Remove the blade and mix in the breadcrumbs.

Remove the roasting tin from the oven and place the racks in the tin. Cook for 5 minutes, then remove and – carefully so as not to burn your hands – press the mixture onto the lamb meat. Return the lamb to the oven and continue to cook for 20 minutes or until golden and crusty.

Serve with gratin potatoes (see below).

GRATIN POTATOES

SERVINGS: 4 | **PREP TIME: 30 MINS** | **COOK TIME: I HOUR** | **SKILL LEVEL: I (EASY)**

INGREDIENTS

60 g (2 oz) butter, plus more for greasing gratin dish

1 kg (2¼ lb) potatoes, thinly sliced

½ tsp chopped fresh thyme

1 clove garlic, thinly sliced

250 ml (9 fl oz) double cream

GF, V

METHOD

Pre-heat the oven to 200°C/400°/gas 6.

Brush a gratin dish with some melted butter. Next, layer the potatoes, thyme, garlic, salt and pepper in the dish until all the ingredients are used, finishing off with some of the thyme and seasoning on the top. Pour the cream over and cook in the oven for 50–60 minutes, or until the potato is tender and the top is nicely browned. Serve.

DRY-AGED PORK WITH SOUTH INDIAN SPICES

Recipe by **ISAAC McHALE**, The Clove Club, Bethnal Green, London

SERVINGS: 2–4 | PREP TIME: 30 MINS | COOK TIME: 1 HOUR | SKILL LEVEL: 2 (MODERATE)

INGREDIENTS

For the curry paste
350 g (12½ oz) white onion
oil, for frying
5 g (1 medium-sized clove) garlic
5 g (4 cm/1¾ in knob) fresh ginger, peeled
5 g (about 1) fresh green chilli (including seeds if wished)
5 g (about 1) fresh red chilli (including seeds if wished)
8 g (¼ oz) fresh turmeric
15 g (½ oz) lemongrass
15 g (½ oz) coriander seeds
30 g (1 oz) coriander stems (leaves removed)

1 tbsp fresh kaffir lime leaves
1 tbsp fresh curry leaves
5 black cardamom pods
10 green cardamom pods
1 tsp black peppercorns
50 g (1½ oz) desiccated coconut
15 g (½ oz) coconut oil

For the sauce
25 g (1 oz) coconut oil
400 ml (14 fl oz) coconut milk
100 g (3½ oz) curry paste (see above)
50 ml (1½ fl oz) lime juice
50 g (1½ oz) yoghurt

For the salt mix
50 g (1½ oz) ground cinnamon
50 g (1½ oz) fennel seeds
25 g (1 oz) green ground cardamom
2 cloves
250 g (9 oz) Maldon salt

2 best dry-aged pork chops you can buy
sunflower oil, for frying
10 fresh curry leaves
wilted spinach, to serve

GF

METHOD

Pre-heat the oven to 200°C/400°F/gas 6.

For the paste, dice and sweat down the onion in a little oil with a pinch of salt, without adding colour, until soft and tender. Meanwhile, finely dice the garlic, ginger, chillies and turmeric and finely slice the lemongrass. Lightly toast the coriander seeds and finely chop the coriander stems. Chop up the lime leaves and curry leaves.

Combine all of the above in a mortar and pestle and crush together with the remaining ingredients, apart from the coconut oil, to make a paste – this is hard work yet worth it, but if you don't have a large enough mortar and pestle or the energy, you can blitz it in a food processor.

Melt the coconut oil and gently fry the paste, gently cooking it all together to meld the flavours and so on. After 4–8 minutes of cooking, let the mixture cool down.

To make the sauce, melt the coconut oil and 50 ml (1½ fl oz) of the coconut milk together and boil it until it 'cracks' – that is, until the fat splits out and the milk solids of the coconut milk start frying in the coconut oil – then add the 100 g (3½ oz) of curry paste and cook out on a medium heat, stirring all the time, for 2 minutes. Add the remaining coconut milk and bring to the boil. Cook out for 10 minutes, then remove the mixture from the heat and blend in the lime juice and yoghurt.

Meanwhile, roast the pork chops for 15 minutes until well golden and a little pink still. Leave to rest, loosely covered in tinfoil.

Crush the salt mix in a mortar and pestle.

Pour 5 cm (2 in) of sunflower oil into a saucepan and heat until the oil is shimmering. Carefully lower in the curry leaves and fry for 1 minute until crisp, then remove onto paper towel.

Serve the pork, whole or carved, with a spoonful of the sauce, and the curry leaves, and some wilted spinach. Serve the salt mix on the side for people to season their own plate.

TIP

Freeze any remaining curry paste, well sealed, for up to 3 months.

MARCO PIERRE WHITE
CHEF, RESTAURATEUR, AUTHOR & TV PRESENTER

This roast woodcock recipe has to be one of the finest comfort dishes you'll ever taste, and takes under half an hour to make. Once upon a time the woodcock, that little wading bird with an exceptionally long beak, was highly popular on our tables. After trying this, I think you'll agree it's time for a resurgence in its popularity.

M. P. W.

Corsham,
Wiltshire

ROAST WOODCOCK ON TOAST WITH WILD MUSHROOMS

Recipe by **MARCO PIERRE WHITE**, chef, restaurateur, author & TV presenter, Corsham, Wiltshire

SERVINGS: 2 | PREP TIME: 45 MINS | COOK TIME: 25 MINS | SKILL LEVEL: 2 (MODERATE)

INGREDIENTS

2 woodcocks, whole, plucked, with head and innards
clarified butter (or ghee)
approx. 50 g (1½ oz) foie gras (or chicken liver pâté)
½ shallot, finely chopped
approx. 100 g (3½ oz) wild mushrooms
2 slices bread (to your taste)

METHOD

Pre-heat the oven to 200°C/400°F/gas 6.

When the oven has reached the required temperature, it's time to start cooking. Place the woodcocks in a roasting tin and spread a little clarified butter or ghee (or unsalted butter) over them.

Place the tin on the top shelf of the hot oven and let the birds roast for 12–15 minutes. Remove from the oven and allow them to rest in the tin.

Using a teaspoon, remove each bird's intestines, heart, liver and gizzard. Discard the gizzards.

Chop the intestines, hearts and livers into a very fine paste. Combine with an equal amount of foie gras (or chicken liver pâté) and the shallot. That's a game pâté like you've never tasted!

Pre-heat the grill to medium-high.

Clean the wild mushrooms with a tea towel or paper towel and lay them on a baking tray. Brush with melted butter and place under the grill for 2 minutes.

Trim the crusts from the bread. Toast the bread, butter it and spread the game pâté on top. Flash it under the grill for about 45 seconds, or until the pâté is cooked.

Place the woodcocks on a chopping board and remove the heads. Using a heavy kitchen knife, split each bird's head down the middle, lengthways and through the beaks.

Place the toast in a large dish or pan and lay the roasted woodcocks, back to back, on top of the toast. Put the split heads on the birds, and garnish with the grilled mushrooms. Serve.

CHICKEN TIKKA MASALA PIE

Recipe by **ATUL KOCHHAR**, Benares (Mayfair) and Sindhu (Marlow), London

SERVINGS: 4–6 | **PREP TIME: 45 MINS PLUS RESTING/MARINATING** | **COOK TIME: 1 HOUR 15 MINS**
SKILL LEVEL: 2 (MODERATE)

INGREDIENTS

For the first marinade
1 clove garlic, peeled
1 cm (½ in) piece of fresh ginger, peeled
1 tsp chilli powder
juice of ½ lemon
1 kg (2¼ lb) boneless chicken thighs,
  chopped into bite-sized pieces

For the second marinade
250 g (9 oz) Greek-style yoghurt
1 tsp garam masala
1 tsp ground coriander
50 ml (1½ fl oz) vegetable oil
½ tsp ground cinnamon

½ tsp chilli powder
½ tsp dried fenugreek leaves
2 tsp gram flour

For brushing
a small knob of butter, melted
2 tsp lime juice
1 tsp chaat masala or garam masala

For the pastry
250 g (9 oz) plain flour, plus extra
  for dusting
1 tsp sea salt
250 g (9 oz) cold, unsalted butter

For the masala
1 small onion, peeled
10 cloves garlic, peeled
vegetable oil
6 cm (2½ in) piece of fresh
  ginger, peeled
3 level tsp ground coriander
3 level tsp chilli powder
3 level tsp turmeric
3 level tsp garam masala
2 large bunches fresh
  coriander, leaves picked
3 ripe tomatoes

METHOD

For the first marinade, finely grate the garlic and ginger and place in a bowl. Add the chilli powder, lemon juice and chicken, then set aside to marinate for 30 minutes.

For the second marinade, add all of the ingredients to the bowl containing the chicken, mix together well and leave to marinate in the refrigerator for a further 4–6 hours.

Pre-heat the barbecue to hot, or the oven to 200°C/400°F/gas 6. Skewer the marinated chicken pieces and cook over the barbecue or in the oven for 15 minutes or until cooked through. Brush with a mixture of butter, lime juice and chaat masala or garam masala and set aside.

For the pastry, sieve the flour and salt into a bowl. Cube the butter, then rub it in with your fingertips until the mixture resembles breadcrumbs. Add up to 50 ml (1½ fl oz) cold water, and slowly and gently mix into a dough until just combined but not wet. Dust the dough with flour, wrap in clingfilm and leave to rest in the refrigerator for 30 minutes.

Turn the oven down to 160°C/325°F/gas 3. For the masala, chop the onion and garlic, then add with a little vegetable oil to a pan over a medium heat and sauté for 5 minutes until soft. Finely grate the ginger into the pan and cook for 2 minutes until golden.

Stir through the spices, then chop the coriander and tomatoes and add to the pan, stirring to combine. Stir for a couple more minutes until everything is cooked through. Toss the chicken in the masala.

Roll out the pastry to just under ½ cm (¼ in) thick. Line the base of a pie dish (roughly 20 cm x 20 cm x 6 cm/ 8 in x 8 in x 2½ in) with pastry, reserving some for the lid. Add the chicken filling to the dish. Lay the second piece of pastry on top, seal the edges, trim off any excess and poke a small hole in the top. Bake in the oven for 35–40 minutes, or until the pastry is golden and the filling is hot.

TRADITIONAL ROAST RIB OF BEEF

Recipe by **PIPPA MIDDLETON**, food enthusiast, Chelsea, London

SERVINGS: 8 | **PREP TIME: 15 MINS PLUS RESTING** | **COOK TIME: VARIES** | **SKILL LEVEL: 1 (EASY)**

This recipe for roast rib of beef, which comes from my first book, Celebrate, *is the ultimate Sunday lunch dish. Roast beef and Yorkshire pudding is a quintessential British combination, well known from the middle of the 18th century when the French started referring to the English as "les rosbifs". Rib of beef is one of the tastiest cuts as it's cooked on the bone, which also makes for a flavoursome gravy. Ask the butcher to trim the bones for a neat finish. I like to cheat a little and use shop-bought fresh or frozen Yorkshire puddings. Remember to remove the meat from the fridge half an hour before cooking to allow it to come to room temperature.*

INGREDIENTS

3- to 4-bone trimmed rib of beef, 3 kg (6¾ lb) (approx.)

4–6 tbsp Dijon mustard

For the horseradish dressing

100 g (3½ oz) hot horseradish sauce

4 tbsp crème fraîche

a squeeze of lemon juice

For the gravy

4 tbsp plain flour

800 ml (1½ pints) good-quality beef stock

200 ml (7 fl oz) red wine

METHOD

Pre-heat the oven to 220°C/425°F/gas 7. Place the beef rib in a large roasting tray and spread the mustard all over the meat. Season well with salt and pepper. Roast in the pre-heated oven for 20 minutes, then reduce the heat to 170°C/325°F/gas 3 and roast for the remaining calculated cooking time (see roasting times below). Baste with the roasting juices occasionally. Once the meat is cooked to your preference, remove it from the oven, transfer it to a board and cover with tinfoil. Reserve the roasting juices. Allow the meat to rest for at least 25–30 minutes. Combine the horseradish sauce, crème fraîche and lemon juice in a bowl. Season to taste.

To make the gravy, drain all but 3–4 tablespoons of fat from the roasting tray. Place the tray on the hob over a medium heat and stir in the flour. Once combined, gradually whisk in the stock and red wine. Continue to whisk until smooth and allow to reduce until thickened. Season with salt and pepper to taste, add the roasting juices and strain before serving. Serve with a red claret, accompanied by the horseradish dressing and gravy.

ROASTING TIMES FOR BEEF ON THE BONE

For rare, allow 12 minutes per 450 grams (1 lb), plus 15 minutes.

For medium, allow 16 minutes per 450 grams (1 lb), plus 20 minutes.

For well done, allow 20 minutes per 450 grams (1 lb), plus 25 minutes.

Check and baste the meat frequently and adjust the timings for your particular oven.

POT-ROAST GUINEA FOWL WITH WILD MUSHROOMS, PRUNES & THYME

Recipe by **ADAM BYATT**, Trinity, Clapham Old Town, London

SERVINGS: 4 | **PREP TIME: 10 MINS** | **COOK TIME: 50 MINS** | **SKILL LEVEL: 1 (EASY)**

This dish is a very simple one-pot wonder that is versatile enough to use with chicken, turkey, goose or duck, and can be ready in less than an hour. It simply relies on first-rate cookery and seasoning to deliver the perfect result.

INGREDIENTS

100 g (3½ oz) prunes

1 Earl Grey tea bag

8 guinea fowl thighs

olive oil, for frying

2 shallots, thinly sliced

½ bunch thyme

2 cloves garlic, left whole

250 g (9 oz) wild mushrooms (chanterelles, girolles, ceps – or use cultivated), washed, cleaned and dried

200 ml (7 fl oz) good-quality brown chicken stock

12 new potatoes

50 g (1½ oz) butter, plus a knob

a handful of chopped parsley, to garnish

GF

METHOD

Pre-heat oven to 170°C/150°C fan/gas 3½. Place the prunes in a bowl with the Earl Grey tea bag. Pour boiling water over and leave to stand for 1 hour.

Meanwhile, lay the guinea fowl thighs, skin-side down, in a cold, heavy-based non-stick frying pan with a drizzle of olive oil and plenty of seasoning. Place this over a low heat and simmer gently for 10 minutes until the thighs begin to crisp. Turn them over and seal the flesh on the other side. After 6 minutes, remove the thighs from the pan and set aside.

Add the shallots, thyme and garlic to the pan and sweat gently for 5 minutes, then add the mushrooms and cook until soft. Pour in the chicken stock and allow it to come slowly to the boil.

Meanwhile, sauté the potatoes in a good glug of hot olive oil until evenly golden, then add the 50 g (1½ oz) butter, season well and place in the pre-heated oven. Cook for 15 minutes.

Place the guinea fowl thighs back into the mushroom pan, skin-side up on top of the mushrooms, and slowly simmer for 15 minutes until cooked through. Remove the thighs from the pan again, remove the bone from each and cut them in half, and leave them to rest.

Add the knob of butter and the chopped parsley to the mushroom mix, adjust the seasoning and pour into the centre of a deep bowl/plate, or serve straight from the dish with the boneless thighs on top, placing a sautéed potato and half a prune between each thigh.

GRILLED LAMB NECK, MINTED FLAGEOLET BEANS & GARLIC CRUMBS

Recipe by **TOM OLDROYD**, Oldroyd, Islington, London

SERVINGS: 2 | **PREP TIME: 30 MINS PLUS MARINATING OVERNIGHT** | **COOK TIME: 1 HOUR 10 MINS**
SKILL LEVEL: 1 (EASY)

INGREDIENTS

For the grill
a good glug of oil
3 cloves garlic, crushed
1 sprig rosemary, leaves picked
300 g (10½ oz) trimmed middle lamb neck (ask your butcher)
a knob of butter

For the pot
200 g (7 oz) dried flageolet beans, soaked overnight in cold water and then drained
½ medium-sized onion
½ leek (the greener end)
½ stalk celery

½ carrot
3 bashed cloves garlic
1 bay leaf

For the beans
½ medium-sized onion, finely diced
½ leek (the whiter end), finely diced
½ carrot, finely diced
½ stalk celery, finely diced
2 cloves garlic, finely diced
3 sprigs thyme, leaves removed
about 25 ml (1 fl oz) olive oil
about 50 ml (1½ fl oz) double cream
1 small handful of chopped mint

For the crumbs
2 slices of day-old bread, toasted (in the toaster is fine)
1 small handful of parsley, roughly chopped
zest of ½ lemon
1 fat clove garlic, finely grated
olive oil

METHOD

Mix together the oil, garlic and rosemary leaves; coat the lamb and marinate overnight. Remove your marinated lamb neck from the fridge well before grilling.

Put the beans, vegetables, garlic, bay leaf and enough cold water to cover them by 2–3 cm (1–1¼ in) in a large pot. Bring to the boil and skim off any impurities that float to the surface. Simmer until the beans are almost cooked, about 40 minutes, topping up the water when necessary. Remove from the heat, discard the vegetables and herbs, and season the beans. Of course you can omit this stage if you would rather use tinned flageolet beans (one 375 g/13 oz tin should suffice).

In a heavy-based pan, sweat the diced vegetables, thyme and seasoning in the olive oil. When starting to stick, add the beans with a little of the cooking liquid. Add the double cream and chopped mint. Bring to a simmer, then remove from the heat. Check the seasoning.

For the crumbs, place the bread, parsley, zest and garlic in a food processor and blitz until well combined, adding a spoonful of olive oil at a time to help.

Heat a griddle pan (or a frying pan will do). Season and oil the lamb neck and cook for 3 minutes on each side. Add a knob of butter for the last 30 seconds. Remove the neck to a warm plate to rest for 2 minutes. Slice into 2 cm (¾ in) slices and place on top of the warm flageolet beans. Sprinkle some breadcrumbs over.

THOMASINA MIERS
TV PRESENTER, CHEF, AUTHOR & COLUMNIST

For me, cooking is all about spending time with family and friends. Both the dishes I've chosen are the type of things I would cook at home – just put the food out and let people help themselves. The Pork Pibil is great just slammed on the table, with some tortillas on the side so people can make their own tacos. It's convivial, fun, sharing food.

Fitzrovia, London

PORK PIBIL

Recipe by **THOMASINA MIERS**, TV presenter, chef, author & columnist, Fitzrovia, London

SERVINGS: 8-10 | PREP TIME: 30 MINS PLUS MARINATING OVERNIGHT | COOK TIME: 3-4 HOURS
SKILL LEVEL: 1 (EASY)

This is our bestselling dish at Wahaca and one of my favourite recipes from Mexico. It comes from the Yucatán, with achiote, a spicy paste made from the ground red berries of the annatto tree, turning the marinade brick red and the habanero chilli (also Yucatecan) giving it a lovely touch of fire. You can buy achiote online or from specialist shops. If you prefer your food not too hot, simply leave the chilli out. We use neck end of pork, which is marbled with delicious pork fat to melt into the sauce. For the tastiest, most tender pork, marinate the day before cooking. In the Yucatán, the pink pickled onion relish is used to accompany Pork Pibil, which is probably the most popular item on our menu at Wahaca. The red onions, which are marinated in fresh lime juice, fresh orange juice and habanero chilli, turn a brilliant neon pink colour, which the Yucatecans use to brilliant effect in many dishes. This is also great on grilled chicken and with slow-cooked black turtle beans.

INGREDIENTS

1 tsp allspice berries
2 tsp freshly ground cumin seeds
½ tsp cloves
1 tsp peppercorns
100 g (3½ oz) achiote paste
3 tbsp cider vinegar
1 medium-sized onion, coarsely chopped
3 fat cloves garlic, coarsely chopped
a large bunch fresh oregano (or 1 tsp dried)
3 fresh bay leaves
2 tbsp sea salt
3 tbsp olive oil
juice of 6 oranges (about 450 ml/16 fl oz)
2 kg (4½ lb) neck of pork
1 habanero or Scotch bonnet chilli, de-seeded and finely chopped
50 g (1½ oz) butter

For the pink pickled onions
2 red onions, thinly sliced
juice of 2 limes
juice of 1 orange
1 habanero or Scotch bonnet chilli, very finely chopped
freshly chopped coriander, to serve

METHOD

Warm the spices in a dry frying pan for a few minutes and then grind to a fine powder in a mortar and pestle or spice grinder. Add them to an upright blender with the achiote, vinegar, onion, garlic, herbs, salt and olive oil and pulse to start breaking up the achiote. Slowly pour in the orange juice with the motor running to get a smooth paste.

Pour about two-thirds of the marinade over the pork, ensuring that it is thoroughly coated. Cover and refrigerate overnight. Freeze your remaining marinade or keep it fresh for a week in the fridge (and try it with something else, like barbecued chicken).

Pre-heat the oven to 130°C/265°F/gas ½.

Transfer the pork and its marinade to a large casserole dish with the chopped chilli and the butter. Bring to simmering point, cover with tinfoil and a tight-fitting lid, and transfer to the oven. Cook for about 4 hours or until the pork is soft and falling apart.

While the pork is cooking, prepare the pink pickled onions. Cover the onion slices with boiling water and soak for 10 seconds. Drain and then add the lime and orange juices and chopped chilli (leave out half the chilli if you are not great with very hot food).

Season well and, using your hands, massage the chilli in the marinade and leave to marinate for several hours. Now, scrub your hands meticulously or you will suffer the ferocious heat of the habanero! Scatter with chopped coriander just before serving. This relish will keep for several days in the fridge.

Serve chunks of pork in deep bowls with rice or steamed potatoes, lots of sauce and piles of the pink pickled onions on top.

GF

ROAST JERUSALEM ARTICHOKES & CHICKEN WITH ANCHOVY, WALNUT & PARSLEY RELISH

Recipe by **DIANA HENRY**, food writer & columnist, London

SERVINGS: 4 | **PREP TIME: 15 MINS** | **COOK TIME: 1 HOUR** | **SKILL LEVEL: 2 (MODERATE)**

Here, anchovies are not disguised — you know you're eating them — but I am totally hooked on salty-sweet-savoury combinations. Cooks tend to think anchovies are good with lamb, but they work really well with chicken, too.

INGREDIENTS

For the chicken

900 g (2 lb) Jerusalem artichokes

5 tbsp extra-virgin olive oil

8 skin-on, bone-in chicken thighs, or a mixture of joints

juice of 1 lemon

For the relish

1 fat clove garlic, chopped

1 tsp sea salt flakes

150 g (5 oz) walnut pieces

5 anchovy fillets, drained of oil and chopped

75 ml (2 fl oz) extra-virgin olive oil

1 tsp white balsamic vinegar

4 tbsp finely chopped flat-leaf parsley leaves

DF, GF

METHOD

Pre-heat the oven to 200°C/400°F/gas 6. Scrub the Jerusalem artichokes well. You don't need to peel them (the skin looks good and has a nice nutty flavour). Cut them in half lengthways and put them in a steamer. Cook for about 10 minutes, then pat them dry.

Heat half the oil in a roasting tin on the hob. Tumble in the Jerusalem artichokes and shake them around to coat in the oil. Brush the rest of the oil on the chicken joints and put these into the tin too, making space for them among the artichokes. Season well and squeeze on the lemon juice. Roast for 35–40 minutes, shaking the pan every so often. The vegetables should be tender and caramelized in patches and the chicken golden and cooked through.

Meanwhile, make the relish. Put the garlic and salt flakes into a mortar and grind to a paste. Add the walnuts and anchovies and pound until you have a mixture that is partly puréed, partly chunky. Stir in the oil, vinegar, some pepper and the parsley. Either serve the relish on the side (that way people get to choose how much they have), or spoon it over the chicken and artichokes.

HARDEEP SINGH KOHLI
CHEF, COMIC & TV PRESENTER

I suppose my interest in food stems from the fact that it's about communing – it's about bringing people together. I'm much less interested in food when it's just me on my own. Around the dinner table we fall in love, we raise families, we do business. For me, food is central to everything we do. *Hardeep*

Regent's Canal, London

OVERNIGHT ROAST PORK BELLY WITH PEARS & THYME

Recipe by **HARDEEP SINGH KOHLI**, chef, comic & TV presenter, Regent's Canal, London

SERVINGS: 6–8 | **PREP TIME: 30 MINS** | **COOK TIME: 9½ HOURS (OR OVERNIGHT)** | **SKILL LEVEL: 1 (EASY)**

INGREDIENTS

1 pork belly (2½–3 kg/
  5½–6½ lb)

3 tbsp rapeseed oil

2 tbsp sea salt

2 leeks

2 carrots

4 sticks celery

8 peppercorns

12 bunches of thyme, of which
  4 should be stripped of leaves

560 ml (1 pint) perry (or pear
  cider)

5 firm pears: 4 halved and cored,
  1 finely diced

DF, GF

METHOD

Set the oven to the highest setting. Pop the kettle on. On buying your belly, have your butcher remove it from the bone. Keep the bone and bring it home. Also, have them remove the skin, having first scored it in a criss-cross fashion.

Place the skin in the sink and pour boiling water over it. Carefully dry the skin, thoroughly. Rub a tablespoon of oil and then the sea salt into the scored flesh. Place the skin in an oiled roasting tin and put in the oven. It should take only 30 minutes for the skin to become crackling. Remove the crackling and allow to cool. Turn the oven down to 120°C/250°F/gas ½.

Slice the leeks, carrots and celery in half lengthways. Lay them in the bottom of a roasting tin with the peppercorns. On top, lay the rib bones, 8 sprigs of thyme and then drizzle a tablespoon of oil over. Tuck the veg in under the ribs. Lay the pork belly on top, oil and drizzle the rest of the oil, and scatter the remaining salt over.

Pour 350 ml (12 fl oz) of the perry into the roasting tin. Cover in tinfoil and pop into the oven for anything between 9 and 11 hours. At 90 minutes before the end of cooking, add the halved pears. Roast uncovered for the final hour and a half.

Remove the pork from the oven. Carefully lift the pork and the pears out and keep warm. Discard the cooked veg. They have served us well. Add the remaining perry, deglaze the tin and reduce the liquor by half. Immediately before serving, add the remaining thyme leaves and finely diced pear.

PIGEON & MELLOW GARLIC PURÉE

Recipe by **SAM & SAM CLARK**, Moro and Morito restaurants, North London

SERVINGS: 4 | **PREP TIME: 20 MINS** | **COOK TIME: 15 MINS** | **SKILL LEVEL: 1 (EASY)**

The less you cook garlic, the more aggressive the flavour. The longer you cook it, the mellower it will be. For a more punchy purée, therefore, cook the garlic in the milk for only 10 minutes. At Morito we also serve this purée with lamb's kidneys or slivers of salted anchovy and a Morito roll or two.

INGREDIENTS

For the garlic purée

3 heads new-season garlic, peeled
300 ml (10½ fl oz) whole milk
1 tbsp extra-virgin olive oil

For the pigeon (or lamb's kidney)

4 pigeon breasts (or 4 lamb's kidneys)
50 g (1½ oz) butter
½ tbsp shredded flat-leaf parsley

GF

METHOD

Place the garlic in a small saucepan and cover with the milk. Simmer for 10 minutes, until the garlic is just soft. Add the olive oil and some salt to the pan. Using a hand-held blender, purée the garlic with the milk until smooth. Check the seasoning and keep warm.

If you are using lamb's kidneys, peel off the thin membrane. Slice each kidney in half lengthways and snip out as much white gristle as possible with scissors. Then cut each half into bite-sized pieces.

To sear the pigeon breasts or lamb's kidneys, put a frying pan over a medium to high heat and add the butter. When it begins to foam, season the pigeon breasts or kidneys well with salt and pepper and add to the pan. Sear the pigeon for 3–5 minutes on either side, depending on size, until caramelized. Set aside to relax for a few minutes, then slice, transfer to a plate and pour over any pan juices. The kidneys require less time – probably about 3 minutes in total. They should still be pink in the middle. Sprinkle over the parsley and serve with the warm purée on the side, and some toast.

OVEN-ROASTED LOIN OF LAMB WITH PEAS, BROAD BEANS, GEM LETTUCE & PANCETTA, SERVED WITH GARLIC ROSEMARY POTATOES

Recipe by **KAREN TAYLOR**, home economist for *The Great British Menu* and *MasterChef*, Old Basing, Hampshire

SERVINGS: 2 | **PREP TIME: 30 MINS** | **COOK TIME: 1¼ HOURS** | **SKILL LEVEL: 1 (EASY)**

INGREDIENTS

300 g (10½ oz) loin of lamb
olive oil, for sealing

For the garlic rosemary potatoes
300 g (10½ oz) new potatoes
1 tbsp olive oil
2 cloves garlic, crushed, peeled
1 large sprig rosemary, picked

For the peas, broad beans, gem lettuce & pancetta
a knob of unsalted butter
100 g (3½ oz) pancetta, cubed
100 g (3½ oz) peas, fresh or frozen
100 g (3½ oz) podded broad beans
125 ml (4 fl oz) chicken stock
1 little gem lettuce, shredded

GF

METHOD

Pre-heat the oven to 180°C/350°F/gas 4. Boil the potatoes until tender; drain and cut in half lengthways.

Season the lamb loin with salt and pepper. In a large, ovenproof, non-stick frying pan, heat some olive oil until hot and sear the loin on all sides. Remove from the frying pan and set to one side.

Add a further tablespoon of olive oil to the frying pan, along with the halved potatoes, garlic cloves and picked rosemary sprig. Sauté until the potatoes are golden-brown on all sides.

Lay the seared lamb loin on top of the potatoes and cook in the pre-heated oven for 10–15 minutes, depending on the thickness of the loin – longer if a more well-done result is preferred.

Meanwhile, heat the butter in another frying pan and fry the pancetta cubes until crisp. Add the peas, broad beans and stock, and cook for 2–3 minutes. Add the shredded gem lettuce and season with salt and pepper.

Remove the lamb and potatoes from the oven. Allow the meat to rest for at least 10 minutes before carving into thick slices. Serve with the garlic rosemary potatoes and spoonfuls of the peas and broad beans.

FILLET OF BEEF
WITH BASIL & LEMON COURGETTES

Recipe by **NIGEL SLATER**, food writer & TV broadcaster, Highbury, London

SERVINGS: 8 | PREP TIME: 15 MINS PLUS RESTING AND DRAINING | COOK TIME: 45 MINS
SKILL LEVEL: 1 (EASY)

INGREDIENTS

2 tbsp white peppercorns

2 tbsp black peppercorns

2 tsp sea salt flakes

olive oil

700 g (1 lb 8 oz) fillet of beef

2 large or 4 small courgettes

2 plump cloves garlic

8–10 bushy sprigs thyme,
  leaves picked

a good handful of basil leaves

½ large lemon, to squeeze

DF, GF

METHOD

Lightly crush the peppercorns (I use a mortar and pestle). They should resemble fine gravel rather than powder. Tip the ground peppercorns onto a plate and mix in the sea salt flakes. Lightly oil the fillet of beef, then roll it in the salt and pepper, pressing down firmly so that the meat is encrusted.

Wipe the courgettes, then cut them into thick, matchstick-shaped strips. Toss them in a little salt and set them aside in a colander to drain for 20 minutes. This will prevent them becoming 'wet' during roasting. Drain them, pat them dry with paper towel, then add a tablespoon of olive oil. Peel and crush the garlic and add to the courgettes with some ground black pepper and the leaves from the thyme sprigs, then toss gently so that the courgettes are evenly oiled and seasoned. Set the oven at 230°C/450°F/gas 8.

Tip the courgettes into a roasting tin and place the peppered beef on top. Roast for 10 minutes, then lower the heat to 180°C/350°F/gas 4 and continue to cook for a further 25 minutes. Remove the meat from the tin, place on a warm plate, cover with tinfoil and leave to rest for 10 minutes. Return the courgettes to the oven; you want them to be tender and golden.

When the courgettes are ready, add the basil leaves, roughly torn, and toss gently, taking care not to break them up. Squeeze over a little lemon juice, then place on a warm serving plate.

Slice the beef very thinly, place on top of the courgettes, season with a little sea salt and serve.

TIP

If you want something to go with this, I would sauté some potatoes.

RICHARD BERTINET
CHEF & BAKER

I've been teaching people to cook and bake
for more than 10 years now, and the more
I teach, the more I love it. Just the magic of it
all: making my students realize they can create
something special, and seeing the confidence
they get from having a go at home. *Richard*

*Bath,
Somerset*

DUCK PIE

Recipe by **RICHARD BERTINET**, chef & baker, Bath, Somerset

SERVINGS: 12 | **PREP TIME: OVER ABOUT 24 HOURS** | **COOK TIME: 3 HOURS** | **SKILL LEVEL: 2 (MODERATE)**

This is a fantastic, rich, open pie that is finished with a little sherry or port jelly poured into it after baking. It is served cold, topped with roasted beetroot and shallots, so it looks quite spectacular. You can find beetroot in all sorts of colours and stripes in good greengrocers or farm shops, so have fun with the topping. I promise it is much simpler to make than it sounds; you just need to allow plenty of time. Ideally, start the night before: make the pastry and line the tin, then put the meat in a bowl to marinate, and keep both in the fridge overnight. If you're pushed for time, a couple of hours in the fridge for both is fine, but note that once you have made the pie, cooled it for 2 hours, then poured in the jelly, it will need to go back into the fridge to set for another 4–5 hours. For deep game and pork pies like this I always dust the greased tin with flour, which seems to help the finish of the pastry.

INGREDIENTS

For the pastry
250 g (9 oz) plain flour
5 g (1 tsp) salt
125 g (4½ oz) butter, straight from the fridge, bashed with a rolling pin between butter wrappers or greaseproof paper
1 egg
35 g or ml (1¼ oz or fl oz) cold water
butter or baking spray, for greasing tin
flour, for dusting

For the filling
200 g (7 oz) pork belly
200 g (7 oz) pork shoulder
200 g (7 oz) duck leg meat
200 g (7 oz) duck liver, diced
6 juniper berries
2 tsp whole allspice
1 tsp whole green peppercorns
1 tsp sweet smoked paprika
1 large sprig thyme, leaves only
200 ml (7 oz) sherry or port
18 small shallots, unpeeled
light olive oil or rapeseed oil
1 smoked duck breast
2 large eggs
150 ml (5 fl oz) single cream
sea salt and freshly ground black pepper

For the jelly
3 gelatine leaves
200 ml (7 fl oz) good-quality chicken stock
100 ml (3½ fl oz) sweet sherry or port

For the topping
3 medium-sized golden (or striped) beetroot
3 medium-sized red beetroot
a few sprigs of rosemary and thyme
olive oil

METHOD

Make the pastry. In a bowl, mix the flour with the salt. Cover the butter well with flour and tear it into large pieces. With both hands, scoop up the flour-covered butter and flick your thumbs over the surface, pushing away from you, as if you are dealing a pack of cards. Keep the butter coated in flour so they don't become sticky. Stop mixing when the shards of butter are the size of your little fingernail. Tip the egg into the flour mixture, add the water and mix everything together. Using a spoon or a plastic scraper, scrape around the sides of the bowl and pull the mixture into the centre until it forms a very rough dough that shouldn't be at all sticky. While it is still in the bowl, press down on the dough with both thumbs, then turn the dough clockwise a few degrees and press down and turn again. Repeat this a few times, then turn the pastry out onto a work surface and fold the pastry over itself and press down until the pastry looks like plasticine, and looks homogenous. Pick up the pastry and tap each side on the work surface to square it off so that when you come to roll it, you are starting off with a good shape rather than raggedy edges. Then wrap the pastry in greaseproof paper and rest it in the fridge for at least 1 hour, preferably several or, better still, overnight.

Trim and dice the pork belly and shoulder, duck leg meat and liver and place in a bowl. Add the juniper berries, spices, thyme and sherry or port, stir, then leave to marinate for at least 2–3 hours, but preferably overnight, in the fridge. Give the bowl a shake from time to time.

Lightly grease a 20 cm (8 in) loose-bottomed square or round cake tin and tip in a little flour. Tilt the tin around so that every surface is lightly dusted, then tip out the excess. Remove the pastry from the fridge and roll it out on a very lightly floured surface to form a square or circle about 5 mm (¼ in) thick and twice the size of your tin (i.e. 40 cm/16 in square or in diameter). Lift the pastry over the tin and gently line it. Place it back into the fridge for at least 30 minutes, or until the meat has finished marinating.

When you are ready to make the pie, pre-heat the oven to 180°C/350°F/gas 4.

Put the unpeeled shallots in a pan with enough light olive oil or rapeseed oil to cover, and simmer very slowly for 10–15 minutes until they are soft and can be easily pierced with the tip of a knife. Leave to cool, then slice off the base and squeeze from the other end so that the shallots pop out of their skins. Keep the shallot flesh to one side.

Dice the smoked duck breast, then set aside.

Remove the marinated meat from the fridge and put it through a mincer (use the largest hole), or chop finely with a large knife.

Mix the eggs and cream together in a bowl, stir in the minced meat, add the diced duck breast and season. To test that it is seasoned to your liking, take a little bit of the mixture and fry it in a pan. Make sure it is cooked through, then taste it and adjust the seasoning if necessary. Now mix in half of the shallots.

Recipe continues next page

Take your pastry case out of the fridge and fill it with the meat mixture. Cover the top with a piece of greaseproof paper to stop the pastry browning too quickly; place on a baking tray and bake for 1½–1¾ hours, or until the meat is cooked through. During the baking, rotate the pie and move it around the oven if necessary, so that the pastry is evenly baked. You can test this by inserting a metal skewer into some pieces of meat and checking that the skewer comes out piping hot. For the last 30 minutes, remove the greaseproof paper. Take the pie from the oven and leave it to cool for at least 2 hours.

To make the jelly, soak the gelatine leaves briefly in cold water, just long enough to soften them. Squeeze out the excess water.

Heat the chicken stock and sherry or port in a pan, then add the squeezed gelatine. Stir well until the gelatine has dissolved. Remove from the heat and leave to cool a little, but not too much or the jelly will start to get too thick to pour.

Now take the cold pie (still in its tin). You will notice that the meat has separated a little from the pastry case, so pour the sherry jelly into the gap and over the top of the meat. Put the pie in the fridge so that the jelly sets. This will take 4–5 hours, but the pie will be at its best after 24 hours (it will keep in the fridge for up to a week if you don't want to eat it straight away).

Before serving, heat the oven again to 200°C/400°F/gas 6.

Wash the unpeeled beetroot and put them whole into a pan of water. Bring to the boil, then lower the heat and simmer for about 20 minutes, until you can slide the tip of a knife into the beetroot but there is still a bit of resistance. Lift out and, when cool enough to handle, cut into wedges, leaving the peel on and any bits of root or stalk – these give the wedges character and will make the topping of your pie look even more eye-catching. Place in a baking tin with the rosemary and thyme, drizzle with a little olive oil, and roast in the oven for about 25 minutes, or until tender. Remove and allow to cool.

When the jelly has set, ease the whole pie carefully from the tin, arrange the beetroot wedges and reserved shallots on top, and serve.

PAS

RISO

& SI

TA,

TTO

DES

RUTH ROGERS MBE,
WITH SIAN WYN OWEN & JOSEPH TRIVELLI
THE RIVER CAFÉ

The best ingredients come from the season they are associated with – peas in the spring, mushrooms in the autumn, melons in early May. This risotto reminds me of summer or maybe late spring; I can imagine eating it in Sardinia while on a sailing trip.

Hammersmith,
London

RISOTTO CON PISELLI, LIMONE E RICOTTA

PEA, RICOTTA & LEMON ZEST RISOTTO

Recipe by **RUTH ROGERS** MBE, The River Café, Hammersmith, London

SERVINGS: 6 | **PREP TIME: 20 MINS** | **COOK TIME: 30 MINS** | **SKILL LEVEL: I (EASY)**

INGREDIENTS

1½ litres (2¾ pints) chicken stock

Maldon salt and freshly ground black pepper

3 kg (6¾ lb) fresh young peas (podded weight 1½ kg/3 lb 6 oz)

2 tbsp fresh mint leaves

3 cloves garlic, peeled, 2 chopped

200 g (7 oz) unsalted butter

500 g (1 lb 2 oz) spring onions, roughly chopped

400 g (14 oz) Carnaroli or Arborio rice

2 tbsp torn fresh basil leaves

150 ml (5 fl oz) dry vermouth

250 g (9 oz) fresh ricotta, lightly beaten

finely grated zest of 2 washed lemons

50 g (1½ oz) Parmesan, freshly grated

GF

METHOD

Heat the chicken stock to boiling and check for seasoning. Bring a medium-sized saucepan of water to the boil, and add ½ tablespoon salt, the peas, half the mint and the whole garlic clove. Simmer for 3–4 minutes or until the peas are al dente. Drain, keeping back 150 ml (5 fl oz) of the water. Return the peas, mint and garlic clove to this water and put aside.

Melt 150 g (5 oz) of the butter in a large, thick-bottomed saucepan; add the spring onion and soften. Add the chopped garlic, then the rice, stirring for about 2–3 minutes to coat each grain. Add a ladleful of hot stock and stir, adding another when the rice has absorbed the first. Continue stirring and adding stock for 10 minutes or until the rice is not quite al dente.

Add half the peas, keeping back the cooked garlic and mint and their liquor. In a food processor, mash together the remainder of the peas, mint and garlic with the liquor, then add to the risotto and combine. Stir in the basil. Add the vermouth, about 2 tablespoons of the ricotta, and the remaining butter. Cook briefly to wilt the basil and melt the butter. The rice should be al dente.

Serve with the remaining ricotta over each portion, sprinkled with lemon zest, salt, pepper and Parmesan.

VERMICELLI WITH PRAWNS, TOMATO & BASIL

Recipe by **THEO RANDALL**, Theo Randall at the InterContinental, Mayfair, London

SERVINGS: 4 | **PREP TIME: 10 MINS** | **COOK TIME: 15 MINS** | **SKILL LEVEL: 1 (EASY)**

Vermicelli is a very underused pasta and cooks remarkably quickly — this kind of dish can be made from start to finish in less than 20 minutes. It's delicious in summer, when lovely, ripe plum tomatoes are available.

INGREDIENTS

1 tbsp olive oil, plus extra
  to serve
1 clove garlic, finely sliced
1 dried chilli
2 tbsp chopped basil
300 g (10½ oz) ripe plum
  tomatoes, skinned,
  de-seeded and chopped
500 g (1 lb 2 oz) peeled
  raw prawns, de-veined
  and cut in half lengthways
400 g (14 oz) vermicelli

DF

METHOD

Heat the oil in a large, heavy-based frying pan; add the garlic, chilli and half the basil and cook gently until the garlic is soft. Add the tomatoes and cook vigorously for 5–7 minutes, until the sauce has become thicker and the flavour is concentrated. Remove from the heat, add the prawns and let them cook in the residual heat of the sauce. Season to taste.

Cook the pasta in a large pan of boiling salted water until al dente — it will cook very quickly. Drain and add to the sauce, then toss well and cook gently for 2 minutes. Finish with the remaining basil and a good dash of olive oil.

PASTA & GREENS WITH GOAT'S CHEESE

Recipe by **HUGH FEARNLEY-WHITTINGSTALL**, River Cottage, Devon

SERVINGS: 4 | **PREP TIME: 10 MINS** | **COOK TIME: 10 MINS** | **SKILL LEVEL: 1 (EASY)**

However much you love your leaves — and I bow to no one in my devotion — there are probably times when you find you have just a bit too much greenery in the fridge, at least some of which needs using up rather urgently. I make this quick pasta dish at precisely such moments. It works with almost-on-the-turn raw greens as well as leftover cooked greens; simply adjust the cooking time accordingly.

INGREDIENTS

300 g (10½ oz) pasta shapes, such as penne, fusilli or farfalle

1 tbsp rapeseed or olive oil, or a knob of butter

2 shallots, finely diced

2 cloves garlic, halved and finely sliced

100–200 ml (3½–7 fl oz) chicken or veg stock, or water

200–250 g (7–9 oz) shredded cooked spring greens, Savoy cabbage, kale or Brussels sprouts, or a few handfuls of uncooked leaves, such as spinach or rocket, tough stems removed, trimmed and shredded

3 tbsp crème fraîche

about 100 g (3½ oz) soft goat's cheese

½ tsp dried chilli flakes (optional)

a small handful of basil leaves, roughly chopped (optional)

2 tbsp roughly chopped walnuts or pine nuts, lightly toasted (optional)

METHOD

Bring a large saucepan of water to the boil and salt it well. Add the pasta and cook according to the packet guidelines, until al dente.

Meanwhile, heat the oil or butter in a frying pan over a low heat. Add the shallots and sauté gently for a few minutes until softened, then add the garlic and fry for a minute.

Now pour in the stock or water: if the greens are already cooked, add 100 ml (3½ fl oz) of liquid; if they're not, add 200 ml (7 fl oz).

Toss in the shredded greens and stir. If using uncooked greens, cover with a lid and simmer for a few minutes until just tender; for cooked greens, just heat through with the lid off.

Remove from the heat, stir in the crème fraîche and season well with salt and pepper.

When the pasta is cooked, drain and add to the creamy greens. Crumble in the goat's cheese and add the chilli flakes, basil and/or toasted nuts, if using. Toss to combine.

Divide between warmed bowls and serve.

VARIATION

Punchier version: gently fry a diced onion in a little olive oil until soft. Add a few anchovy fillets with some of their oil and a diced green or red fresh chilli. Fry until the anchovies break up. Toss with the pasta, cooked greens and soft goat's cheese, or scatter over lots of grated hard goat's cheese or other well-flavoured hard cheese.

ROTOLO DI SPINACI AL BURRO E FORMAGGIO

SPINACH & PASTA ROLL WITH MELTED BUTTER & PARMESAN

Recipe by **ANNA DEL CONTE OMRI**, food writer, Shaftesbury, Dorset

SERVINGS: 6 | PREP TIME: 45 MINS PLUS RESTING | COOK TIME: 1¼ HOURS
SKILL LEVEL: 2 (MODERATE)

This is a lovely vegetarian dish consisting of a roll of homemade pasta stuffed with spinach and ricotta, the most traditional of all vegetarian pasta fillings. The pasta must be rolled out by hand, but it is not too difficult to handle, being made with only 2 eggs. I recommend adding a teaspoon of oil to the dough to make it easier to stretch and roll thin. For the same reason, I also suggest making a dough you would roll out by machine.

INGREDIENTS

500 g (1 lb 2 oz) baby spinach leaves or 1 kg (2¼ lb) fresh bunch spinach

sea salt

2 tbsp finely chopped shallots

150 g (5 oz) unsalted butter

300 g (7 oz) fresh ricotta

100 g (3½ oz) freshly grated Parmesan

¼ tsp ground nutmeg

1 free-range egg yolk

2 cloves garlic, peeled and bruised

a small sprig of fresh sage

For the pasta

200 g (7 oz) Italian '00' flour

2 free-range eggs

1 tsp olive oil, for rolling the pasta

METHOD

If you are using bunch spinach, discard any wilted or discoloured leaves, the roots and the long stems. Wash very well in a basin in several changes of cold water. The baby leaves only need one wash. Cook with just the water that clings to the leaves in a covered pan with sea salt until tender, then drain. Squeeze the spinach lightly in your hands to remove most of the moisture. Set aside.

In a frying pan, sauté the shallot with 45 g (1½ oz) of the butter over a medium heat. Chop the spinach coarsely by hand and when the shallot turns pale gold in colour, add it to the pan. Sauté for 5 minutes, turning the spinach over and over to insaporire – take up the flavour. You will find that all the butter has been absorbed.

Transfer the contents of the frying pan to a mixing bowl, and add the ricotta, half the grated Parmesan, the nutmeg, and, last of all, the egg yolk. Mix all the ingredients with a fork until they are all well blended. Taste and check seasoning.

Make the pasta dough. Put the flour on the work surface and make a well in the centre. Break the eggs into the well. Beat them lightly with a fork and draw the flour in gradually from the inner wall of the well. When the eggs are no longer runny, draw in enough flour to enable you to knead the dough with your hands. You may not require all the flour; push some to the side and add only what is needed. Alternatively you might need a little more from the bag, which you should keep at hand. Work until the flour and eggs are thoroughly amalgamated and then put the dough to one side and scrape the worktop clean.

Proceed to knead the dough by pressing and pushing with the heel of your palm, folding it back, giving it half a turn and repeating these movements. Repeat the movements for about 7–8 minutes. Wrap the dough in clingfilm and let it rest for at least 30 minutes, though you can leave it for up to 3 hours.

Roll out a rectangle of roughly 30 cm x 25 cm (12 in x 10 in) in size. Spread the filling over the pasta, starting about 5 cm (2 in) in from the edge near you. The filling should cover all but a 5 mm (¼ in) border all around the sheet, and a larger border near you. Fold this border over the filling, and continue to fold until you have rolled up all the pasta. Wrap the pasta roll tightly in muslin, tying the two ends securely with string.

Use a fish kettle or other long, deep pan that can hold the roll and 3–4 litres (5–7 pints) of water. Bring the water to the boil, add 1 tablespoon of salt, then put in the pasta roll and cook at a gentle but steady simmer for 25 minutes after the water has come back to the boil. Lift the roll out, using the fish retriever in the kettle or two fish slices, and place on a wooden board. Unwrap the roll as soon as you can, without burning your hands, and set aside to cool a little, which will make slicing easier.

Pre-heat the oven to 200°C/400°F/gas 6.

Cut the roll into 1 cm (½ in) slices. Generously butter a large oven dish and lay the slices on it, overlapping a little.

Heat the remaining butter in a heavy frying pan with the garlic cloves and the sage. When the butter begins to turn a lovely golden colour, draw it off the heat. Remove and discard the garlic and the sage and then spoon the sauce evenly over the roll.

Cover the dish with tinfoil and place in the oven until the roll is hot – about 10–20 minutes, depending on how hot it was when it went into the oven. Remove the dish from the oven and uncover it. Serve, handing the remaining Parmesan around separately.

TIPS

The rotolo can be made up to 2 days in advance and refrigerated, wrapped in tinfoil.

Once cooked, allow the rotolo to cool if you have time, because (like any other food) it becomes easier to slice. I use an electric carving knife, which I find one of the most useful tools. It is invaluable for slicing a roulade like this, or a stuffed fish, or a piece of braised meat that would otherwise tend to crumble.

After experimenting with different sauces to serve with the rotolo, I have come to the conclusion that the best, as so often, is the simplest: melted butter and Parmesan.

SAUSAGE, RADICCHIO & LEMON GNOCCHI

Recipe by **JAMES MARTIN**, chef & TV presenter, Malton, North Yorkshire

SERVINGS: 4 | PREP TIME: 30 MINS | COOK TIME: 2 HOURS | SKILL LEVEL: 2 (MODERATE)

A great chef mate of mine — Stephen Terry — runs a fab place called The Hardwick in Abergavenny, Wales. If it's a nice day, I often take one of the old cars for a spin and go there for lunch. This was a dish I saw Stephen make and it's so good that I've nicked it both for this book and for me at home. It's very clever cooking from a top-class chef, using just a hint of spice, but the lemon calms it down. Trust me, you will like it.

INGREDIENTS

For the gnocchi

4 large floury potatoes

olive oil, for the potatoes

4 tbsp rock salt

75 g (2½ oz) '00' flour, plus more for dusting

1 egg yolk

25 g (1 oz) Parmesan, finely grated, to finish

For the sauce

4 good-quality pork sausages, skins removed, roughly chopped

50 g (1½ oz) unsalted butter

2 shallots, finely chopped

2 cloves garlic, finely chopped

1 tsp dried chilli flakes, or to taste

300 ml (10½ fl oz) chicken stock

100 ml (3½ fl oz) double cream

25 g (1 oz) capers, rinsed, roughly chopped

2 tbsp roughly chopped flat-leaf parsley leaves, plus more to serve

finely grated zest of 2 unwaxed lemons

1 large head of radicchio, cut into wedges through the root

1 tbsp olive oil

50 g (1½ oz) fresh white breadcrumbs

METHOD

For the gnocchi, pre-heat the oven to 170°C/340°F/gas 3½. Rub the potatoes with a little oil, then place on top of the rock salt on a baking tray. Bake in the oven for 1½ hours, or until tender. When cooked, remove from the oven and set aside until cool enough to handle.

Cut the potatoes in half and scoop out the flesh, then pass through a potato ricer or sieve into a large bowl. Add the flour and egg yolk, season, then mix lightly until it forms a soft dough. Tip onto a floured work surface, divide into quarters and roll each into a long sausage. Cut into 2 cm (¾ in) pieces and lightly pinch each in the middle.

Once all the gnocchi are cut, drop them into a large saucepan of boiling salted water. When the gnocchi bob to the surface, they are ready. Remove with a slotted spoon and place in a bowl of ice water to cool.

To make the sauce, heat a frying pan until medium hot, add the sausage meat and half the butter and fry until golden-brown all over. Add the shallots, garlic and chilli flakes and cook for 2 minutes.

Pour in the chicken stock and simmer until it is reduced by half and the sausage meat is cooked through. Add the cream, drained gnocchi, capers, parsley and lemon zest and simmer for 2 minutes.

Heat a griddle pan until hot, toss the radicchio with the olive oil, then char on the griddle pan for 1 minute on each side.

Heat a small frying pan until medium hot, add the remaining butter and, when it's foaming, add the breadcrumbs and fry until golden. Season with salt and pepper. Tip the crumbs onto paper towel to cool.

Place the radicchio onto a serving plate, then spoon the gnocchi and sauce over the top. Finish with some Parmesan and a sprinkling of crunchy breadcrumbs.

CHILLI & PARMESAN POLENTA WITH BASIL OIL, GREEN BEANS, SMASHED HAZELNUTS, LEMON ZEST & EDIBLE FLOWERS

Recipe by **CAT ASHTON**, Paradise by Way of Kensal Green, Queen's Park, London

SERVINGS: 4–6 | **PREP TIME: 25 MINS PLUS COOLING** | **COOK TIME: 35 MINS** | **SKILL LEVEL: 1 (EASY)**

INGREDIENTS

For the basil oil

1 large bunch basil leaves
1 clove garlic
a pinch of salt
125 ml (4 fl oz) olive oil

For the polenta

625 ml (1 pint 4 fl oz) vegetable stock
125 g (4½ oz) coarse polenta, plus extra for dusting
75 g (2½ oz) unsalted butter
75 g (2½ oz) Parmesan, grated
zest of ½ lemon
½ tsp chilli flakes
oil, for frying

For the salad

400 g (14 oz) green beans
100 g (3½ oz) blanched hazelnuts, roasted
1 tbsp olive oil
¼ tsp chilli flakes
100 g (3½ oz) wild rocket
zest of ½ lemon

To garnish

1 punnet edible flowers (marigolds, violas, nasturtiums)

GF

METHOD

For the basil oil, place the basil, garlic and salt in a food processor and blitz quickly until finely chopped. With the motor running, slowly pour in the oil, season, and set aside in a cool place for the flavours to develop.

For the polenta, bring the stock to the boil in a large pot with salt to taste, and whisk in the polenta grains. Cook on a low heat for about 8 minutes, stirring often so it doesn't stick to the bottom. Add the butter, Parmesan, lemon zest and chilli flakes and season to taste.

Pour the mixture into a shallow tray lined with greaseproof paper and dust with some extra polenta once cool. Cut into rectangles, or any desired shape.

For the salad, blanch the green beans in a large pot of salted boiling water for about 2 minutes. Drain and cool quickly in a bowl of ice water to prevent them from cooking. This will keep them bright green and tender. Smash the hazelnuts with the olive oil and chilli flakes and set aside.

Heat a little oil in a large frying pan, and cook the portioned polenta on a medium heat until crisp. Warm the green beans and toss with the rocket, zest and smashed nuts. Place on top of the polenta, spoon over the basil oil, and garnish with the edible flowers.

RISOTTO OF COURGETTE & CRAB

Recipe by **MATT TEBBUTT**, TV presenter & consultant chef to Schpoons & Forx, Bournemouth, Dorset

SERVINGS: 4 | **PREP TIME: 15 MINS** | **COOK TIME: 40 MINS** | **SKILL LEVEL: 1 (EASY)**

INGREDIENTS

1 white onion, diced
1 clove garlic, smashed
1 small fennel bulb, diced
extra-virgin olive oil
200 g (7 oz) Arborio rice
125 ml (4 fl oz) white wine
  or vermouth
1½ litres (2⅔ pints) hot fish,
  vegetable or light chicken
  stock
10 small courgettes, sliced
  on the angle, with flowers
  where possible
30 g (1 oz) unsalted butter
250 g (9 oz) white crabmeat
200 g (7 oz) brown crabmeat
1 large spoon crème fraîche
1 lemon, to squeeze
2 tbsp chopped dill

GF

METHOD

In a large, shallow-sided pan, throw in the onion, garlic and fennel along with a glug of olive oil. Season with salt and cook for 5–10 minutes to soften.

Add the rice and stir to coat the grains in the olive oil. Give it 1 minute in the pan without any liquid, then add the wine and allow the rice to absorb it all before following it with one ladleful of the hot stock.

Continue to add the hot stock, bit by bit, for about 15–20 minutes. At this stage taste the rice – it should still have a bite to it. Now chuck the sliced courgettes in and stir through, reserving the flowers for the end.

Just before serving, stir in the butter and the white and brown crabmeat. Add the spoon of crème fraîche and the lemon juice. The risotto may need a little more salt. Add the courgette flowers, roughly chopped, and the dill. Taste, adjusting the seasoning if necessary, and serve with enough liquid so that the rice just about holds its weight before collapsing.

MALTAGLIATI WITH RED MULLET

Recipe by **MITCH TONKS**, The Seahorse, Dartmouth, Devon

SERVINGS: 4 | **PREP TIME: 45 MINS PLUS RESTING** | **COOK TIME: 15 MINS** | **SKILL LEVEL: 2 (MODERATE)**

Maltagliati are just small triangles of flat pasta that are perfect with this sauce. We first ate this simple but perfect recipe at La Pinetta restaurant on the Tuscan coast. It's a wonderful place right on the beach, serving some of the best seafood we have eaten; the cooking is very traditional and very precise. Luciano, an ex-fisherman, chef and patron, understands fish in the way we do; when it's all you cook, you get to know every quality of every species — how scorpion fish can make the texture of soups like no other and where to look for the best meat on them behind the gills, and how the head of the red mullet releases stickiness when gently poached. It's these small but subtle differences that make a dish taste in a way you can't quite put your finger on. As ever in all the greatest fish restaurants, the fish is of the best quality you can imagine and the cooking is so simple you couldn't guess how it was cooked. For us, it's the finest cooking there is.

INGREDIENTS

For the pasta
200 g (7 oz) '00' pasta flour
6 egg yolks
a dash of olive oil
fine semolina, for sprinkling

100 ml (3½ fl oz) extra-virgin
   olive oil
4 or 5 very thin slices white
   onion
1 small dried peperoncini,
   crushed into 1 tbsp olive oil
1 whole red mullet, about
   300 g (10½ oz), cleaned
   and scaled
100 ml (3½ fl oz) fish stock
   made with just a fish head
   or bone (monkfish or turbot
   is ideal)
a good pinch of sea salt
1 ripe tomato, chopped
1 tbsp chopped parsley

GF

METHOD

First, make the pasta. Place the flour on a board and make a well in the centre. Add the egg yolks and the olive oil, then use a fork to incorporate the ingredients into the flour to make a dough. Knead the dough for 10–15 minutes, then wrap in clingfilm and allow to rest in the fridge for an hour.

Roll the pasta dough into thin sheets, either by hand or with a pasta machine, then cut the sheets into small uneven triangles about the size of the palm of your hand. Place them on a tray and sprinkle with fine semolina to stop them sticking together. Set aside.

Make the sauce by heating the olive oil in a large, lidded frying pan over a medium heat. Add the onion and peperoncini and fry for 2–3 minutes until softened. Place the whole fish in the pan and add a ladleful of the fish stock. Add the salt, then cover with a lid and poach the fish over a low heat for about 6–7 minutes.

Once the fish is cooked, use two spoons to fillet the fish in the pan then take the meat off the bones. Remove the central bone and any small bones, then discard the cheek of the mullet and then the head. Add a little more stock if needed, and bring the sauce to the boil so that the oil and stock emulsify.

Meanwhile, cook the pasta in lots of boiling salted water for 3–4 minutes until just al dente. Drain, reserving a tablespoon of the cooking water, then add the pasta to the sauce, together with the reserved cooking water. Add the tomato and parsley, then taste and season – you want the sea! Toss everything together until the only sauce left is what's clinging to the pasta, and serve.

SPAGHETTI AGLIO, OLIO E PEPERONCINO
SPAGHETTI WITH PEPERONCINO & GARLIC

Recipe by **ANGELA HARTNETT** MBE, Murano, Mayfair, London

SERVINGS: 2 | PREP TIME: 10 MINS | COOK TIME: 10 MINS | SKILL LEVEL: 1 (EASY)

This very simple Italian standby can be put together quickly after a busy day at work because it uses just store-cupboard basics. Beware: the peperoncino can be very spicy.

INGREDIENTS

240 g (9 oz) dried spaghetti
2–3 tbsp olive oil
1 clove garlic, finely sliced
2 peperoncino (dried red chillies), crushed
1–2 tbsp chopped fresh flat-leaf parsley
freshly grated Parmesan, to serve

DF

METHOD

Bring a large pan of salted water to the boil. Add the spaghetti and stir as it starts to cook. Boil for 7–8 minutes, or according to packet instructions, until the pasta is al dente.

Meanwhile, heat the olive oil in a large, deep frying pan, add the garlic and peperoncino and cook for 30 seconds, until soft but without colouring. Remove from the heat and set aside.

Drain the cooked spaghetti and toss with the garlic and peperoncino.

Stir in the chopped parsley, season to taste with salt and freshly ground black pepper and scatter with Parmesan before serving immediately.

JUN TANAKA
THE NINTH

I chose this rabbit recipe because lasagna is
a comforting dish that everyone loves, but I'm
making it with an ingredient that isn't quite so
familiar. When you take a bite you have the rich
béchamel sauce then the gentle gamey flavour of
the rabbit, and it works beautifully well with the
tomato compote and the chicken mousse.

Jun

*Fitzrovia,
London*

RABBIT LASAGNA

Recipe by **JUN TANAKA**, The Ninth, Fitzrovia, London

SERVINGS: 6 | **PREP TIME: 2½ HOURS PLUS RESTING/MARINATING/CHILLING** | **COOK TIME: 2 HOURS**
SKILL LEVEL: 2 (MODERATE)

This has been on the menu at The Ninth from the day we opened and has become one of our signature dishes. It's the combination of a comforting and familiar recipe with an unusual ingredient that makes this dish so popular. It's not only delicious but also the layers of pasta with the rabbit mousse and melted béchamel give a wonderful mouthfeel!

INGREDIENTS

For the pasta dough
300 g (10½ oz) '00' flour
salt
3 egg yolks
2 whole eggs
1 tbsp olive oil

For the rabbit filling
6 rabbit legs
30 g (1 oz) coarse sea salt
5 g (1 tsp) black peppercorns
1 sprig thyme or rosemary
2 cloves garlic, sliced
100 ml (3½ fl oz) white wine
1½ litres (2¾ pints) duck fat
1 shallot, finely chopped

50 g (1½ oz) celeriac, finely chopped
½ carrot, finely chopped
25 ml (1 fl oz) olive oil

For the chicken mousse
200 g (7 oz) boneless chicken breast,
  cut into pieces
1 egg white
1 whole egg
350 ml (12½ fl oz) double cream

For the béchamel
80 g (2½ oz) butter
80 g (2½ oz) plain flour
500 ml (18 fl oz) milk
140 g (5 oz) Parmesan, grated

20 g (4 tsp) Pommery mustard
10 g (2 tsp) Dijon mustard

For the tomato compote
50 ml (1½ fl oz) olive oil
1 onion, finely chopped
2 cloves garlic, crushed
1 tsp thyme leaves
½ tbsp tomato purée
100 ml (3½ fl oz) white wine
500 g (1 lb 2 oz) canned
  tomatoes, drained and seeds
  removed
1 tsp sugar
25 ml (1 fl oz) red wine vinegar

METHOD

To make the pasta dough, place the flour and salt in a food processor and slowly add the eggs and oil until it starts to come together. Take out of the food processor and knead until it forms a dough. Wrap in clingfilm and rest for 1 hour.

To make the rabbit filling, place the rabbit legs into a plastic container, add the salt, black peppercorns, thyme or rosemary, garlic and white wine. Cover with clingfilm and leave in the fridge for 24 hours. Wash the rabbit legs under cold water, dry, and place in a saucepan. Cover with the duck fat and simmer for an hour or until the meat is falling off the bone. Cool down, drain and remove the meat and place in a bowl. Chop the meat.

Sweat the finely chopped shallot, celeriac and carrot in olive oil for 5 minutes and add to the rabbit meat.

To make the chicken mousse, place the chicken breast in a food processor, blend until smooth and slowly add all the egg. Take the mix out the blender and pass through a drum sieve. Take a bowl of ice and place another bowl on top of the ice. Add the sieved chicken mix in the chilled bowl and slowly add the double cream, continuously folding in with a spatula. Season and mix until the cream has completely blended in.

Add enough chicken mousse to bind the rabbit mixture. To test, take a little mix, wrap in clingfilm and steam for 5 minutes. Taste and add seasoning if necessary, and more cream if it is too dense.

For the pasta sheets, roll out the pasta to setting 1 on the pasta machine. Cut four rectangular pieces 15 cm x 25 cm (6 in x 10 in) and blanch in boiling salted water.

To build the lasagna, place a sheet of pasta on a chopping board, add 300 g (10½ oz) of rabbit mousse and spread evenly across the pasta. Add another sheet of pasta and repeat the process, finishing with a sheet of pasta.

To make the béchamel, melt the butter in a saucepan, add the flour and cook for a few minutes. Slowly pour the milk in and whisk until smooth. Add 40 g (1½ oz) Parmesan and the mustards. Season to taste and cool down. Once it is cool, spread an even layer over the top of the lasagna. It should be ½ cm (¼ in) thick. Chill in the fridge for 30 minutes to 1 hour. Cut the lasagna into 7 cm (3 in) squares and cover the top with the remaining Parmesan.

To make the tomato compote, pour the olive oil into a saucepan. Add the chopped onion and garlic and sweat for 10 minutes. Add the thyme and tomato purée and cook for a further 2 minutes. Pour the white wine in and reduce until most of the wine has evaporated. Add the canned tomatoes and sugar, and simmer for 30 minutes. Season to taste and add the vinegar.

To serve, place the lasagna in a steamer for 10 minutes, then place under a pre-heated medium grill until golden-brown. Spoon some tomato compote onto a plate and place the lasagna on top.

RISOTTO CON FUNGHI

RISOTTO WITH MUSHROOMS

Recipe by **ANTONIO CARLUCCIO OBE, OMRI**, chef & food writer, Wandsworth, London

SERVINGS: 4 | **PREP TIME: 10 MINS PLUS SOAKING** | **COOK TIME: 35 MINS** | **SKILL LEVEL: 1 (EASY)**

It's not by chance that I chose this recipe for the book, because a mushroom risotto is one of my preferred risottos. In Italy every family goes mushroom picking in autumn. The entire family goes and the children are taught how to sort the poisonous mushrooms from the other ones. And now I go mushroom picking in Britain — I pick them and I cook them, and I'm continuing what I started to do as a child.

INGREDIENTS

2 litres (3½ pints) chicken or vegetable stock

4 tbsp olive oil or 50 g (3½ oz) unsalted butter

1 onion, very finely chopped

300 g (10½ oz) firm button mushrooms, finely sliced

50 g (1½ oz) dried ceps, rehydrated (see tip below) and chopped

350 g (12½ oz) Carnaroli or Arborio rice

60 g (2 oz) Parmesan, grated

80 g (2½ oz) unsalted butter

GF

METHOD

Put the stock in a pan, bring to the boil and keep at a low simmer.

Heat the olive oil or butter in a large pan over a low heat, add the onion and fry until soft, about 10 minutes. Add the button mushrooms and the ceps and cook for 5 minutes, until soft and lightly browned.

Add the rice and stir for a minute or two, then add one or two ladles of boiling stock. Stir continuously over the heat, adding stock a ladleful at a time as each addition is absorbed. After 18–20 minutes, check for the required al dente texture – the rice should be tender but with a firm bite in the centre, and the risotto should be moist.

Remove the pan from the heat, add the Parmesan and unsalted butter and stir in well. Season to taste and serve on warm plates. Buon appetito.

TIP

To rehydrate dried ceps, cover them in water and soak for about 20 minutes. Pick the mushrooms out of the water into a sieve set over a bowl. Then very carefully strain the water, preferably through muslin. This will remove any dust that may have come off the mushrooms. The liquid will taste intensely mushroomy, and can be used in addition to the stock to add extra mushroom flavour to this risotto.

COURGETTE NOODLES WITH AVOCADO PESTO

Recipe by **ELLA MILLS**, entrepreneur & founder of Deliciously Ella and The MaE Deli, London

SERVINGS: 4 | **PREP TIME: 20 MINS** | **COOK TIME: 5–10 MINS** | **SKILL LEVEL: 1 (EASY)**

This is one of my favourite speedy weekday suppers. It only takes 10 minutes and requires almost no chopping, which I love! Courgette noodles are the best pasta replacement as they have the exact same texture, but they're a little lighter and packed full of vitamins. They taste incredible tossed in this minty avocado and Brazil nut sauce with a heap of sautéed mushrooms on the top.

INGREDIENTS

For the noodles
4 courgettes
2 dozen (24) chestnut
   mushrooms
olive oil, for drizzling

For the avocado pesto
1 mug Brazil nuts
   (approx. 120 g/4½ oz)
4 avocados
4 tbsp olive oil
a large handful of fresh
   mint leaves
juice of 4 limes

DF, GF, V

METHOD

For the noodles: start by making the courgette noodles, by simply putting the courgettes through your spiralizer. Alternatively, cut them into long matchsticks with a knife. Place the noodles to one side and begin preparing the mushrooms.

Cut the mushrooms into thin slices, drizzle them with olive oil, and then gently heat them in a frying pan for about 5 minutes, until they're nice and soft.

For the avocado pesto: while the mushrooms cook, place the Brazil nuts in a food processor and blend for a minute or two, until they're totally crushed. Then add in the avocado flesh, olive oil, mint leaves, lime juice and a sprinkling of salt and pepper, and blend again.

Either mix the noodles and sauce together in a bowl raw and then add the mushrooms, or add the sauce and noodles to the mushrooms in the frying pan and gently heat for a couple of minutes to warm the dish up and soften the noodles a little.

ANNA DEL CONTE OMRI
FOOD WRITER

I learned to cook in my mother's kitchen, and not just from my mother but from our cook as well. My brother and I loved our cook very much – she played with us and cooked with us. I can remember her giving us a bit of gnocchi to make, and letting us put the little pieces in a meat roll.

Anna

Shaftesbury, Dorset

CONCHIGLIE ROSSE RIPIENE DI SPAGHETTINI IN INSALATA

RADICCHIO LEAVES FILLED WITH THIN SPAGHETTI

Recipe by **ANNA DEL CONTE OMRI**, food writer, Shaftesbury, Dorset

SERVINGS: 12 AS AN ANTIPASTO, 6 AS A FIRST COURSE | PREP TIME: 25 MINS | COOK TIME: 10 MINS SKILL LEVEL: 1 (EASY)

Remember that cold pasta must be more al dente than hot pasta. This is a perfect antipasto for a summer party. I prefer olives with the stone to the pitted sort, because they have more flavour, but if your guests don't like spitting, buy good-quality olives without any stuffing and with as little dressing as possible. The dressing must be made by you.

INGREDIENTS

4 or 5 large radicchio heads
450 g (1 lb) spaghettini
sea salt
120 ml (4 fl oz) extra-virgin
    olive oil
60 g (2 oz) flat-leaf parsley
2 cloves garlic, peeled
2 dried chillies
freshly ground black pepper
225 g (8 oz) black olives
5 tbsp capers, rinsed
8 hard-boiled eggs

DF, V

METHOD

Cut the cores out of the radicchio heads and unfurl the outside leaves very gently so that they remain whole. Keep the rest of the radicchio for a salad. Wash the leaves, dry very thoroughly and place them on one or two large dishes. You will need 12 large leaves.

Cook the spaghettini in plenty of salted water. It cooks quite quickly, and when serving it cold you should drain it when you think it is still on the undercooked side. Drain and refresh it under cold water. Drain again and then transfer to a large bowl. Pat dry with paper towel. Toss with half the oil and allow to cool.

About 2 hours before you want to serve the pasta, chop together, by hand or in a food processor, the parsley, garlic and chillies. Add the mixture to the spaghettini and toss thoroughly with the rest of the oil. Taste and add salt and pepper if necessary.

Fill each radicchio leaf with a forkful or two of spaghettini. Sprinkle the olives and the capers over it. Cut the eggs into segments and garnish each leaf and the dish with them.

TIP

The radicchio leaves can be prepared up to 1 day in advance and kept in the fridge in a covered container. The pasta can be cooked and partly dressed with the oil up to 8 hours ahead, but it must be finished off no longer than 4 hours in advance.

PANZANELLA

Recipe by **RUTH ROGERS** MBE, The River Café, Hammersmith, London

SERVINGS: 6 | **PREP TIME: 40 MINS PLUS RESTING** | **COOK TIME: 20 MINS** | **SKILL LEVEL: 2 (MODERATE)**

Panzanella is a traditional Tuscan summer salad. At its most simple it is just strong white bread, green peppery olive oil and delicious ripe summer tomatoes. The addition of peppers, anchovies, capers and olives makes it more delicious and interesting.

INGREDIENTS

3 stale ciabatta loaves (roughly 150 g/5 oz each)

1 kg (2¼ lb) fresh plum tomatoes

4 cloves garlic, peeled and crushed to a paste with a little sea salt

sea salt and freshly ground black pepper

at least 250 ml (8 fl oz) Tuscan extra-virgin olive oil

4 tbsp red wine vinegar

3 red peppers

3 yellow peppers

2 fresh red chillies (optional)

100 g (4 oz) salted capers

100 g (4 oz) salted anchovies

150 g (5 oz) black olives, pitted

1 large bunch basil

DF, V

METHOD

Cut the bread into rough, thick slices, and place in a large bowl.

Skin, halve and de-seed the tomatoes into a sieve set over a bowl, to retain the tomato juice. Season the juice with the garlic and some black pepper, then add 250 ml (8 fl oz) of the olive oil and 2–3 tablespoons of the red wine vinegar. Pour the seasoned tomato juice over the bread and toss until the bread has absorbed all the liquid. Depending on the staleness of the bread, more liquid may be required, in which case add more olive oil.

Grill the peppers whole until blackened all over, then skin, de-seed and cut into eighths lengthways. If using, grill the chillies until blackened, then skin, de-seed and chop finely.

Rinse the salt from the capers and soak in the remaining red wine vinegar. Separate the anchovies into fillets.

In a large dish, make a layer of some of the soaked bread, and top with some of all the other ingredients, then cover with another layer of bread and continue until all the bread and other ingredients have been used. The final layer should have the peppers, tomatoes, capers, anchovies and olives all visible. Leave for an hour at room temperature before serving with more extra-virgin olive oil.

ROQUEFORT, PEAR & CHICORY SALAD WITH WALNUT OIL

Recipe by **SIMON HOPKINSON**, chef, food writer & TV presenter, Brook Green, London

SERVINGS: 2 | **PREP TIME: 5 MINS** | **SKILL LEVEL: 1 (EASY)**

Of all blue cheeses, Roquefort will always remain my favourite. I will take a small slice of Stilton — or even better, Stichelton — at Christmas, or maybe a thick wedge of sweetly savoury Fourme d'Ambert when in a good French restaurant. And I am very fond of a fine and creamy Gorgonzola or Dolcelatte, from time to time. But Roquefort, the king of blue cheeses, takes the biscuit. Anyway, here is a very fine, very simple salad: all at once fresh, crisp, salty, sweet and fragrantly oily — and just perfect when using Roquefort that is cool and crumbly. Use either the red-leafed or traditional white chicory, here.

INGREDIENTS

2–3 heads of chicory, separated into leaves and put to soak in ice water

1 large, ripe pear, peeled and thinly sliced

100–125 g (3½–4½ oz) Roquefort, crumbled

a squeeze of lemon juice

2–3 tbsp walnut oil

GF, V

METHOD

Dry the chicory leaves (a spinner is best, here) and neatly arrange on a serving dish, inner curved sides uppermost. Evenly distribute the pear in and among the leaves, crumble the cheese over and add a touch of lemon juice. Trickle the walnut oil over and add a grind of pepper. Serve forthwith.

ENGLISH ASPARAGUS
WITH GARLIC & GINGER BUTTER

Recipe by **MARK SARGEANT**, chef, food writer & restaurateur, Folkestone, Kent

SERVINGS: 4 | **PREP TIME: 10 MINS** | **COOK TIME: 10 MINS** | **SKILL LEVEL: 1 (EASY)**

At six weeks, the season for English asparagus is unfairly short, but that just means you have to eat it as often as possible. It's grown all over the country and is delicious, but in my experience the best asparagus comes from East Anglia. You can add the same flavourings to a hollandaise sauce, but I prefer warm, salty butter melted all over, as here.

INGREDIENTS

600 g (1 lb 5 oz) English asparagus, trimmed of the woody ends

100 g (3½ oz) salted butter

2 cloves garlic, peeled and crushed

a small knob of fresh ginger, peeled and grated

zest and juice of 1 lemon

GF, V

METHOD

Cook the asparagus spears in a large pan of boiling salted water until they are just tender with a very slight crunch. This should take no more that 3–4 minutes. Carefully remove them from the pan and drain well, then place on a serving dish and keep warm.

In a small pan, melt the butter and add the garlic, ginger, lemon zest and juice, then season well. Keep stirring for a couple of minutes, to allow the flavours to infuse and to cook the ginger and garlic, before pouring the sauce over the asparagus.

SLAW WITH PEARS, TOASTED HAZELNUTS & BUTTERMILK DRESSING

Recipe by **SKYE GYNGELL**, Spring, Covent Garden, London

SERVINGS: 6 | **PREP TIME: 15 MINS** | **COOK TIME: 5 MINS** | **SKILL LEVEL: 1 (EASY)**

There is nothing quite like a really good coleslaw. It makes for an excellent side, especially with grilled meats or rich, slow-cooked dishes such as shoulder of pork. It's easy to prepare and, unlike most salads, really benefits from being dressed a couple of hours in advance to allow time for the flavours to develop and mellow. You can add and subtract ingredients as you like, but I think this salad needs both a nutty crunch and a little fruity sweetness to make it really interesting. The dressing, which includes buttermilk and cider vinegar, gives it a creamy, yet gutsy, finish.

INGREDIENTS

120 g (4½ oz) shelled and
    skinned hazelnuts
¼ red cabbage, cored
¼ white cabbage, cored
1 bulb fennel, peeled
3 firm, ripe pears
a bunch of flat-leaf parsley,
    leaves only

For the dressing
1 organic free-range
    egg yolk
½ tbsp Dijon mustard
1½ tsp honey
1 tbsp good-quality cider
    vinegar
180 ml (6 fl oz) mild-tasting
    extra-virgin olive oil
2 tbsp buttermilk

GF, V

METHOD

Pre-heat the oven to 180°C/350°F/gas 4. Spread the hazelnuts out on a baking sheet and toast them on the middle shelf of the oven for 4–5 minutes. Remove from the oven and allow to cool, then chop roughly.

Finely slice both the red and the white cabbage into thin ribbons and place in a bowl. Remove the tough, fibrous outer layer from the fennel, cut the bulb in half lengthways and then slice very finely. Add to the cabbage.

Halve the pears, remove the cores and then slice finely. Add to the bowl of cabbage and fennel, toss lightly and season well with salt and plenty of freshly ground black pepper. Set aside while you make the dressing.

Put the egg yolk, mustard, honey and vinegar into a small bowl. Season with a little salt and pepper and stir vigorously to combine. Now whisk in the olive oil slowly – almost drip by drip to begin with – increasing the flow slightly once the dressing begins to homogenize. Continue until all the oil is incorporated. Stir in the buttermilk, then taste and adjust the seasoning as necessary.

Pour the dressing over the salad with the hazelnuts and parsley, and mix together gently but thoroughly, using your fingertips. Set aside in a cool place for an hour or two before serving.

ARTICHOKE VINAIGRETTE

Recipe by **SYBIL KAPOOR**, chef, food writer & broadcaster, London

SERVINGS: 4 | **PREP TIME: 10 MINS** | **COOK TIME: 30–45 MINS** | **SKILL LEVEL: 1 (EASY)**

Large artichokes are commonly sold in Britain during the summer months. Although we've grown them for many centuries they're still regarded as an essentially foreign and rather exotic dish. You can serve these artichokes warm with melted butter or hollandaise sauce, or tepid with mayonnaise or vinaigrette.

INGREDIENTS

4 large-sized globe artichokes

1 tsp Dijon mustard

sea salt and freshly ground black pepper, to taste

½ tsp caster sugar

1 tbsp good-quality sherry vinegar

1 tbsp lemon juice

6 tbsp mild extra-virgin olive oil

DF, GF, V

METHOD

Fill a very large non-reactive saucepan, with a lid, with enough boiling unsalted water to hold the artichokes comfortably. It is common practice to acidulate the water to prevent discolouration, but I think it imbues the artichoke with an unpleasant flavour and isn't necessary.

Drop the artichokes into the briskly boiling water, stem-side down; cover and return to the boil. A medium-sized artichoke will take around 30 minutes to cook; a large specimen, nearer 45 minutes. A globe artichoke is cooked when you can easily pull a leaf from its base.

Drain the artichokes upside-down in a colander before serving warm or at room temperature. You will need to remove the pad of fine white fibres or 'choke' at the heart of each artichoke as eating it can cause choking. You can remove it at this stage by opening up the artichoke and scraping it out with a teaspoon or, easier still, leave it for your guests to remove once they've reached the heart.

To make the vinaigrette, place the mustard in a bowl. Season with salt, pepper and the sugar, then gradually whisk in the vinegar, lemon juice and olive oil.

To serve: place each artichoke on a large plate with a small bowl of sauce alongside. You will also need to supply a small bowl of warm water with a slice of lemon for your guests to clean their fingers, and a knife and fork to enable them to eat the heart.

WARM NEW POTATO SALAD
WITH MINT LEAVES & CHIVES

Recipe by **ELISABETH LUARD**, food writer, Brynmeheryn, Wales

SERVINGS: 4 | PREP TIME: 10 MINS | COOK TIME: 20 MINS | SKILL LEVEL: 1 (EASY)

INGREDIENTS

500 g (1 lb 2 oz) new potatoes,
  halved or quartered

5 tbsp extra-virgin olive oil

2 tbsp orange wine vinegar

sea salt flakes, to taste

½ tsp black peppercorns,
  crushed in a mortar and pestle

a handful of fresh mint leaves,
  torn

about 5 chive stems, with
  flowers

DF, GF, V

METHOD

Bring the potatoes to the boil in a pan of cold water and cook for 15 minutes, until tender. Drain and allow to cool slightly, then tip into a serving dish and drizzle the oil and vinegar over, as well as plenty of sea salt flakes and the black pepper. Toss through the herbs and flowers. Serve.

MARCUS WAREING
TREDWELL'S

Aubergines are a fantastic vegetable that absorb
flavours really well. They do release a lot of
liquid when cooked, though, so it's important
to chargrill the slices until they're really golden,
otherwise the additional flavours will become
diluted when serving.

Marcus

Covent Garden,
London

HARISSA-GLAZED AUBERGINE WITH COCONUT & PEANUTS

Recipe by **MARCUS WAREING**, Tredwell's, Covent Garden, London

SERVINGS: 4 | PREP TIME: 20 MINS | COOK TIME: 30 MINS | SKILL LEVEL: 1 (EASY)

INGREDIENTS

2 aubergines
3 tbsp olive or rapeseed oil
1 tsp flaked sea salt, plus extra
150 g (5 oz) dairy-free coconut
  yoghurt
grated zest and juice of 1 lime
50 g (1¾ oz) rose harissa
30 g (1 oz) agave syrup
1 tsp lemon juice
75 g (2½ oz) roasted and salted
  peanuts, roughly chopped
½–1 red chilli, finely sliced
coriander cress or salad cress

DF, GF, V

METHOD

Pre-heat the oven to 200°C/180°C fan/400°F/gas 6. Heat a chargrill pan until hot.

Slice each aubergine lengthways into six long strips. Brush with the oil and season with the salt.

Chargrill both sides of the aubergine slices until deep golden. You may need to do this in a couple of batches depending on the size of your pan.

Transfer to a foil-lined baking tray and finish cooking in the oven for 15 minutes.

Mix together the coconut yoghurt, lime zest and juice, and a good pinch of salt. Set aside.

Mix together the harissa, agave syrup, 4 teaspoons of water and lemon juice. Season with salt and, when the aubergine is cooked, brush the harissa mix liberally over the top of each strip. Return to the oven for 5 minutes.

To serve, place the aubergine slices on a large plate and dot the coconut yoghurt around. Scatter over the peanuts, chilli and cress.

CHICKPEA, OLIVE & RAISIN TAGINE

Recipe by **MINA HOLLAND**, food writer, Camden, London

SERVINGS: 6 | **PREP TIME: 30 MINS PLUS OVERNIGHT SOAKING** | **COOK TIME: 1 HOUR**
SKILL LEVEL: 1 (EASY)

If I was faithful to Moroccan naming traditions, this would be called a Chickpea, Olive and Raisin Cast Iron Casserole Pot, after the vessel in which it is cooked – like 'tagine' and 'kedra'. But that would be long-winded, and that's the opposite of this incredibly straightforward dish. Chickpeas – which I think of as almost meaty – are its backbone, and the caramelized onions, carrots, honey and dried fruits give it a sweetness that's offset by the acidic preserved lemons, umami olives and aromatic spices. There's real complexity of flavour which can make it a conveniently low-effort showstopper!

INGREDIENTS

800 g (1 lb 12 oz) chickpeas

50 g (1½ oz) unsalted butter

a pinch of saffron infused in
    2 tbsp boiling water

4 onions: 1 grated, the others
    sliced into feathers

3 tsp ground cinnamon

2 tsp ground ginger

½ tsp grated nutmeg

1 tsp salt

1 tsp ground black pepper

4 carrots, peeled and cut into
    2 cm (¾ in) chunks

200 g (7 oz) raisins
    (I like to use golden ones)

approx. 350 g (12½ oz) pitted
    green olives

1 tbsp honey

1 tbsp extra-virgin olive oil

1 preserved lemon, pulp removed
    and sliced very finely

1 big handful of whole almonds,
    toasted

1 tsp ras el hanout
    (North African spice mix)
    (optional)

GF, V

METHOD

Soak the chickpeas in water overnight.

In a deep-sided pan or casserole dish, place half the butter, the saffron water, grated onion, cinnamon, ginger, nutmeg and seasoning and heat over a low heat. It will quickly come together into a paste-like consistency, the onion beginning to dissolve, and will be fragrant.

Add the chickpeas and cover with water to ½ cm (¼ in) above the chickpeas. Cover, turn up the heat, bring to the boil, then simmer for 30 minutes before adding the feathered onions. Simmer for a further 20 minutes.

Pre-heat the oven to about 120°C/250°F/gas ½.

Check the seasoning of this broth, then add the carrots, raisins and olives and simmer until the carrots are tender (i.e. they hold their shape but are not crunchy).

Remove the vegetables, chickpeas and raisins and place in a heatproof dish. Cover this with tinfoil and place in the warm oven. Leave the liquor in the pan.

Add the honey, the olive oil and the rest of the butter to the broth; bring to the boil and simmer until it reduces and thickens.

Take a serving dish and arrange the vegetables and chickpeas on it. Spoon the broth over, then sprinkle with preserved lemon pieces, almonds and a little ras el hanout, if using, for extra spice and prettiness. Serve with couscous, rice and, if you fancy an injection of dairy goodness, some goat's cheese or feta crumbled on top.

SHAVED RAW BRUSSELS SPROUT SALAD WITH HAZELNUTS, POMEGRANATE & PUMPKIN SEEDS

Recipe by **LORRAINE PASCALE**, chef & TV presenter, London

SERVINGS: 4 | PREP TIME: 15–20 MINS | COOK TIME: 20 MINS | SKILL LEVEL: 1 (EASY)

There is only one thing which is not quite super-easy with this dish, and that is the cutting of the nutrient powerhouses that are brussels sprouts. I have recently dusted off my food processor and put one of those attachments on it that usually just stay on the top shelf of the cupboard. However, who would have thunk it but these attachments actually make the whole job so much easier and you can chop the whole lot in a few minutes! If, however, you do not have one of these machines, then put your favourite music on and enjoy slicing your sprouts.

INGREDIENTS

75 g (2½ oz) pumpkin seeds

500 g (1 lb 2 oz) Brussels sprouts, outer leaves removed

100 g (3½ oz) roasted hazelnuts, roughly chopped

1 x 400 g (14 oz) can Puy or green lentils, drained (or a 250 g (9 oz) pack of ready-to-eat Puy lentils)

75 g (2½ oz) raisins

150 g (5 oz) pomegranate seeds (from 1 large pomegranate)

For the dressing

6 tbsp extra-virgin olive oil

3 tbsp balsamic vinegar

DF, GF, V

METHOD

Put a medium-sized frying pan on a medium-high heat and dry-fry the pumpkin seeds for 2–3 minutes, until toasted and just beginning to pop. Remove and tip onto a small plate to cool.

Mix the dressing ingredients together in a really large bowl and season well with salt and pepper. Very thinly slice the sprouts by hand (or I like to use the slicing attachment on my food processor for a speedier job).

Toss the pumpkin seeds, sprouts, hazelnuts, lentils, raisins and all but a handful of pomegranate seeds into the dressing, giving it a good mix all together.

Spoon the salad out onto a large serving platter, sprinkle the remaining pomegranate seeds over the top and serve.

CREAMY KALE & CELERIAC

Recipe by **NIKKI DUFFY**, freelance food writer & editor, Suffolk

SERVINGS: 2 AS A MAIN, 4 AS A SIDE DISH | **PREP TIME: 20 MINS** | **COOK TIME: 45 MINS**
SKILL LEVEL: 1 (EASY)

I absolutely love leafy veg and this dish is a fantastic way to showcase one of my favourite kinds: delicious, dark-green kale or cavolo nero. I enjoy eating this on its own, but it also makes a great partner to simply cooked meat: pan-cook pigeon breasts, chicken breasts or lamb leg steaks, then let them rest for a few minutes before pouring their juices over the veg, then slicing the meat and serving it alongside or on top.

INGREDIENTS

1 celeriac, about 600 g
  (1 lb 5 oz)

1 red onion, sliced

1 clove garlic, thickly sliced

leaves from a couple of sprigs
  of thyme

2 tbsp olive oil, plus a little
  extra

250 g (9 oz) curly kale or
  cavolo nero

4 tbsp crème fraîche

1 tsp English mustard

20 g (1½ oz) Parmesan or
  another hard, grainy cheese,
  finely grated

GF

METHOD

Pre-heat the oven to 190°C/375°F/gas 5.

Remove the rough outer skin from the celeriac. Cut the celeriac into roughly 2 cm (¾ in) slices, then cut each slice into large bite-sized chunks. Put these in a medium-sized roasting dish – 25 cm x 20 cm (about 10 in x 8 in) is ideal. Add the red onion, garlic, thyme leaves, olive oil and some salt and pepper. Toss everything together well. Roast for about 40 minutes, stirring halfway through, or until the celeriac is tender and starting to turn golden-brown.

Meanwhile, bring a large pan of lightly salted water to the boil. Tear the kale or cavolo nero leaves from their stalks and drop them into the boiling water. Cook for about 3 minutes, until the leaves are wilted but not soft. Drain, reserving the cooking water, then chop the leaves roughly and put them back in the warm saucepan.

Combine the crème fraîche, mustard, half the grated Parmesan and a little salt and pepper. Add 2–3 tablespoons of the kale cooking water to loosen the mixture a little. Stir this into the wilted kale.

When the celeriac is done, add the kale/cavolo nero and the creamy liquor to the roasting dish. Stir well and make sure the veg is spread out in a roughly even layer. Sprinkle on the remaining Parmesan and trickle on a little more olive oil. Return to the oven for 5 minutes, and then it's ready to serve.

CAULIFLOWER WITH
A SEVILLE ORANGE DRESSING

Recipe by **JOSÉ PIZARRO**, restaurateur, Bermondsey, London

SERVINGS: 4 AS A SIDE DISH | PREP TIME: 15 MINS PLUS MARINATING | COOK TIME: 5 MINS
SKILL LEVEL: 1 (EASY)

The cauliflower is not a vegetable from the New World. Along with broccoli (to which it is closely related), the cauliflower probably originated in Syria. The first mention of its cultivation in Spain dates from the twelfth century. Cauliflower is a strange vegetable – it's been available to chefs for a very long time and yet doesn't offer many ways in which to be cooked. However, this is an outstanding warm salad, and is an excellent accompaniment to roast chicken; the simple dressing works equally well with broccoli. When Seville oranges aren't in season, use sour Valencia oranges plus the juice of one lemon.

INGREDIENTS

2 cloves garlic
1 tsp sea salt
4 tbsp Seville orange juice
1 medium-sized cauliflower
4 tbsp extra-virgin olive oil
a small bunch of coriander

DF, GF, V

METHOD

Use a mortar and pestle to crush the garlic cloves and salt to make a thick paste. Scrape this into a large bowl and stir the orange juice through. Leave for 30 minutes to let the flavours mingle.

Break the cauliflower up into florets – each about the size of a golf ball – and steam for 5 minutes, until cooked but still a bit crunchy. Transfer to a serving dish straight away and fold the orange and garlic dressing through. Drizzle the olive oil over, then leave to cool a little until warm.

Just before serving, roughly tear some coriander leaves with your fingers and stir them in.

WARM BUTTERNUT SQUASH SALAD
WITH LABNEH & CHILLI

Recipe by **JAMES RAMSDEN**, food writer & restaurateur, Homerton, London

SERVINGS: 4–6 | PREP TIME: 30 MINS PLUS HANGING OVERNIGHT | COOK TIME: 45 MINS
SKILL LEVEL: I (EASY)

Labneh is yoghurt that has been strained of all its whey, leaving the thick, almost cheesy, curd behind. It needs a day or two to reach its peak, so if you're making this at more of a run, just use a really thick Greek-style yoghurt.

INGREDIENTS

500 g (1 lb 2 oz) natural,
   unsweetened yoghurt
1 small butternut squash
   or pumpkin
olive oil
a few sprigs of thyme,
   leaves only
1 fresh red chilli,
   de-seeded and finely
   chopped

For the dressing
a large bunch of parsley,
   leaves only
1¼ tsp ground coriander
1 clove garlic, peeled and
   crushed to a paste
juice of ½ lemon
100 ml (3½ fl oz) olive oil

GF, V

METHOD

1–2 days ahead: line a bowl with a clean tea towel. Tip the yoghurt in, add a pinch of salt, then tie the towel up with string and hang from a cupboard handle over the bowl.

Up to 1 day ahead: pre-heat the oven to 200°C/400°F/gas 6. Wash the squash but don't peel it (the skin is delicious) and cut it into rounds, discarding the seeds. Toss with olive oil, salt, pepper and thyme, and roast for 45 minutes. Leave to cool; chill overnight if necessary.

Up to 1 hour ahead: make the dressing by chopping the parsley finely and mixing it with the ground coriander, garlic, lemon juice, olive oil and salt and pepper, or whizz everything together in a blender.

30 minutes ahead: if necessary, warm the squash in a medium oven (180°C/350°F/gas 4). If the oven's already on for something else, do it at that temperature, keeping an eye on it if it's particularly hot.

Dinnertime: place the chunks of squash on a plate and top with a dollop of labneh. Scatter with chopped chilli and a generous splash of the parsley dressing, then serve.

TIPS

Use goat's milk yoghurt instead, to produce lovely goat's curd. Also delicious just spread on toast.

Perk up leftover labneh with herbs and garlic for a sort of homemade Boursin.

ALMODROTE DE BERENJENA
AUBERGINE FLAN

Recipe by **CLAUDIA RODEN**, food writer, North London

SERVINGS: 4–6 | **PREP TIME: 30 MINS** | **COOK TIME: 1¾ HOURS** | **SKILL LEVEL: 1 (EASY)**

This is one of the best-loved and most distinctive Jewish dishes of Turkey, the one everyone mentions as the favourite. A similar dish of mashed aubergine, eggs and cheese is mentioned in the records of the Court of the Inquisition in Spain as one that gave away Christian converts attached to their Jewish faith. The only similar dish I found is the Papeton d'Aubergines of Provence. Is there a link and a story? A mixture of feta and Kashkaval cheese is traditionally used, but other cheeses, like Cheddar and Gruyère, are used also (by Turkish Jews in England) with very pleasing effect.

INGREDIENTS

2 kg (4½ lb) aubergine
2 large slices bread,
  crusts removed
150 g (5 oz) feta
6 eggs, lightly beaten
150 g (5 oz) grated
  Kashkaval or Gruyère
5 tbsp sunflower oil

V

METHOD

Pre-heat the oven to 180°C/350°F/gas 4. Roast the aubergines for 45 minutes and allow to cool, then peel them. Put them in a colander and press with your hand to squeeze out as much of the juice as you can, then chop the flesh with two knives or, as is also the custom in Turkey, mash it with a wooden spoon. Do not use a food processor – that would change the texture.

Soak the bread in water until wet, then squeeze it dry. In a bowl, mash the feta with a fork. Add the eggs, bread, Kashkaval or Gruyère cheese (reserving 2–3 tablespoons) and 4 tablespoons of oil. Beat well. Add the aubergine and mix well. Pour the mixture into an oiled baking dish, sprinkle the top with the remaining oil and cheese, and bake for 45 minutes to 1 hour, until lightly coloured.

VARIATION

For Almodrote de Kalavasa, use boiled and chopped courgettes instead of aubergines.

ANGELA HARTNETT MBE
MURANO

My inspiration for cooking has always been my family. I was brought up with Irish-Italian heritage, and food was very important. We ate together as a family, we talked around the dinner table and sat there for hours. And I love the simplicity of Italian food – it's all about not messing with the produce. Nature's done amazing work; we really don't have to do too much after that.

Angela

Mayfair, London

DEEP-FRIED COURGETTE FLOWERS

Recipe by **ANGELA HARTNETT** MBE, Murano, Mayfair, London

SERVINGS: 4 | PREP TIME: 25 MINS | COOK TIME: 30 MINS | SKILL LEVEL: 1 (EASY)

Courgette flowers are very trendy in London restaurants these days, but are only in season over summer (July and August). They're so easy to cook – just dip in batter and put straight into a deep-fat fryer a few at a time. Tempura flour makes the lightest batter, and is widely available in supermarkets.

INGREDIENTS

vegetable oil, for deep-frying
100 g (3½ oz) tempura flour
150 ml (5 fl oz) ice-cold sparkling
    mineral water
50 g (1½ oz) '00' flour, for dusting
12–15 courgette flowers with
    stems, cut in half lengthways

DF, V

METHOD

Pre-heat a deep-fat fryer or a large pan of oil to 180°C/350°F/gas 4.

Put the tempura flour in a bowl and sit it over another bowl filled with ice water. (This helps to keep the batter mix cold, and therefore as light as possible.) Slowly pour in the sparkling water while whisking lightly, ideally with chopsticks. The last thing you want to do here is overwork the batter – lumps are fine.

Put the '00' flour in a large dish and add some salt and freshly ground black pepper. Toss the courgette flowers briefly in the seasoned flour, then plunge them straight into the tempura batter. Fish them out and lower carefully into the hot oil. It's best to do this in small batches so as not to overload the pan and reduce the temperature of the oil. Fry until light golden in colour.

Using a slotted or wire spoon, carefully remove the flowers from the oil and drain on paper towel. Season with salt and serve immediately.

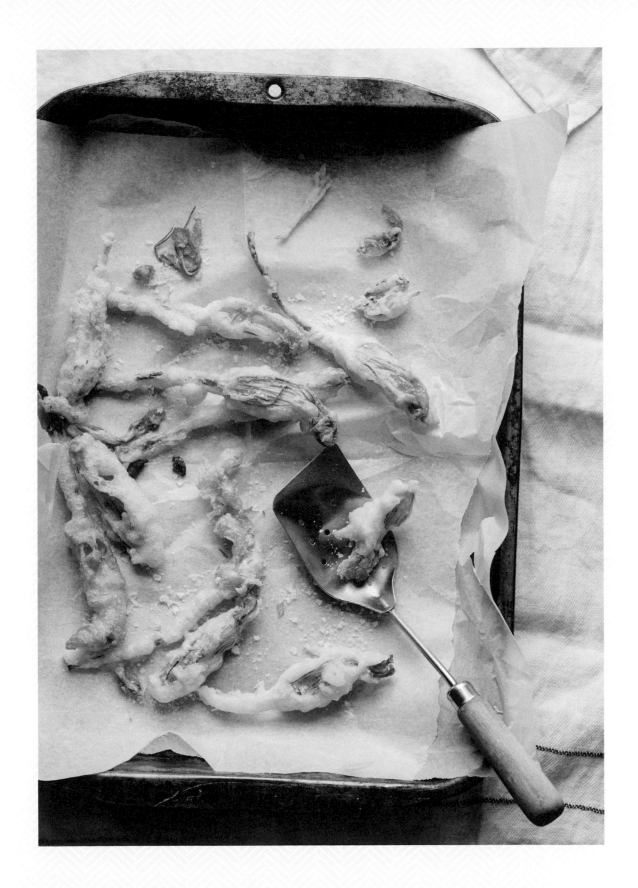

CHOPPED SALAD

Recipe by **ELEANOR MAIDMENT**, food writer, Kensal Green, London

SERVINGS: 2 | **PREP TIME: 20 MINS** | **COOK TIME: 20 MINS** | **SKILL LEVEL: 1 (EASY)**

Chopped salads are something you see on menus across the US, but less so in the UK. I love them as they're packed full of good things and completely versatile – any finely shredded leaves can make up the base (I love cavolo nero) and you can adjust the other veg according to the seasons (asparagus and broad beans are perfect to celebrate an early British summer). A little sweetness (like pomegranate seeds) and crunch (chopped nuts) are essential, too. And the burnt tomato dressing brings it all together nicely, though just a lick of extra-virgin olive oil and balsamic vinegar works if you're pushed for time.

INGREDIENTS

For the burnt tomato dressing
200 g (7 oz) cherry tomatoes
1 clove garlic, finely sliced
½ red onion, finely sliced
¼ lemon, finely sliced
4 tbsp olive oil

200 g (7 oz) tenderstem broccoli,
   trimmed and cut into 3 cm
   (1¼ in) pieces
200 g (7 oz) podded broad beans
100 g (3½ oz) sugar snap peas,
   halved
a handful of basil leaves,
   shredded
a handful of flat-leaf parsley
   leaves, roughly chopped
a handful (roughly 30 g/1 oz)
   of pomegranate seeds
   (or dried cranberries)
a handful (roughly 30 g/1 oz)
   of pecans, roughly chopped
   (or any other nuts or seeds)
100 g (3½ oz) soft goat's cheese

GF, V

METHOD

Pre-heat the oven to 220°C/425°F/gas 7–8.

Start by making the dressing. Toss the tomatoes in a small roasting tray with the garlic, onion, lemon and oil; season and roast for 20 minutes, stirring halfway through. You want them to be charred and slightly blistered, so return to the oven if they're not quite there. Crush everything together with the back of a fork and set aside to cool slightly.

Meanwhile, blanch the tenderstem broccoli and broad beans in boiling water for 2 minutes. Drain, refresh under cold water and pat dry; slip the beans from their skins.

In a large bowl, toss together the broccoli, broad beans, sugar snap peas and herbs with the warm dressing (you can leave the salad to sit and marinate at this point for 1–2 hours). Season and fold through most of the pomegranate seeds, pecans and goat's cheese. Transfer to plates or a large platter and scatter the remaining seeds and cheese over before serving.

FARRO WITH ROASTED LEEKS & SMOKY-SWEET ROMESCO

Recipe by **ANNA JONES**, cook, stylist & food writer, Hackney, London

SERVINGS: 4–6 (WITH LEFTOVER ROMESCO) | **PREP TIME: 10 MINS** | **COOK TIME: 55 MINS** | **SKILL LEVEL: 1 (EASY)**

If I had my way, this smoky, tangy-sweet Catalan sauce would find its way into a meal a day. The recipe will make enough for this dinner plus an extra jam-jar-full to keep in the fridge for a week or so. Farro is one of my favourite grains – it has a chewy, almost gummy texture that is so pleasing. Farro is much lower in gluten than most grains, so if you have a mild sensitivity to gluten it might be okay for you. It's available in most wholefood shops and good supermarkets. If you can't get your hands on farro, then pearl barley or bulgur wheat would also work, as would quinoa if you prefer it. Just adjust the cooking times accordingly. Use the best jarred Spanish red peppers you can find – piquillo are the ones to look out for. If you can't find baby leeks, normal leeks are fine too. Just wash, trim, halve them lengthways and cut them into 3 cm (1¼ in) lengths.

INGREDIENTS

For the romesco

100 g (3½ oz) blanched almonds

50 g (1¾ oz) hazelnuts

olive oil, for frying

2 slices stale, good-quality white bread (about 40 g/ 1½ oz), torn into chunks

2 cloves garlic, peeled and finely chopped

1 tsp sweet smoked paprika

1 x 220 g (8 oz) jar roasted red peppers, drained

6 tbsp extra-virgin olive oil

2 tbsp sherry vinegar

1 small dried chilli, crumbled, or a pinch of dried chilli flakes

a generous pinch of saffron strands

1 tbsp tomato purée

1 butternut squash, de-seeded and cut into rough chunks

12 whole baby leeks, washed

1 unwaxed lemon

200 g (7 oz) farro (or another grain)

a few sprigs of fresh flat-leaf parsley, leaves picked

DF, V

METHOD

Pre-heat the oven to 200°C/180°C fan/400°F/gas 6. First, make your romesco sauce. Scatter the nuts on a baking tray and roast in the hot oven for 10–15 minutes, until golden. While they are roasting, heat a little olive oil in a pan and fry the bread until golden-brown all over. Add the garlic and smoked paprika and cook for a further minute, then remove from the heat.

Leaving the oven on, transfer the nuts and toasted bread to a food processor. Add the peppers and blitz until you have a coarse paste – you still want a nice bit of texture. Tip the whole lot into a mixing bowl, stir in the olive oil, vinegar, crumbled chilli, saffron and tomato purée. Season to taste and mix well, adjusting the favours if need be. Romesco is about a balance of punchy flavours. Too thick? Add a little water. Too sweet? Add a little vinegar. Too sharp? Add a little oil to soften. Leave to one side to mellow.

Next, put the squash on a large roasting tray with the leeks. Drizzle some olive oil over, grate the zest of the lemon over and season. Roast in the oven for 40 minutes until the squash is golden and the leeks are sweet. Meanwhile, cook the farro in salted boiling water for 35–40 minutes, until it is soft but still has a good gummy bite.

Drain the farro, toss with the roasted squash and leeks and a good few tablespoons of the romesco, and finish off with a generous sprinkling of parsley.

TIPS

Ways to use romesco:
· spread on toast and topped with a slick of goat's cheese for a quick snack
· as a dip for baby carrots and spring veg
· as a marinade for barbecued veg
· piled onto roasted veg for extra flavour
· tossed through cooked noodles with pan-fried greens
· stirred into a bowl of brown rice and topped with a poached egg
· next to your morning eggs
· with flat-bread and feta for a quick, simple lunch
· spooned on top of a bowl of soup.

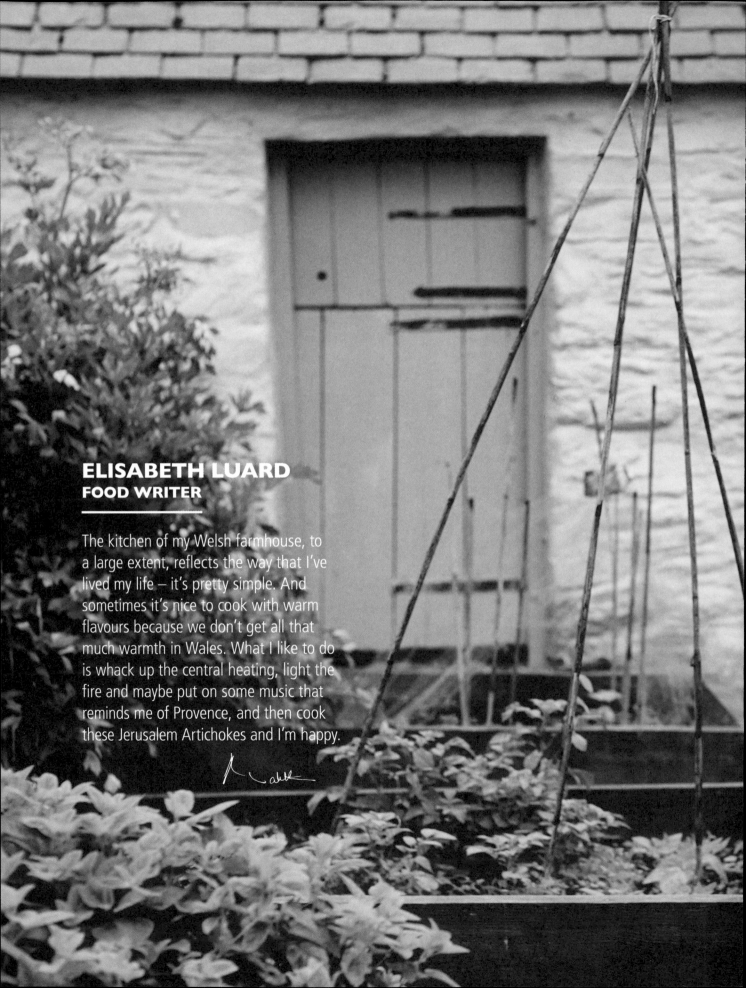

ELISABETH LUARD
FOOD WRITER

The kitchen of my Welsh farmhouse, to a large extent, reflects the way that I've lived my life — it's pretty simple. And sometimes it's nice to cook with warm flavours because we don't get all that much warmth in Wales. What I like to do is whack up the central heating, light the fire and maybe put on some music that reminds me of Provence, and then cook these Jerusalem Artichokes and I'm happy.

Brynmeheryn,
Wales

JERUSALEM ARTICHOKES
WITH OLIVES & THYME

Recipe by **ELISABETH LUARD**, food writer, Brynmeheryn, Wales

SERVINGS: 4 | **PREP TIME: 10 MINS** | **COOK TIME: 45 MINS** | **SKILL LEVEL: 1 (EASY)**

Jerusalem artichokes, the tubers that form on the root of a member of the sunflower family, thrive in the same marginal conditions as the potato – which, in a nutshell, means my corner of mid-Wales. It's no relation to the leaf artichoke, which is the flower bud of a large thistle – confusion arose over the name when the tuber was first introduced from the Americas via the garden of Seville, where it is known as the girasol (turn to the sun), hence 'Jerusalem'. While it makes an acceptable soup, it is even better with olives and thyme, as they like it in Provence.

INGREDIENTS

about 500 g (1 lb 2 oz)
  Jerusalem artichokes
2–3 tbsp olive oil
1–2 tbsp black olives, pitted
  or not, as you please
juice and finely grated zest
  of 1 unwaxed lemon
1–2 sprigs thyme
a generous glass of white wine
a pinch of freshly grated nutmeg
a pinch of freshly ground pepper
1–2 cloves garlic, finely chopped
1 tbsp finely chopped parsley
1 tbsp fresh breadcrumbs

DF, V

METHOD

If the artichokes are freshly dug and the skins are tender, there is no need to peel them. If the roots are elderly and the skins a little tough – test with a sharp fingernail – pop them in boiling salted water for 10 minutes, after which you'll find them easy to skin.

Chop the artichokes, skinned or not, into walnut-sized pieces; rinse and transfer to a saucepan in which they don't rattle around. Add the olive oil, olives, lemon juice and zest, thyme, wine and just enough water to barely cover.

Bring to the boil, then turn down the heat and season with nutmeg and pepper (no salt – the olives are quite salty enough). Cover tightly and leave to simmer gently until the roots are perfectly tender, 25–30 minutes, and the liquid has almost disappeared.

Stir in the garlic, parsley and breadcrumbs and re-heat for a minute or two, until the garlic softens and the crumbs have absorbed the juices and begun to fry a little, before serving.

BALSAMIC ROASTED RED ONION TARTE TATIN WITH TARRAGON

Recipe by **LORRAINE PASCALE**, chef & TV presenter, London

SERVINGS: 4 | **PREP TIME: 45 MINS** | **COOK TIME: 30 MINS** | **SKILL LEVEL: 2 (MODERATE)**

I made my first tarte tatin at Leiths School of Food and Wine when I started out as a chef. I loved the magic of the finished product when it was turned upside down to reveal dark golden-brown caramelized apples. With this red onion version, once cooked these alliums take on a savoury sweetness that I balanced out with the aniseed hint of tarragon. When peeling the onions, I try not to take off too many of the outer layers of the skin as that is where most of the nutritional goodness is.

INGREDIENTS

a knob of unsalted butter

2 Medjool dates, pitted and very, very finely chopped (or 1 tbsp date paste)

6 tbsp good-quality balsamic vinegar

3 sprigs fresh thyme

600 g (1¼ lb) red onions, peeled and cut into wedges

leaves from 1 bunch of fresh tarragon, roughly chopped

For the pastry

225 g (8 oz) plain or wholemeal spelt flour, plus extra for dusting

75 g (2½ oz) unsalted butter

1 egg

a pinch of salt

V

METHOD

Put the butter in a 20 cm (8 in) non-stick, ovenproof frying pan over a medium heat and allow to melt. Add the dates and cook them down for a minute or two, until they start to break down a little. If you are using date paste, then just put it in and stir. (There is no need to cook it for a minute or two, just proceed to the next step.)

Add the balsamic vinegar and thyme sprigs and continue to cook for a couple of minutes until reduced slightly. Add the onions and cook them for about 10 minutes, stirring frequently, until caramelized.

Meanwhile, pre-heat the oven to 180°C/160°C fan/350°F/gas 4.

To make the pastry, place all of the ingredients in a food processor and whizz them together until they start to form a smooth ball of dough. If using plain spelt flour, add 3 tablespoons of water to help bring it together. If using wholemeal flour, you will need to add a further 1–2 tablespoons of water.

Alternatively, to make by hand, put the flour and butter into a large bowl. Pick up bits of the mixture with the tips of your fingers and rub your thumb into your fingers to blend the ingredients together, allowing them to fall back into the bowl. Keep doing this until the mixture resembles fine breadcrumbs. Lightly beat the egg in a small bowl and stir into the crumbs really well with a small knife, until lumps start to form. Add the water (as above) to bring it together.

Lightly dust a clean surface with flour and roll out the pastry to a 20 cm (8 in) circle that is about two-thirds the thickness of a pound coin (about 2 mm).

Once cooked, remove the onion from the heat, stir all but a tablespoon of the tarragon through and season with salt and pepper. Then place the circle of pastry on top, tucking the excess pastry down the sides so everything is nice and snug. Transfer to the oven and cook for 25–30 minutes or until the pastry is cooked through and just turning golden.

Once cooked, remove from the oven and carefully invert onto a plate. Sprinkle with the remaining tarragon and serve. Great with some greens or a crisp salad.

TIP

Swap the herbs if you're not too fond of the anise hit of tarragon – parsley, basil and coriander make for more-than-worthy substitutes.

BAK & DES

ING
SERTS

RICHARD CADDICK
WITH ARTHUR CADDICK
HOME BAKER

————————

I started baking bread about 20 years ago,
and it was really inspired by my grandfather.
We used to go round there for Sunday lunch
and in the afternoon he'd always bake a loaf
of wholemeal bread, and it became part of
the family tradition. These days I really enjoy
baking for the family and for friends.

Richard

Bristol

EDWARD'S BURGER BUNS

Recipe by **RICHARD CADDICK**, home baker, Bristol

SERVINGS: 4 | **PREP TIME: 30 MINS** | **COOK TIME: 30 MINS** | **SKILL LEVEL: 2 (MODERATE)**

These buns are named after our fourth child. I made them for my wife on the night she came home from hospital with him. They're a sweet bun, softer than a bread roll but with more substance than brioche. The perfect combination. Because of the sweetness they are very versatile and can be shaped into fingers and iced, or have currants and spices thrown into the mix and used as hot cross buns – I've included the variations here. These are best eaten the same day but will freeze well in plastic zip-lock bags.

INGREDIENTS

The dough
500 g (18 oz) strong white bread-making flour
150 g (5¼ fl oz) cold semi-skimmed milk
150 g (5¼ fl oz) hot water
16 g (½ oz) instant yeast (or 2 sachets)

10 g (2 tsp) salt
100 g (3½ oz) sugar
50 g (1½ oz) butter
1 egg (if you're new to making bread and not used to sticky doughs then you can leave this out to start with, they'll still taste just as good!)

To add before baking
1 extra egg, beaten, for the wash
nigella, poppy or sesame seeds for the top (optional)

V

METHOD

Mix: mix all the dough ingredients in a large bowl until everything is combined. Leave for 10 minutes, then gently tuck the dough underneath itself from the edges – working all the way around the bowl a couple of times. Repeat this every 10 minutes for 40 minutes. You'll find the dough is quite sticky at first, but each time you tuck the mixture under it gets more elastic and you eventually end up with a smooth ball of dough.

Rise: cover the bowl with a shower cap (or clean plastic bag) and leave the dough to rise until almost doubled in size.

Scale: once risen, weigh the dough on scales and divide the weight by 10. Then use the scales to divide the dough into 10 equal pieces. Weighing the dough may seem like a faff, but it means each bun will look the same and, more importantly, cook in exactly the same time.

Shape: the dough can be quite wet and it's tempting to add lots of extra flour. Try to resist and handle the dough lightly, dipping your fingers in a little flour instead.

Shape each piece of dough into a ball. The simple way to do this is to hold a piece in one hand, then take a piece of dough from the edge, pull it over and push it into the middle. Repeat this all the way around. Alternatively, cup your hand over a piece of dough on the work surface and move your hand in a small circular pattern with the tips of your fingers lightly touching the dough in contact with the work surface. This will push the dough underneath itself and you'll start to see a smooth ball appear.

Proof: put baking paper onto two trays and place five balls on each tray. This makes sure that as they rise and bake they don't join together. Cover loosely with a plastic bag or bin liner and leave to double in size.

Bake: heat the oven to 200°C/400°F/gas 6.

Brush each bun with the beaten egg and sprinkle with seeds, if using. Bake in the pre-heated oven for 20 minutes, turning the tray once. Leave to cool, then cut in half and toast before serving.

VARIATIONS

For iced buns, divide into 20 pieces and shape into fingers. Once baked, top with a simple water-based icing.

For hot cross buns, swap out 50 g (1½ oz) flour for wholemeal and add 150 g (5 oz) raisins, 1 tablespoon mixed spice, 1 teaspoon ground ginger and 1 teaspoon ground cinnamon. Once you've shaped the buns and let them rise, pipe a mixture of 100 g (3½ oz) water and 100 g (3½ oz) flour in crosses on top of the dough. Once baked, brush with diluted apricot jam for a good shiny and sticky finish (see overleaf).

BASIC FLAPJACKS

Recipe by **FRANCES QUINN**, baker & designer, Market Harborough, Leicestershire

SERVINGS: 4 | PREP TIME: 5 MINS | COOK TIME: 20 MINS | SKILL LEVEL: I (EASY)

INGREDIENTS

50 g (1½ oz) butter, roughly
    chopped
50 g (1½ oz) golden caster
    sugar
1 tbsp golden syrup
100 g (3½ oz) porridge oats

V

METHOD

You will need a 15 cm (6 in) round, loose-bottomed tin, greased and base-lined.

Pre-heat the oven to 180°C/160°C fan/350°F/gas 4.

Put the butter, sugar and golden syrup in a saucepan. Set it over a medium heat and warm, stirring occasionally, until the butter has melted and the sugar has dissolved. Take the saucepan off the heat and stir in the oats, combining everything thoroughly.

Transfer the mixture into the prepared tin and spread out evenly using the back of a spoon or spatula.

Bake for 12–15 minutes or until golden-brown around the edges. Leave to cool in the tin.

TIPS

Although they are delicious on their own, flapjacks needn't be plain. I enjoy them coated with chocolate. In fact, this 15 cm round one can be made into something like a giant Chocolate Hobnob! Just cover it in 50 g (1¾ oz) melted chocolate and use a palette knife to create biscuit markings on top.

I also love citrus zest in my flapjacks to give a really fruity flavour, and often substitute marmalade or honey for the golden syrup.

CHOCOLATE BREAD PUDDING WITH BACON CUSTARD

Recipe by **DAN DOHERTY**, chef & author, Hackney, London

SERVINGS: 8–10 | PREP TIME: 1½ HOURS | COOK TIME: 30 MINS | SKILL LEVEL: 1 (EASY)

This is such a simple dessert, but we have pimped it with bacon. I've no idea why it works, but it just does. Don't be put off by the bacon — the smoky, salty edge that it gives really complements the rich, sweet pudding. Give it a go...

INGREDIENTS

For the pudding
140 ml (5 fl oz) double cream
800 ml (1 pint 9 fl oz) milk
40 g (1½ oz) milk chocolate, roughly chopped
40 g (1½ oz) dark chocolate (70 per cent cocoa), roughly chopped
4 egg yolks
140 g (5 oz) caster sugar, plus extra for dusting
150 g (5 oz) unsalted butter, plus a little extra for greasing
1 loaf good-quality white bread, sliced

For the custard
6 rashers smoked streaky bacon
150 ml (5 fl oz) milk
150 ml (5 fl oz) double cream
2 egg yolks
35 g (1¼ oz) caster sugar

METHOD

Pre-heat your oven to 140°C/275°F/gas 1 and butter an ovenproof dish approximately 28 cm x 23 cm (11 in x 9 in).

To make the pudding, put the cream and milk in a saucepan and bring to the boil, then add the chocolate and whisk in until melted. Remove from the heat. Whisk together the egg yolks and sugar in a bowl, then pour in the chocolate cream. Whisk well, then strain.

Use the butter to butter the bread, then layer the slices in the dish, with ladles of the chocolate custard in between. Press down with your fingers to make sure it is all soaked properly. Dust the top with a few pinches of sugar, and place in the oven for 30 minutes.

In the meantime, make your custard. Put the bacon into a medium-sized saucepan and caramelize over a medium heat, pouring away any fat that comes out. When it's all brown, add the milk and cream and bring to the boil. Lower the heat and allow to infuse over a low heat for 30 minutes.

In a bowl, whisk together the egg yolks and sugar. Bring the cream back to the boil, and strain. Slowly pour the cream onto the yolk mix and stir well. Pour back into the pan and heat gently until it thickens a little — taking care not to let it scramble and go lumpy.

Serve the pudding with the custard poured over and around.

CHERRY CLAFOUTIS

Recipe by **RAYMOND BLANC OBE**, Belmond Le Manoir aux Quat'Saisons,
Great Milton, Oxfordshire

SERVINGS: 4 | **PREP TIME: 30 MINS PLUS 2 HOURS MACERATING** | **COOK TIME: 30–35 MINS**
SKILL LEVEL: I (EASY)

Clafoutis is one of the great classics of French family cuisine. This dessert often features on our menus, both at Belmond Le Manoir and at Brasserie Blanc. It is very easy to prepare and I would go so far as to say it is foolproof. Other stone-fruits, such as peaches, plums and apricots, or indeed figs, work just as well.

INGREDIENTS

For the cherries

450 g (1 lb) best-quality cherries (such as Montmorency or Morello), stoned

50 g (1½ oz) caster sugar, plus extra for sprinkling

2–3 tbsp kirsch, to taste (optional)

For preparing the dish

10 g (⅓ oz) unsalted butter, melted

30 g (1 oz) caster sugar, plus extra to finish (optional)

For the batter

2 organic/free-range medium-sized eggs

45 g (1½ oz) caster sugar

½ tsp vanilla extract

20 g (¾ oz) unsalted butter

20 g (¾ oz) plain flour

50 ml (1½ fl oz) whole milk

75 ml (2½ fl oz) whipping cream

a pinch of sea salt

Equipment

a 20 cm (8 in) round ceramic or cast-iron baking dish (5 cm/2 in deep)

a cherry stoner

V

METHOD

To prepare the cherries: gently mix together the cherries, sugar and kirsch, if using, in a bowl. Leave to macerate for 2 hours (see tips).

Pre-heat the oven to 180°C/350°F/gas 4.

To prepare the dish: brush the inside with the melted butter. Add the sugar and tilt the dish to coat the sides and base evenly; shake out the excess.

To make the clafoutis: in a large bowl, whisk together the eggs, sugar and vanilla until creamy. Meanwhile, melt the butter in a small pan until it turns a pale hazelnut colour – this is called a beurre noisette (see tip below). Add the flour to the egg and sugar mixture and whisk until smooth, then slowly incorporate the milk, cream, salt and beurre noisette. Stir in the cherries with their juice and then pour into the prepared baking dish.

To cook the clafoutis: bake in the oven for 30–35 minutes until the clafoutis has risen slightly and a knife inserted in the middle comes out clean (see tip below). Leave to stand for about 10 minutes. Sprinkle with caster sugar, if using, and serve just warm.

TIPS

While macerating, the sugar slowly permeates the fruit and intensifies the taste.

The foaming butter will turn a hazelnut colour at 150–155°C (302–311°F), i.e. beurre noisette. This butter will lend a wonderful roundness and nutty flavour to the clafoutis.

The centre is always the last part to cook, so you must test it. Note that a dip in the middle suggests the clafoutis is undercooked.

BLACKCURRANT & CHOCOLATE LAYER

Recipe by **NIKKI DUFFY**, freelance food writer & editor, Suffolk

SERVINGS: 4 | PREP TIME: 40 MINS PLUS CHILLING | COOK TIME: 25 MINS | SKILL LEVEL: 1 (EASY)

Blackcurrants, in season in the summer months of July and August, are one of my favourite fruits. They have a strong but exquisite flavour that is almost spicy, and that pairs well with dark chocolate. This recipe includes several different elements, but they can all be prepared ahead of time and the assembled dish chilled overnight. It's definitely a no-pressure pud.

INGREDIENTS

For the blackcurrant layer
250 g (9 oz) blackcurrants
a squeeze of lemon juice
up to 100 g (3½ oz) caster
  sugar

For the chocolate layer
25 g (1 oz) cocoa powder
50 g (1½ oz) caster sugar
100 ml (3½ fl oz) water

For the cream/yoghurt layer
200 ml (7 fl oz) double cream
200 ml (7 fl oz) plain full-fat
  yoghurt
2 tbsp caster sugar

To finish
50 g (1½ oz) skinned hazelnuts
1 tbsp Demerara sugar

GF, V

METHOD

Put the blackcurrants in a saucepan with 50 ml (1½ fl oz) water. Bring to a simmer and cook for a few minutes, stirring once or twice, until the fruit has broken down and you have a chunky, juicy mix. Push this through a sieve to remove the currant skins and seeds. Add the lemon juice to the warm purée, then sweeten it by stirring in caster sugar. Start by adding 50 g (1½ oz), then stir in more until the purée is sweet but still tastes fruity and fresh. Leave to cool and then chill.

To make the chocolate layer, put the cocoa and sugar in a small pan with the water. Bring to the boil, whisking constantly, then let the mixture simmer for about 1 minute – again, stirring often – so that it thickens. Leave to cool and then chill.

When you're ready to assemble the puds, put the cream, yoghurt and caster sugar in a mixing bowl and use a hand-held electric whisk to beat the mixture until it holds soft peaks.

Choose four wine glasses or tumblers. Divide half the blackcurrant purée between the four glasses. Add a couple of spoonfuls of the creamy mixture to each glass. Trickle on a layer of chocolate sauce. Add a second layer of the creamy mixture, using it all up this time, then finish the dishes with the rest of the blackcurrant purée. Chill for at least a few hours – up to 24.

Shortly before serving, toast the hazelnuts in an oven pre-heated to 180°C/350°F/gas 4 for 5–6 minutes, until golden and fragrant. Put the nuts in a mortar and pestle with the Demerara sugar and bash together roughly so that the nuts are broken up but not pulverized. (Alternatively, do this in a food processor.) Leave to cool, then sprinkle over the puddings and serve.

CHOCOLATE GUINNESS CAKE

Recipe by **NIGELLA LAWSON**, food writer & TV presenter, London

SERVINGS: 12 | **PREP TIME: 15 MINS** | **COOK TIME: 1 HOUR** | **SKILL LEVEL: 1 (EASY)**

INGREDIENTS

For the cake
250 ml (9 fl oz) Guinness
250 g (9 oz) unsalted butter
75 g (3 oz) cocoa powder
400 g (14 oz) caster sugar
150 ml (5 fl oz) sour cream
2 eggs
1 tbsp real vanilla extract
275 g (9¾ oz) plain flour
2½ tsp bicarbonate of soda

For the topping
300 g (10½ oz) Philadelphia
  cream cheese
150 g (5 oz) icing sugar
125 ml (4 fl oz) double or
  whipping cream

V

METHOD

Pre-heat the oven to 180°C/350°F/gas 4, and butter and line a 23 cm (9 in) springform tin.

Pour the Guinness into a large, wide saucepan, add the butter – in spoonfuls or slices – and heat until the butter's melted, at which time you should whisk in the cocoa and sugar. Beat the sour cream with the eggs and vanilla and then pour into the brown, buttery, beery pan and finally whisk in the flour and bicarb.

Pour the cake batter into the greased and lined tin and bake for 45 minutes to an hour. Leave to cool completely in the tin on a cooling rack, as it is quite a damp cake.

When the cake's cold, sit it on a flat platter or cake stand and get on with the icing. Lightly whip the cream cheese until smooth, sieve over the icing sugar and then beat them both together. Or do this in a food processor, putting the unsieved icing sugar in first and blitzing to remove lumps before adding the cheese.

Add the cream and beat again until it makes a spreadable consistency. Ice the top of the black cake so that it resembles the frothy top of the famous pint.

ROSIE BIRKETT
FOOD WRITER

This seasonal take on a very classic dessert is inspired by where I live, on the edge of the Walthamstow Marshes nature reserve. There is so much wild food growing here and every year, I love watching the seasons bestow their fleeting gifts on the landscape – from gorgeous fragrant elderflower to wild cherries and, later in the year, juicy blackberries we all fight the parakeets for. *Rosie*

Hackney, London

FIG LEAF & CHERRY BRÛLÉE

Recipe by **ROSIE BIRKETT**, food writer, Hackney, London

SERVINGS: 4 | PREP TIME: 30 MINS | COOK TIME: 30 MINS | SKILL LEVEL: 2 (MODERATE)

There is a huge fig tree by the canal on the route where I walk my dog, and I always bag a load of the younger, furrier leaves, which smell so good and almondy. They're brilliant for infusing custards and creams, and their almond notes work beautifully with British cherries.

INGREDIENTS

3 young, fresh fig leaves
  (not the waxy, older ones)
290 ml (½ pint) double cream
50 g (1½ oz) cherries, plus
  4 whole cherries to serve
1 tbsp cherry liqueur or kirsch
4 egg yolks (Burford Browns
  make for the best colour)
2 tbsp golden caster sugar
2 tbsp Demerara sugar

GF, V

METHOD

Rip the fig leaves and then place them in a pan with the cream. Heat the cream until just before it boils, when tiny little bubbles are starting to emerge at the edge of the pan. Allow to stand and infuse for at least 20 minutes, then discard the fig leaves.

Setting aside the 4 whole cherries, put the remaining cherries into a pan with the liqueur and cook over a medium heat for about 3 minutes, until they're softening and have released some of their juice. Divide between 4 ramekins.

Pre-heat the oven to 170°C/150°C fan/gas 3. Prepare a warm bain marie by filling a high-sided roasting tray with boiling water, high enough that it will almost cover your ramekins but leaving about 2 cm (¾ in) from the top of them free.

Whisk the egg yolks and caster sugar together until pale, then slowly pour in the cream, stirring. Transfer to a jug and pour the mixture through a sieve into the ramekins on top of the cherries and place the ramekins into the bain marie. Bake in the oven for 20–25 minutes, or until a skin forms on top of the custard and it wobbles slightly when you shake the dishes. Allow to cool and then refrigerate for at least 5 hours.

Top each ramekin with the Demerara sugar, to a thickness of about 2 mm (⅛ in), then use a blow-torch to brûlée the top by sweeping the flame across the surface in an even motion until the sugar caramelizes into a nice crisp layer. Alternatively, top them evenly with the sugar in a slightly thicker layer of about 5 mm (¼ in) and then brûlée under a hot grill. Serve immediately.

EASTERN MESS

Recipe by **SABRINA GHAYOUR**, chef & food writer, London

SERVINGS: 6 | **PREP TIME: 10 MINS** | **SKILL LEVEL: 1 (EASY)**

Having spent almost all of my life in England, I am no stranger to Eton Mess. I like to believe that it was first created as a happy accident in a failed attempt at strawberry pavlova at Eton College, although this is largely believed to be a myth. Over the years, I have made versions using every fruit imaginable and have added a variety of flavours to the cream. I won't mind admitting that some were less successful than others. This Eastern version is perfumed with Persian rose-water and combined with raspberries, basil and delicate pistachio slivers which give a little crunch to every bite.

INGREDIENTS

600 ml (21 fl oz) double cream

3 tbsp icing sugar

1 tsp vanilla bean paste, or the seeds scraped from 1 vanilla pod

2 tbsp rose-water

6 ready-made meringues, broken slightly if large

450 g (1 lb) raspberries

a handful of Greek basil leaves or torn basil leaves

75 g (2½ oz) pistachio nut slivers or chopped pistachio nuts (optional)

For the raspberry sauce

225 g (8 oz) fresh raspberries

1 tbsp icing sugar (you may need more if using raspberries out of season)

1 tbsp rose-water

a squeeze of lemon juice

GF, V

METHOD

Using an electric hand whisk, whip the double cream, icing sugar, vanilla paste or seeds and rose-water together in a mixing bowl until soft peaks form. You don't want the cream to be too loose or too stiff, so keep an eye on the consistency. With the whisk set on a high speed, it should take about 3 minutes or so.

To make the sauce, mash the raspberries to a purée with the icing sugar, rose-water and lemon juice in a bowl until the mixture is completely smooth. Pass the mixture through a sieve to remove the raspberry seeds.

Choose either a large platter or individual serving dishes. Now layer the cream mixture, meringues and raspberries in the serving dish(es), drizzling on the sauce and scattering over the basil leaves and pistachios, if using, as you go. Decorate the top layer with a little drizzle of sauce and a final scattering of basil leaves and pistachios, if using. Serve immediately.

CARAMELIZED RADICCHIO & WINTER RHUBARB ROUND

Recipe by **ROSE PRINCE**, food writer, journalist & cookery school owner, Winterborne Houghton, Dorset

MAKES: 2 X 500 G (I LB 4 OZ) LOAVES | PREP TIME: 2½ HOURS PLUS RESTING OVERNIGHT & PROVING
COOK TIME: I¼ HOURS | SKILL LEVEL: 2 (MODERATE)

Radicchio is a bitter-flavoured leaf but if very slowly cooked, it becomes as sweet as fruit and can be added to fruity breads – it is sometimes added to panettone in Italy. In this instance it is kneaded into an enriched dough with winter rhubarb to make a loaf with an interesting pinkish-buff-coloured crumb. This has a wet dough that collapses into a flattish, round bread; a wonderful bread to eat with hard cheeses, slices of apple and chutney.

INGREDIENTS

For the sponge ferment

3 g (⅛ oz) fresh yeast
  (or 2 g/⅓ tsp dried)

150 ml (5 oz) water

150 g (5 oz) strong white
  flour

For the filling

300 g (9 oz) pink winter
  (forced) rhubarb, cut into
  4 cm (1½ in) pieces

300 g (9 oz) radicchio leaves,
  shredded

a knob of butter

For the dough

1 quantity sponge ferment
  (see above)

3 g (⅛ oz) yeast

180 g (6½ oz) Italian '00'
  white flour, plus extra for
  dusting

60 ml (4 tbsp) extra-virgin
  rapeseed oil

5 g (1 tsp) sea salt

Equipment

2 x baking sheets:
  1 lined with baking paper
  (for the rhubarb);
  1 lightly greased

V

METHOD

Put all the sponge ferment ingredients into a bowl, mix well and leave to ferment for 1 hour at room temperature.

The rhubarb and radicchio can be prepared ready to use in the next stage – allowing cooling time. Pre-heat the oven to 200°C/400°F/gas 6. Put the rhubarb on the lined baking sheet, 1 cm (½ in) apart. Bake for about 30 minutes, until it is roasted but is not browning. Some juice will leach out and evaporate.

Put the radicchio in a frying pan with the butter and 1 tablespoon of water, and cook over a very low heat for about 15 minutes, until the radicchio is dark brown and tastes sweet. It must not burn, but it will lose its red colour.

Put the dough ingredients, including the sponge ferment, into the bowl of an electric stand mixer and beat for about 10 minutes. Remove the dough from the bowl to a floured worktop using dough scrapers. Scatter the rhubarb and radicchio over two-thirds of the surface.

Fold into three, like a letter, using floured dough scrapers to lift the dough. Pat the dough gently then fold again. Repeat one more time. Put the dough back into the bowl, cover with clingfilm and place in the fridge overnight.

The following day, take the dough from the fridge; it will be bubbly and firm. Scrape it out of the bowl onto the worktop, then lift one edge with a scraper, bringing it into the centre. Repeat, working around the piece of dough, by which time you will have a neat round shape.

Pick up the dough, turn it over so that the smooth side is uppermost, and place it on the greased baking sheet. Dust it with a light covering of flour, if it is not already quite floury. Leave to prove for 45 minutes, until well risen.

Pre-heat the oven to 220°C/425°F/gas 7. Before baking, make a series of shallow slashes on the surface of the round with a blade, like a windmill. Bake for 20–30 minutes or until pale brown and airy. Cool on the baking sheet, then eat sliced.

MITCH TONKS
THE SEAHORSE

The thing I love most about restaurants is the instant satisfaction you get from giving other people a good time. I come from the old school of hospitality. For me, just watching people's faces when they have that first mouthful; seeing a table engrossed in conversation; hearing the noise levels in the room — that's when you know you've really, really cracked it. A great night in a restaurant is such a joy.

Mitch

Dartmouth,
Devon

FIGS ROASTED WITH GRAPPA & AMARETTO GELATO

Recipe by **MITCH TONKS**, The Seahorse, Dartmouth, Devon

SERVINGS: 4 | **PREP TIME: 1 HOUR PLUS CHURNING** | **COOK TIME: 35 MINS** | **SKILL LEVEL: 2 (MODERATE)**

In the summer when we have ripe black or green figs from Provence, we love to cook this dish. The marriage of butter, honey, grappa and sugar is a lovely combination. This gelato is one of Jake Bridgwood's (chef at The Seahorse) creations. He goes quiet when he's on to something and starts making things in between service — 'Taste this, chef,' he says — and it's a magnificent recipe! This ice cream is best eaten within a week.

INGREDIENTS

For the amaretto gelato
10 egg yolks
400 g (14 oz) caster sugar
750 ml (1 pint 7 fl oz) full-fat milk
1 whole vanilla pod, split in half lengthways and seeds scraped out
750 ml (1 pint 7 fl oz) double cream
210 g (7½ oz) amaretti biscuits, crushed

For the figs
8 fresh figs
100 g (3½ oz) unsalted butter, softened
honey, for drizzling
75 ml (2½ fl oz) grappa
a splash of amaretto, to serve

V

METHOD

Using an electric mixer, whisk the egg yolks and sugar together until light and fluffy.

In a small saucepan, bring the milk and vanilla pod and seeds to just below the boil, then remove from the heat and leave to infuse for 5–10 minutes.

Pour the infused milk over the egg mixture and stir with a whisk to combine, then pour back into the pan and cook for 4–5 minutes until thickened slightly; ideally, use a thermometer and heat to 80°C (176°F). Pass the mixture through a fine sieve, then allow to cool.

Once cool, stir in the cream and crushed amaretti biscuits, then churn in an ice cream machine according to the manufacturer's instructions. Keep the ice cream in the freezer until needed.

Pre-heat the oven to 220°C/425°F/gas 7.

Cut a cross in the top of each fig and place them in an ovenproof dish so that they are nice and snug. Put a pinch of soft butter into the cuts in the figs, then drizzle liberally with the honey.

Pour a little grappa over each fig and roast in the oven for 10–15 minutes, until the figs are soft and you have a lovely sticky syrup in the base of the dish. Sometimes the syrup may need a little more cooking; if so, pour it into a pan and boil for 1–2 minutes to reduce slightly.

Serve the figs with a good scoop of amaretto gelato and a spoonful of the syrup over the top. Pour a small splash of amaretto over the ice cream when serving.

BABAS IN PINK GRAPEFRUIT SYRUP

Recipe by **ROSE PRINCE**, food writer, journalist & cookery school owner, Winterborne Houghton, Dorset

MAKES: 12 | **PREP TIME: 40 MINS PLUS PROVING** | **COOK TIME: 30–45 MINS** | **SKILL LEVEL: 2 (MODERATE)**

Babas are yeasty buns, made from a very rich dough, which are baked in small moulds then soaked in syrup. The classic version of this French baking phenomenon includes fat raisins in the dough and lots of rum in the syrup. I love it but it found no friends among the children. We devised something simpler, and more, well, babyish, so appetising sold packed in jars with syrup. Serve as a pudding with whipped cream, or vanilla ice cream.

INGREDIENTS

For the dough
200 ml (7 fl oz) cold milk
14 g (½ oz) dried yeast
300 g (10½ oz) plain flour
2 eggs
2 egg yolks
15 g (1 tbsp) caster sugar
1 tsp salt
90 g (3 oz) unsalted French butter, cold from the fridge, cut into small ½ cm (¼ in) dice

For the syrup
500 ml (18 fl oz) pink grapefruit juice, freshly squeezed
600 g (1 lb 5 oz) caster sugar

Equipment
12 baba moulds or a 12-hole muffin tray, lightly greased with butter

V

METHOD

It is better to make this dough in an electric stand mixer. First, combine the milk, yeast and one-third of the flour in the bowl, then leave for 20 minutes until bubbling and active. Beat in all the remaining ingredients of the dough, except the butter; add this, bit by bit, with the mixer on high speed.

Once the butter has been incorporated, continue to beat for 5 minutes. The dough will be wet but elastic in appearance and texture. Cover the bowl with clingfilm and leave to rise, either in the fridge overnight or for 1–1½ hours in a draught-free spot.

Pre-heat the oven to 180°C/350°F/gas 4. Stir the yeast batter to knock it down in size. Using two tablespoons, one to scoop and the other to shape, spoon enough dough into each baba mould or muffin recess to fill it just over half full.

Leave the babas in a draught-free spot to prove for 30–45 minutes. When they have doubled in size, bake them until puffed, crisp and golden.

In the meantime, while the dough is rising, boil the grapefruit juice and sugar together for about 5 minutes until the mixture is reduced to a syrup. Put the babas in a tall jar, and pour the syrup over the top.

PRUE LEITH CBE
RESTAURATEUR, CATERER & FOOD WRITER

If I have a food philosophy, it is simply that food is meant
to make you happy. You have to enjoy it; if it becomes
stressful or you get too anxious about getting it right,
that's no good. You want to cook things that make you
feel comfortable, things you can enjoy cooking and eating.
I think food is all about pleasure.

PRUE

Chastleton,
Gloucestershire

NORMANDY TART
MADE WITH A FOOD PROCESSOR

Recipe by **PRUE LEITH CBE**, restaurateur, caterer & food writer, Chastleton, Gloucestershire

SERVINGS: 8–10 | **PREP TIME: 45 MINS PLUS CHILLING** | **COOK TIME: 45 MINS** | **SKILL LEVEL: 2 (MODERATE)**

This is one of my favourite recipes — it's so classic, it just never, never fails. It's basically pastry on the outside, with this really almondy, creamy, rich filling, and sliced apple halves shoved into it. However badly you make it, it still tastes wonderful.

INGREDIENTS

For the pastry
225 g (8 oz) plain flour
140 g (5 oz) butter
1 egg
a pinch of salt
50 g (1½ oz) caster sugar

For the almond filling
170 g (6 oz) butter
170 g (6 oz) caster sugar
225 g (8 oz) ground almonds
2 eggs
1 tbsp calvados, kirsch, or
  whatever liqueur you like
a few drops almond essence

For the topping
3–5 eating apples,
  depending on size
half a 340 g (12 oz) jar
  of smooth apricot jam,
  warmed with 1 tbsp water
  to a thick syrup

V

METHOD

Set the oven at 200°C/400°F/gas 6 and put a metal tray in it to heat.

Whizz everything for the pastry together until the mixture forms a ball. Roll out between two sheets of polythene or baking paper until big enough to line a 25 cm (10 in) flan ring. Chill for 30 minutes. If the dish is porcelain, bake blind; if metal, don't bother. To bake blind, line the pastry-lined flan ring with baking paper and fill with baking beans. Bake for 10 minutes, then remove the beans and paper and bake for a further 5–10 minutes or until the pastry is light golden all over.

Whizz everything for the filling in the food processor (no need to wash the bowl after making the pastry), then spread in the flan case.

Peel the apples if you like, but no need to. Core them and cut in half from top to stalk end. Slice each half-apple finely, keeping the slices in order. Arrange them on top of the filling.

Set the flan in the middle of the hot oven and bake for 15 minutes. Then paint with hot jam. Reduce the oven temperature to 180°C/350°F/gas 4 and bake for half an hour or so, until the filling is firm and brown. Remove from the oven and give it another brush with the jam if you think it needs it.

To serve: best cooled to tepid or room temperature without refrigeration. If you make it in advance, freeze it and then reheat for 20 minutes at 180°C/350°F/gas 4 and allow to cool. This will crisp up the pastry again.

HOOGIM-JA ICE CREAM

BLACK SESAME SEED ICE CREAM

Recipe by **JORDAN BOURKE**, chef & food writer, & **REJINA PYO**, fashion designer, Alexandra Palace, London

SERVINGS: 2–3 | PREP TIME: 1 HOUR | COOK TIME: 45 MINS | SKILL LEVEL: 1 (EASY)

On a tiny street near Insadong-gil (the tourist mecca of Seoul) and up a flight of winding wooden stairs, we found ourselves, to our delight, in a paper-screened little oasis of calm away from the masses. We had come for iced tea but were unable to resist their black sesame seed ice cream. It was subtle and naturally flavoured, with an almost chewy creaminess, yet made without any dairy at all. It took ages to develop this recipe, but we got there in the end. You must use good-quality, fresh black sesame seeds, otherwise the taste won't be as perfect.

INGREDIENTS

50 g (1½ oz) black sesame seeds
60 g (2 oz) agave syrup
2 x 400 ml (14 fl oz) cans coconut milk
100 g (3½ oz) unrefined sugar or coconut palm sugar

a pinch of sea salt
3 tbsp cornflour

DF, GF, V

METHOD

Put the black sesame seeds in a dry frying pan over a medium heat. The moment they begin to pop and release their aroma, remove them from the heat and cool. Blitz the seeds in a coffee grinder or food processor until finely ground, then place them in a bowl and combine them with the agave syrup to form a paste.

Heat 1 can of the coconut milk, the sugar and the salt in a heavy-based saucepan over a medium-low heat until the sugar has dissolved. In a bowl, slowly whisk the remaining can of coconut milk into the cornflour, ensuring there are no lumps. Add this to the saucepan, mix everything together and cook for 4–6 minutes over a medium-high heat, stirring constantly, until the mixture becomes thick. Use a spatula to stir the mixture, making sure the bottom does not burn or become lumpy.

When thickened, remove the pan from the heat and transfer the mixture to a large bowl. If there are any lumps, pass the mixture through a sieve into a bowl.

Stir the sesame seed paste into the ice cream mixture until combined. Place baking paper onto the surface to prevent a skin forming and leave to cool completely. Refrigerate for 1–2 hours until well chilled. You can speed up this process by placing the bowl in an ice bath.

Churn in an ice cream maker according to the instructions. Alternatively, pour the mixture into a wide, flat (preferably metal) tray and place in the freezer. After 40 minutes, use a fork to mix and break down the ice crystals. Repeat this process twice more, at 40-minute intervals. You can blitz it all in a food processor at the final stage to make it really smooth.

Return to the tray and leave in the freezer to set fully. Remove 15 minutes before serving to give the ice cream a chance to soften.

BAKEWELL PUDDING

Recipe by **GERARD BAKER**, chef, food historian & radio presenter, Roos in Holderness, East Riding

SERVINGS: 6 | **PREP TIME: 20 MINS PLUS RESTING** | **COOK TIME: 1½ HOURS** | **SKILL LEVEL: 2 (MODERATE)**

Mrs Beeton used puff pastry for her Bakewell pudding, but a well-baked shortcrust tart case is a better match, giving a crisp contrast to the rich, silky filling. Use homemade raspberry jam if you have it, or choose a sharp conserve to contrast with the sweet filling.

INGREDIENTS

For the pastry
250 g (9 oz) plain flour
a pinch of salt
125 g (4½ oz) cold unsalted
  butter, cubed or grated
½ tsp lemon juice
100 ml (3½ fl oz) ice water

For the filling
115 g (4 oz) butter
160 g (5½ oz) caster sugar
30 g (1 oz) ground almonds
5 egg yolks
1 egg white
80 g (3 oz) sharp-tasting,
  best-quality raspberry jam

Equipment
a deep 22 cm (9 in) metal
  pie dish
some baking beans

V

METHOD

First make the pastry. If you have a food processor, sift the flour and salt into the bowl and mix. Add the cubed butter and pulse until the mixture resembles fine breadcrumbs. Pour the mixture into a bowl.

If you are working by hand, sift the flour and salt into a bowl and add the butter. Rub the butter and flour between your fingertips until it resembles fine breadcrumbs, working quickly to keep the mixture as cool as possible. If it starts to feel sticky, chill the mixture for 30 minutes before moving on to the next step.

Add the lemon juice to the water and pour two-thirds of this into the flour mixture. Blend well with a fork, stirring quickly but gently. Using your fingertips, bring the dough together. Add more lemon-water as necessary (you may need to use all of it), until everything is evenly mixed and there are no dry lumps of flour. Bring the mixture together into a smooth, supple lump. Carefully form the pastry into a flattened ball, wrap in clingfilm and chill for 20 minutes.

Then, roll the pastry out on a floured surface to a 27 cm (10½ in) round. Place it in the pie dish, leaving the extra pastry hanging over the edge. Line the pastry with a large piece of non-stick baking paper and then fill with baking beans. Leave to rest in a cool place for 10 minutes.

Pre-heat the oven to 200°C/400°F/gas 6.

Place the pastry case on a baking tray and bake for 35 minutes until firm and golden-brown. Remove the beans and paper and return the case to the oven for 5 minutes to bake further and dry slightly. Remove from the oven and set aside. Reduce the oven to 160°C/320°F/gas 3.

Make the filling by melting the butter in a medium-sized saucepan over a low heat. Remove from the heat, and add the sugar, ground almonds and egg yolks and white, beating well to combine.

Spread the jam into the pastry case and carefully pour the filling over. Bake for 15 minutes, then turn the oven down to 140°C/275°F/gas 1 for a further 30 minutes, until the filling is just firm to the touch. Trim the pastry hanging over the rim with a sharp knife, and cool to room temperature before serving.

CHURROS

Recipe by **RICHARD BERTINET**, chef & baker, Bath, Somerset

MAKES: ABOUT 12 | **PREP TIME: 20 MINS** | **COOK TIME: 5 MINS PER BATCH** | **SKILL LEVEL: 2 (MODERATE)**

In Spain, if you try to walk past one of the cafés that specializes in these strips of sugary doughnut, the smell of hot oil and sugar is just impossible to resist. Traditionally, they are made using a churrera, a pump with a special nozzle, which squeezes the churro mixture into hot oil in long, snaking, ridged rings. Once these are fried, they are snipped into short lengths and dusted in sugar and sometimes cinnamon, ready for dipping into the thick hot chocolate that is usually served with them. At home you can use a piping bag, and snip the mixture into shorter, more manageable lengths as you pipe it into the oil. The secret is to fry them slowly at a relatively low temperature so that they get crispy on the outside, without burning, and are well cooked all the way through; otherwise they can be stodgy.

INGREDIENTS

250 g (9 oz) plain flour
½ tsp baking powder
50 g (1½ oz) unsalted butter
5 g (1 tsp) salt
20 g (¾ oz) sugar
vegetable oil, for deep-frying
caster sugar, for dusting
hot chocolate, to serve

V

METHOD

Put the flour and baking powder into a bowl.

Put the butter, salt and sugar in a pan into 250 g or ml (9 oz or fl oz) water. Bring to the boil and boil for 1 minute, then pour the mixture into the flour bowl, beating well until you have a thick batter.

Fit a piping bag with a big star nozzle about 1½ cm (¾ in) in diameter and fill with batter.

Put some oil in a fryer or deep pan (making sure it comes no further than a third of the way up) and heat to 170°C (325°F). If you don't have a thermometer, you can test if it is hot enough by dropping in a little of the mixture – it should sizzle.

With one hand, pipe the mixture into the oil, using the other hand to snip it off every 10–15 cm (4–6 in) with a pair of kitchen scissors. Fry for about 3–4 minutes, turning over regularly until the churros are golden on all sides. Lift out and drain briefly on paper towel.

Put the caster sugar on a large plate. While the churros are still hot, toss them in the sugar and serve with hot chocolate.

VARIATION

Instead of serving hot chocolate for dipping the churros into, you could make a little sauce with 100 g (3½ oz) melted chocolate mixed with 2 tablespoons of double cream.

SUMMER PUDDING

Recipe by **SKYE GYNGELL**, Spring, Covent Garden, London

SERVINGS: 6 | PREP TIME: 10 MINS | COOK TIME: 10 MINS | SKILL LEVEL: 1 (EASY)

Nothing says English summer to me quite like a summer pudding, and I return to this recipe year after year, when our beautiful soft summer fruits are at their peak. I make a sponge rather than use the more traditional stale bread — the extra effort is well worth it. I also use more currants than other fruits, as they keep the sweetness in check.

INGREDIENTS

For the sponge

15 g (½ oz) unsalted butter, plus extra to grease

7 medium-sized organic free-range eggs, separated

375 g (13 oz) caster sugar

a small pinch of salt

360 g (12½ oz) plain flour, sifted

5 tbsp warm water

For the fruit

300 g (10½ oz) blackcurrants

300 g (10½ oz) redcurrants

250 g (9 oz) caster sugar

finely grated zest and juice of 1 lemon, separated

200 g (7 oz) blackberries

200 g (7 oz) raspberries

100 g (3½ oz) strawberries

V

METHOD

For the sponge, pre-heat the oven to 180°C/350°F/gas 4 and grease a 33 cm x 23 cm (13 in x 9 in) baking tin. Melt the butter in a small saucepan over a low heat; set aside to cool. Using an electric mixer, whisk the egg yolks with half the sugar until pale and thick enough to leave a ribbon trail on the surface when the whisk is lifted.

In a separate, clean bowl, whisk the egg whites with the salt and the remaining sugar, whisking in slowly to begin with, then increasing the speed slightly after a minute or two. Continue to whisk until the mixture holds stiff peaks.

Carefully fold the flour into the egg yolk and sugar mix, a third at a time, alternately with the water. Fold in the whisked whites, a third at a time. Finally, fold in the melted butter.

Spread the mixture thinly and evenly in the prepared baking tin. Bake on the middle shelf of the oven for 8–10 minutes or until the sponge is just golden and dry to the touch. Leave in the tin for a few minutes, then turn out and cool on a wire rack while you prepare the fruit.

Place the black- and redcurrants in a saucepan with the sugar and lemon juice and cook over a medium heat until the fruit just starts to release its juices. Remove from the heat and add the rest of the fruit and the lemon zest. Let stand for a few minutes to allow the flavours to develop.

Line a 1-litre (1¾-pint) pudding basin with clingfilm, leaving plenty overhanging all round. Using pastry cutters, cut two rounds of sponge, one to fit the bottom of the basin and one the diameter of the top. Place the smaller disc in the bottom of the basin. Now cut long, tapering strips of sponge and use to line the sides of the basin, overlapping them slightly and pressing tightly to ensure there are no gaps.

Using a slotted spoon, spoon the fruit into the sponge-lined basin, filling it to the brim. Spoon the juices over the top, reserving a few spoonfuls for serving. Lay the other sponge disc on top. Fold over the clingfilm to seal and place a saucer on top that just fits inside the rim of the basin. Weigh down with a can (or something similar) and refrigerate overnight.

To serve, fold back the clingfilm and invert the pudding onto a deep plate. Using a pastry brush, smear any pale areas of sponge with the reserved juice. Serve each portion topped with a dollop of crème fraîche or thick cream.

TARTE FINE AU CITRON

LEMON TART

Recipe by **MICHEL ROUX OBE**, The Waterside Inn, Bray, Berkshire

SERVINGS: 8 | **PREP TIME: 40 MINS PLUS CHILLING** | **COOK TIME: 1⅓ HOURS** | **SKILL LEVEL: 2 (MODERATE)**

INGREDIENTS

For the pâté sablée
(use 350 g/12½ oz)

250 g (9 oz) plain flour

200 g (7 oz) butter, cut into small pieces and softened slightly

100 g (3½ oz) icing sugar, sifted

a pinch of salt

2 egg yolks

butter, to grease

For the filling

5 eggs

180 g (6 oz) caster sugar

150 ml (5 fl oz) double cream

finely grated zest and strained juice of 2 lemons

1 egg yolk mixed with 1 tsp milk, to glaze

V

METHOD

To make the pâté sablée, heap the flour on the work surface and make a well. Put the butter, icing sugar and salt in the centre. With your fingertips, mix and cream the butter with the sugar and salt, then add the egg yolks and work them in delicately.

Little by little, draw the flour into the centre and work the mixture delicately with your fingers until you have a homogeneous dough.

Using the heel of your palm, push the dough away from you three or four times, until it is completely smooth. Roll it into a ball, wrap in clingfilm and refrigerate until ready to use. (It will keep in the fridge for up to a week, or in the freezer for up to three weeks.) This makes about 650 g/23 oz, but you'll only need 350 g/12½ oz.

Lightly butter a 22 cm (9 in) tart tin, about 2 cm (¾ in) deep, and chill on a baking tray. Roll out the pastry to a round, 3–4 mm (⅛ in) thick. Drape it over the rolling pin and unfurl over the tart tin. Line the tin with the pastry, gently tapping it in with a knob of pastry. Trim off the excess pastry around the rim; then, using your index finger and thumb, gently press the pastry edges up the side of the tin to form a fluted lip, about 2 mm (¹⁄₁₆ in). Refrigerate for 20 minutes.

Pre-heat the oven to 190°C/375°F/gas 5.

For the filling, lightly whisk the eggs and sugar in a bowl, without letting the mixture turn pale. In another, chilled, bowl, whisk the cream for a few seconds, then mix it into the eggs. Add the lemon zest and juice, stir briefly, cover with clingfilm and refrigerate.

Line the chilled pastry case with greaseproof paper, fill with baking beans and bake blind for 15 minutes. Remove the beans and paper, leave for a couple of minutes, then brush the base and sides of the pastry with the egg glaze. Bake for a further 5 minutes, until lightly coloured. Remove from the oven and lower the temperature to 150°C/300°F/gas 2.

Lightly whisk the chilled lemon filling, then pour it into the tart case up to the level of the lip. Immediately bake for about 1 hour, until lightly set. Leave for about 5 minutes, then carefully remove the tart from the tin. Leave to cool on a wire rack for at least 4 hours before serving.

Serve the tart as it is, or sprinkled with a generous layer of icing sugar. It is delicious accompanied by red berries when in season.

DARK CHOCOLATE, CHILLI CARAMEL & MACADAMIA NUT TART

Recipe by **THOMASINA MIERS**, TV presenter, chef, author & columnist, Fitzrovia, London

SERVINGS: 6 | **PREP TIME: 45 MINS PLUS CHILLING** | **COOK TIME: 45 MINS** | **SKILL LEVEL: 2 (MODERATE)**

This is a very naughty play on the flavours of a Snickers bar, with layers of chocolate ganache, wickedly good caramel and toasted nuts. The caramel is really dark and not too sweet, flavoured with a hint of chilli and sea salt for a mysterious character.

INGREDIENTS

For the pastry (or use 375 g ready-made all-butter shortcrust pastry)
200 g (7 oz) plain flour
40 g (1½ oz) icing sugar
60 g (2 oz) unsalted butter (cold), diced
60 g (2 oz) lard, diced
1 egg, separated
1 egg white

For the chilli caramel
50 g (1½ oz) macadamia nuts
½ tsp dried chilli flakes
150 g (5 oz) caster sugar
50 g (1½ oz) unsalted butter
75 g (2½ oz) soft brown sugar
3 large tbsp golden syrup
150 g (5 oz) crème fraîche
¼–½ tsp sea salt

For the chocolate ganache
2 eggs
2 egg yolks
70 g (2½ oz) caster sugar
300 g (10½ oz) dark chocolate, broken into small even-sized pieces
200 g (7 oz) unsalted butter, diced
60 g (2 oz) plain flour

V

METHOD

You will need a 30 cm (12 in) round cake tin (or two 20 cm/8 in round cake tins), brushed with melted butter, and a sugar thermometer.

To make the pastry, place the flour, icing sugar, butter and lard in a food processor and pulse a few times until the butter vanishes into the flour. Add the egg yolk and pulse again. In a separate bowl, lightly beat the egg whites. Save a third for brushing the pastry case and whizz the rest into the mixture, little by little, until the pastry comes together into a ball. You may need to add up to a tablespoon of ice water to bind the pastry. Wrap in clingfilm and chill for at least 1 hour.

Roll the pastry 2–3 mm (⅛ in) thick to fill the cake tin and lift it onto the tin. Press down firmly into the sides and corners of the tin; prick all over with a fork and trim away the excess pastry, allowing for a 1 cm (½ in) overhang. Freeze for 30 minutes or chill in the fridge for up to a day.

Pre-heat the oven to 180°C/350°F/gas 4. Press some tinfoil weighed down with baking beans inside the cake tin, ensuring that you fully cover the pastry. Blind-bake for 25 minutes, then remove the baking beans and cut away the pastry overhang. Brush the pastry with the reserved lightly beaten egg white and bake for another 5–10 minutes until the pastry is pale golden.

Turn the oven down to 130°C/265°F/gas ½. Heat the macadamia nuts until they are lightly toasted, then roughly chop them. Sprinkle the chilli flakes into a saucepan with the caster sugar and 25 ml (1 fl oz) water and place over a medium-high heat until the sugar starts to darken in patches. Swirl the sugar around to mix the dark bits into the lighter ones, without stirring. Once the sugar has turned a very dark reddish brown (just before it starts smoking and turning black), add the butter and stir to mix in. Then add the rest of the caramel ingredients except the nuts, and keep stirring to combine until the mixture has reached 110°C (230°F). Remove from the heat and stir in the nuts.

For the ganache, turn the oven down to 170°C/325°F/gas 3.

Whisk the eggs and egg yolks with the sugar until light and fluffy. Place the broken chocolate and the butter in a heatproof bowl over, but not touching, a pan of simmering water. When the chocolate has melted into the butter, fold in the eggs and flour. If the chocolate splits – which it will do if you have overheated it – beat in a few tablespoons of cold cream.

Spoon enough caramel to just cover the bottom of the pastry. Pour over the molten chocolate, bake in the oven for 5–10 minutes until just set, then remove from the oven and leave to cool to room temperature. Serve with lashings of crème fraîche or double cream.

TIP

Making pastry is much, much easier than it sounds and unbelievably quick, whizzed up in moments in a food processor ready to rest in the fridge for an hour, or a few days, as needed.

CORNISH SAFFRON CAKE

Recipe by **ALLEGRA McEVEDY MBE**, chef, writer & broadcaster, London

---

SERVINGS: 10–12 SLICES | **PREP TIME: 45 MINS PLUS PROVING** | **COOK TIME: 1 HOUR**
SKILL LEVEL 1 (EASY)

Having some Cornish blood in my veins, I have no doubt the locals of yesteryear got their mitts on this rarest of spices, weight-for-weight more expensive than gold, by good old-fashioned piratical looting. Well, it would be mad not to take advantage of that craggy coastline full of clandestine caves in which to stash your booty. This recipe makes a brilliant yellow loaf with a nice crust. It's fabulous eaten warm but, like most things Cornish, it's pretty resilient and carries on toasting well for days. The general consensus is that jam is superfluous — even my two-year-old says, "No jam, Mama!"

INGREDIENTS

300 ml (11 fl oz) full-fat milk,
  plus extra for brushing
  on top

¼ tsp saffron threads

500 g (1 lb 2 oz) white bread
  flour (though you can do
  it with plain flour)

150 g (5 oz) cold butter,
  cut into 3 cm (1 in) cubes

a large pinch of salt

80 g (2½ oz) soft light brown
  sugar

¼ tsp ground or grated
  nutmeg

1 x 7 g (¼ oz) sachet fast-
  action yeast

100 g (3½ oz) currants

50 g (1½ oz) candied peel

a generous sprinkling of
  Demerara sugar

V

METHOD

In a saucepan, infuse the milk with the saffron over a low heat for a few minutes, then turn the heat off and cover with clingfilm.

Tip the flour into a large mixing bowl, add the butter cubes and salt and work with your fingertips until it looks like breadcrumbs, then stir in the brown sugar and nutmeg.

Gently warm the milk again, then stir in the yeast. Make a well in the middle of the flour and fill it with the milk. Mix slowly until it comes together in a ball, then tip onto a floured surface and knead for about 10 minutes until it's a smooth dough.

Mix the currants and candied peel together and throw a third in. Knead a couple of times, then do the same with the next third and repeat with the last lot for good random distribution.

Grease a 900 g (2 lb) loaf tin (23 cm x 13 cm x 7 cm/9 in x 5 in x 3 in) and knock the dough into a rough loaf shape. Plop it into the tin with the smoothest part on top, then put the whole thing in a plastic bag and tie loosely. Leave to prove somewhere warmish for 1¼–3 hours, until the dough has risen and springs back up when gently pressed.

Pre-heat the oven to 180°C/160°C fan/gas 4. Brush the top of the loaf with milk and sprinkle with the Demerara sugar, then bake for 45 minutes to 1 hour until well risen and slightly brown. To check it's ready, gently tip the loaf out of the tin and make sure the base is cooked, coloured and sounds hollow when tapped. If it's not there yet, stick it back in the oven and try again in a bit.

Cool on a wire rack for 15 minutes but don't miss the opportunity to slather butter on a slice warm from the oven.

BLOOD-ORANGE MARSHMALLOWS

Recipe by **EDD KIMBER**, baker & food writer, Hackney, London

MAKES: 50–60 | **PREP TIME: 50 MINS PLUS SETTING** | **COOK TIME: 30 MINS** | **SKILL LEVEL: 2 (MODERATE)**

Marshmallows have definitely gone through a revival in France over recent years. No longer just a sweet found in the supermarket, they have turned into a gourmet treat, made in a myriad flavours. I have seen pâtisserie windows decorated with jars full to the brim with marshmallows in a rainbow of colours and flavours. Here, I have used blood-orange juice in place of water to give the marshmallows a wonderfully natural orange flavour. If blood oranges are out of season, you can change the juice — I have used blackcurrant, lemon and raspberry, all with great success.

INGREDIENTS

For the marshmallow
oil, preferably an oil spray, for greasing
425 g (15 oz) caster sugar
1 tbsp liquid glucose

275 ml (10 fl oz) blood-orange juice
10 sheets gelatine
2 large egg whites

For the coating
50 g (2 oz) icing sugar
25 g (1 oz) cornflour

DF, GF

METHOD

Lightly grease a 23 cm x 33 cm (9 in x 13 in) baking tin. Line the tin with a piece of clingfilm, making sure that it overhangs the sides.

Lightly grease the clingfilm. Put the ingredients for the coating in a small bowl and mix together, then dust the inside of the lined tin with this mix, setting the leftover coating aside for later.

Put the sugar, glucose and 125 ml (4 fl oz) of the orange juice in a large pan and bring to the boil over a medium-high heat. Cook, without stirring, until the syrup registers 121°C (250°F) on an instant-read thermometer. Meanwhile, put the remaining orange juice in a small bowl with the gelatine sheets and set aside to soften.

Put the egg whites in a clean, grease-free bowl (this is best done using a free-standing electric mixer). When the syrup reaches 110°C (230°F), whisk the whites on high speed until they hold soft peaks. Leave the syrup to continue heating to 121°C (250°F), then remove from the heat and, with the mixer still running, pour the syrup in a slow stream down the side of the bowl containing the whites, avoiding the beaters.

Put the orange and gelatine mixture in the now-empty pan over a medium heat, stirring until the gelatine has melted. Pour this mixture into the mixer and continue whisking the marshmallow until it is thick and has cooled down slightly, about 5–10 minutes. Scrape the marshmallow mixture into the prepared tin and, using a greased spatula, spread it into an even layer. Dust the top of the marshmallow with more of the coating mixture, then set aside for 2 hours or until the marshmallow has fully set.

Turn the slab of marshmallow out onto a large chopping board and remove the clingfilm. Using a pizza cutter or kitchen scissors, cut first into long strips and then into squares. The cut edges will be sticky, so toss the marshmallows in a little more of the coating, gently shaking the marshmallows in a fine sieve to remove the excess. The marshmallows will keep for up to 1 week in an airtight container.

TIP

Blood-orange juice works well in this recipe, as the juice is a similar viscosity to water. If using other fruits you may need to thin your purée with a little water (before measuring) to make sure that it doesn't burn as it boils.

ALICE HART
CHEF & FOOD WRITER

This recipe is my favourite kind of dessert, because you can make it in advance and then forget about it until the moment you have to get it out of the freezer and scoop it onto the plates. The geranium leaf is a traditional British flavouring often used in preserving – you would put a leaf at the bottom of your jar when making jam. This dish also uses a light honey instead of refined sugar.

Alice

Brighton, Sussex

GERANIUM LEAF FROZEN YOGHURT WITH BERRY RIPPLE

Recipe by **ALICE HART**, chef & food writer, Brighton, Sussex

SERVINGS: 4–5 (MAKES 600 ML) | **PREP TIME: 3 HOURS PLUS STRAINING AND FREEZING**
COOK TIME: 30 MINS | **SKILL LEVEL: 1 (EASY)**

Blame it on romance or nostalgia, but I can't resist the lure of scented leaves or petals to add fragrance to syrups and custards. I have made this with geranium leaves and without; both versions are outstanding, so don't worry at all if you can't easily get hold of any — they just add a hint of Turkish delight. The berry ripple here is tart, to contrast with the soft and velveteen yoghurt, but you may wish to up the honey by a tablespoon or two.

INGREDIENTS

1 kg (2¼ lb) full-fat unsweetened natural yoghurt

6 lemon- or rose-scented geranium leaves

190 g (7 oz) acacia or other mild, floral honey

1 large lemon, juice only

a small pinch of fine salt

300 g (10½ oz) blackberries or black mulberries

GF, V

METHOD

Line a large sieve with muslin and set over a large bowl. Spoon the yoghurt in and put the whole lot in the fridge overnight or for at least 8 hours. If you don't want to do this, simply use 500 g (18 oz) of thick, Greek-style yoghurt and miss out the straining step.

Holding them over a small saucepan, snip the geranium leaves into pieces with scissors. Add 160 g (5½ oz) honey to the pan, along with all but 1 teaspoon of the lemon juice and the salt. Bring to the boil slowly, then reduce the heat and simmer gently until the syrup is reduced by half. Cool off the heat for 10 minutes, then strain into a jug (through a sieve to remove the geranium leaves) and cool completely.

To make the blackberry or black mulberry ripple, put the berries in a saucepan with the remaining honey. Heat through gently, stirring occasionally. Cook over a low to medium heat for 10–15 minutes, until the berries burst, look 'sauce-y' and have reduced down to thicken slightly. Stir in the reserved teaspoon of lemon juice and set aside to cool. Chill until needed.

These three steps can all be done, or started in the case of the yoghurt straining, the night before, or even a couple of days before freezing the yoghurt.

Whisk the cooled syrup into the strained (or Greek) yoghurt. Churn in an ice cream machine, according to the manufacturer's instructions, until the blade stops. Transfer to a freezable container and muddle in the chilled berry mixture with a spoon, being careful not to over-mix and lose the rippled effect. Cover and freeze for 4 hours or overnight.

To make without a machine, pour the yoghurt mixture into a shallow, wide container and freeze for 1 hour, until the mixture freezes in a border around the edge. Break up the ice crystals with a whisk and return to the freezer. Repeat this whisking every 30 minutes, until the yoghurt is evenly set and too thick to whip. This should take about 3 hours in total. At this stage, ripple in the chilled berry mixture, cover and freeze undisturbed for 4 hours or overnight.

Soften in the fridge for 15–20 minutes before scooping.

BLACKBERRY & APPLE RYE GALETTE

Recipe by **DIANA HENRY**, food writer & columnist, London

SERVINGS: 6 | **PREP TIME: 1 HOUR PLUS CHILLING** | **COOK TIME: 1 HOUR** | **SKILL LEVEL: 2 (MODERATE)**

This pastry is so gorgeously autumnal — it's the nutty rye flour in it — and there's plenty of fruit here. You could serve a no-pastry fruity pudding instead: baked apples, or stewed apples and blackberries with yoghurt and a little maple syrup would be lovely.

INGREDIENTS

For the pastry
125 g (4½ oz) rye flour
125 g (4½ oz) plain flour,
  plus more for dusting
a pinch of salt
150 g (5 oz) cold butter,
  cubed
2 tbsp soft light brown sugar
1 egg yolk

For the filling
250 g (9 oz) eating apples
  (about 2)
juice of ½ lemon
finely grated zest of 1 orange
4 tbsp soft light brown sugar
200 g (7 oz) blackberries
85 g (3 oz) hazelnuts

For the glaze
1 egg, lightly beaten
4 tbsp granulated sugar

V

METHOD

Sift the flours together, then tip the grains caught in the sieve back into the mixture. Add the salt and rub in the butter with your fingers until you have small pea-sized lumps. Rub in the sugar too, then add the egg yolk and ½ tablespoon of very cold water, a little at a time, until you can bring the mixture together into a ball. Press this into a disc shape, wrap in clingfilm and chill for an hour.

Unwrap the pastry and roll it out on a lightly floured surface to a circle of about 32 cm (13 in), trying to roll it evenly. Move this onto a baking sheet lined with baking paper. Don't worry if the pastry is crumbly, just patch it up. This is a very forgiving tart because it is free-form.

Peel, core and slice the apples, then put them in a bowl with the lemon juice, orange zest and half the brown sugar. Add the blackberries and toss around with your hands.

Whizz the hazelnuts coarsely in a food processor — you should end up with a mixture that is partly ground, partly chunky — and add the rest of the brown sugar.

Sprinkle the nut mixture onto the pastry, leaving a clear width of about 5 cm (2 in) all the way round. Put the fruit on top, then carefully lift up the edges of the pastry to enclose the fruit all the way round. Again, just patch the pastry together if it breaks, nobody will ever know. Put the galette into the coldest part of the fridge for 30 minutes (or your freezer, if it's big enough, for 10 minutes or so).

Pre-heat the oven to 170°C/340°F/gas 3½.

For the glaze, mix the egg with half the granulated sugar and brush it over the pastry. Sprinkle the remaining sugar over the whole tart.

Bake in the hot oven for 50–60 minutes. The pastry should be golden and crusted with sugar, and the fruit should be tender.

MARCHMONT CAKE

Recipe by **KIM JONES**, cook at Marchmont Estate, Berwickshire, Scotland

SERVINGS: 8–10 | **PREP TIME: 30 MINS** | **COOK TIME: 1½ HOURS** | **SKILL LEVEL: 1 (EASY)**

I have baked this cake in individual portions (in ramekins) and drizzled the glacé icing over when hot from the oven, topped with a walnut and served with crème fraîche on the side (sprinkled with cinnamon) – it is a 'hug' of a winter dessert. A fabulous chef called Sarah Mellish introduced me to this recipe. She has an amazing cookery school in Perthshire, where I had a fabulous (and inspiring) time.

INGREDIENTS

225 g (½ lb) cooking apples
225 g (½ lb) self-raising flour
a pinch of salt
1 tsp ground nutmeg
1 tsp ground cinnamon
110 g (3¾ oz) butter
110 g (3¾ oz) sugar
115 g (3¾ oz) sultanas
  or raisins
2 eggs, beaten
walnut halves, to serve

For glacé icing
150 g (5 oz) icing sugar
about 2 tbsp water

V

METHOD

Pre-heat oven to 180°C/350°F/gas 4. Grease and line a round 23 cm (9 in) tin.

Peel, core and finely slice apples. Sieve flour, salt and spices into a bowl and rub butter in with the fingertips until mixture resembles breadcrumbs. Stir in sugar, sultanas or raisins and apple slices. Gradually beat in eggs.

Place mixture in tin and bake for 1¼–1½ hours until firm to the touch, then cool on a wire rack.

Make the glacé icing by adding water a little at a time, until the icing is drizzling consistency. Drizzle liberally on top of the cake and decorate with walnut halves.

RHUBARB, APPLE
& MAPLE PAN CRUMBLE

Recipe by **ANNA JONES**, cook, stylist & food writer, Hackney, London

SERVINGS: 2 | PREP TIME: 10 | COOK TIME: 10 MINS | SKILL LEVEL: 1 (EASY)

I love desserts but I'm not much of a planner, so it's rare, unless I have people round, that I think to make them in advance – most of the time they are a quick reaction to a craving for something sweet after dinner. So, while I love a crumble, I really only make them on a weekend to have after a big family meal. This is a crumble you can make any night of the week and it's filled with good nutrient-packed stuff and natural coconut sugar, so you can eat it with a smile. Any orchard fruit or stone-fruit would work well here. I like plums and pears in autumn and apricots and apples in summer. Dried fruits like prunes work well, too. And, if you like, a swig of sloe gin or Armagnac would do nicely as well. If you can't get coconut sugar, a soft light brown sugar will work but it won't be as virtuous.

INGREDIENTS

For the fruit
200 g (7 oz) apples (about 2)
200 g (7 oz) rhubarb
2 tbsp coconut sugar
juice of ½ orange

For the crumble topping
a small handful of skin-on
   almonds (about 45 g/1½ oz)
5 tbsp small oats
1 tbsp coconut sugar
a knob of coconut oil or
   butter
1 tbsp maple syrup

V

METHOD

Get all your ingredients together and put two frying pans on a medium heat. Peel the apples and chop into thin slices, then trim the rhubarb and chop it into slices of about the same size. Put both fruits into one of the pans with the sugar and the orange juice and cook for 5 minutes, until soft but still holding their shape.

Roughly chop the almonds. Put the oats and almonds into another pan and toast on a low heat for a few minutes. Add the sugar and stir until the sugar starts to melt a little, then quickly remove from the heat and add the coconut oil or butter, and the maple syrup.

Spoon the fruit into bowls and top with a sprinkling of the crumble. Serve with custard or yoghurt; I like to use coconut yoghurt.

Limerstone,
Isle of Wight

MARY CASE
BEE-KEEPER

I've lived on the Isle of Wight all of my life, and I've kept bees for 33 years. It started off as just an interest, a hobby. But over time it grew and grew and, in the way of these things, it ended up being a business. Once you're hooked on bee-keeping, you can't let it go.

Mary

GRANNY'S HONEY & APPLE CAKE

Recipe by **MARY CASE**, bee-keeper, Limerstone, Isle of Wight

SERVINGS: 8–12 | **PREP TIME: 20 MINS** | **COOK TIME: 40–50 MINS** | **SKILL LEVEL: 1 (EASY)**

As a local producer of honey, I'm able to keep all the batches I produce separate. Every batch is different. So, while the big supermarkets want a consistent product, I'm actually looking for inconsistency. This is one of my favourite baking recipes using honey.

INGREDIENTS

225 g (½ lb) soft margarine, plus extra for greasing

4 cooking apples, peeled, cored and thickly sliced

80 g (2½ oz) clear honey, plus extra to drizzle

3 heaped tsp ground cinnamon

225 g (½ lb) caster sugar

275 g (10 oz) self-raising flour

2 level tsp baking powder

4 eggs

DF, V

METHOD

Pre-heat oven to 180°C/160°C fan/gas 4. Grease a 25 cm x 35 cm (10 in x 14 in) baking tin and line with baking paper.

Make the topping first. Put sliced apples in a bowl, then add honey and cinnamon and mix until apples are well coated. Set aside.

Using an electric mixer, beat margarine, sugar, flour, baking powder and eggs for 2 minutes on full speed. Pour into prepared tin, then lay the honey- and cinnamon-covered apple slices in rows on top of the batter.

Bake on a baking sheet for 40–50 minutes or until golden and cooked through – test this by prodding the cake with a skewer: if it comes out clean, it's ready. Cover with tinfoil if the top is getting too brown.

Remove from the oven and allow to cool in its tin. Once cool, carefully lift out, remove the paper and place on a cooling rack. Slice before or after you do this, and drizzle generously with honey.

FALLEN CHOCOLATE SOUFFLÉ WITH ARMAGNAC PRUNES

Recipe by **DELIA SMITH** CBE, cookery writer & TV presenter, Suffolk

---

SERVINGS: 6–8 | **PREP TIME: 45 MINS PLUS SOAKING OVERNIGHT** | **COOK TIME: 30 MINS**
SKILL LEVEL: 2 (MODERATE)

Yes, it's really true — this soufflé is supposed to puff up like a normal one, but it is then removed from the oven and allowed to subside slowly into a lovely, dark, squidgy chocolate dessert. It is served slightly chilled with a prune and crème fraîche sauce. The only problem I can foresee with this recipe is that someone will write and tell me that their soufflé wouldn't sink! Let me pre-empt that by saying: don't worry, I'm sure it will taste just as good. This also works superbly with prunes in amaretto or port, so use whichever flavour you like best. The prunes soaked in Armagnac and served with crème fraîche make an extremely good dessert in their own right. Also, the soufflé and sauce freeze very well for up to a month.

INGREDIENTS

For the soufflé
225 g (8 oz) dark chocolate
 (70 per cent cocoa solids minimum)
110 g (4 oz) unsalted butter
1 tbsp Armagnac
4 large eggs, separated
110 g (4 oz) golden caster sugar
a little sifted icing sugar, for dusting

For the Armagnac prunes
350 g (12 oz) Californian pitted
 ready-to-eat prunes
150 ml (5 fl oz) Armagnac

For the prune & crème fraîche sauce
150 ml (5 fl oz) crème fraîche
the remainder of the soaked prunes

Equipment
a 20 cm (8 in) round, loose-based cake tin, greased and with a non-stick base liner

GF, V

METHOD

The prunes need to be soaked overnight, so simply place them in a saucepan with 275 ml (½ pint) of water, bring them up to simmering point and let them simmer very gently for 30 minutes.

After that, pour the prunes and their cooking liquid into a bowl and stir in the Armagnac while they're still warm. Leave to cool, then cover the bowl with clingfilm and chill in the refrigerator overnight.

To make the soufflé, pre-heat the oven to 170°C/325°F/gas 3. Meanwhile, break the chocolate into squares and place them, together with the butter, in a bowl fitted over a saucepan containing some barely simmering water (the bowl must not touch the water). Leave it for a few moments to melt, then stir until you have a smooth, glossy mixture. Now remove the bowl from the heat, add the Armagnac and leave to cool.

Next take a large roomy bowl and combine the egg yolks and caster sugar in it. Then whisk them together for about 5 or 6 minutes, using an electric hand whisk — when you lift up the whisk and the mixture drops off making ribbon-like trails, it's ready.

Now count out 18 of the soaked prunes, cut each one in half and combine the halves with the whisked egg mixture along with the melted chocolate. Next you'll need to wash the whisk thoroughly with hot soapy water to remove all the grease, and dry it well. In another bowl, whisk up the egg whites until they form soft peaks. After that, fold them carefully into the chocolate mixture. Spoon this mixture into the prepared tin and bake the soufflé in the centre of the oven for about 30 minutes or until the centre feels springy to the touch. Allow the soufflé to cool in the tin (it's great fun watching it fall very slowly).

When it's quite cold, remove it from the tin, peel off the paper, then cover and chill for several hours (or it can be made 2 or 3 days ahead if more convenient).

Serve the soufflé dusted with icing sugar and cut into small slices (it's very rich). To make the sauce, simply liquidize the remaining prunes together with their liquid, place the purée in the serving bowl and lightly stir in the crème fraîche to give a slightly marbled effect. Hand the sauce round separately.

ROASTED PLUMS WITH CARDAMOM CARAMEL

Recipe by **TOM AIKENS**, Tom's Kitchen, Chelsea, London

SERVINGS: 4 | PREP TIME: 10 MINS | COOK TIME: 15 MINS | SKILL LEVEL: 1 (EASY)

There is a lovely balance of sweet and spicy flavours in this dish, which is also very quick to make. For me, the British plum is not used enough really. I remember having stewed plums as a child and they weren't great, so with this dish I've tried to make plums the hero.

INGREDIENTS

For the spiced crème fraîche
300 g (10½ oz) crème fraîche
80 g (3 oz) caster sugar
1 tsp ground cinnamon
seeds from a split vanilla pod

2 tbsp muscovado sugar
a large pinch of mixed spice
a small pinch of ground cloves
a large pinch of ground ginger
a pinch of five-spice powder
2 cardamom pods, finely crushed
finely grated zest of 2 oranges
3 tbsp unsalted butter, softened
1 tbsp brioche crumbs
12 ripe plums, cut in half and
   stones removed

V

METHOD

Put the crème fraîche in a bowl with the sugar, cinnamon and vanilla seeds and beat with a wooden spoon for 3–4 minutes.

Pre-heat the oven to 200°C/400°F/gas 6.

Mix the muscovado sugar, spices, orange zest, butter and brioche crumbs in a bowl. Put the plums in a baking tin and add a little of the crumb mixture on each half. Bake in the pre-heated oven for 15 minutes, or place under a hot grill until the plums start to caramelize. Serve hot or cold with spiced crème fraîche.

DAMSON ICE CREAM

Recipe by **STEVIE PARLE**, Dock Kitchen, Ladbroke Grove, London

SERVINGS: 4–8 | PREP TIME: 30 MINS PLUS FREEZING | COOK TIME: 10 MINS
SKILL LEVEL: 2 (MODERATE)

The damson season is short and I always greet it with great excitement. They are so intensely flavoured that they make a really fabulous ice cream. It is very easy to make as it doesn't include a custard.

INGREDIENTS

500 g (1 lb 2 oz) damsons
200 g (7 oz) caster sugar,
  or to taste
250 ml (9 fl oz) double cream
250 ml (9 fl oz) natural
  (unsweetened) yoghurt

GF, V

METHOD

Rinse the damsons, then bring to the boil with 100 ml (3½ fl oz) water in a stainless-steel pan. It probably won't seem like enough water, but it'll be OK. Reduce the heat so that the damsons simmer gently for 10 minutes, until the skins have burst and you have a quantity of deep purple juice.

Push the fruit through a fine sieve with a wooden spoon, pushing until you have nothing left but stones. Return the purée to the heat with the sugar, and heat to dissolve. Leave the purée to cool. Stir in the cream and yoghurt; taste to check the amount of sugar and adjust if necessary (remembering that, when frozen, sweetness is less pronounced).

Churn in an ice cream machine, or freeze in a tray for about 4 hours, whisking every 30 minutes.

Weston,
Northamptonshire

SARAH WEBB
HOME COOK

This Sherry Trifle is my mother's recipe,
and we enjoyed it throughout our
childhood. I now make it for my family
on special occasions. The colours look
gorgeous in a big glass trifle bowl.

Sarah

SHERRY TRIFLE

Recipe by **SARAH WEBB**, home cook, Weston, Northamptonshire

SERVINGS: 8-10 | PREP TIME: 45 MINS PLUS SETTING | COOK TIME: 15 MINS | SKILL LEVEL: 1 (EASY)

You will need a large glass trifle bowl for this recipe.

INGREDIENTS

2 shop-bought jam Swiss rolls or trifle sponges

1 x 340 g (12 oz) jar seedless raspberry jam

a sprinkle of sherry, to taste

1 x 135 g (4¾ oz) pack raspberry jelly cubes

1 punnet (300 g/10½ oz) fresh raspberries or 1 large can raspberries in fruit juice

1 punnet (300 g/10½ oz) fresh strawberries or 1 large can strawberries in fruit juice

2 tbsp custard powder

560 ml (1 pint) milk

2 tbsp caster sugar

up to 560 ml (1 pint) double cream

halved glacé cherries, toasted flaked almonds or plain chocolate curls, to decorate

V

METHOD

Slice the Swiss rolls and cover the top of the slices with raspberry jam. Arrange the slices in the bottom of a trifle bowl and sprinkle with sherry to taste.

Melt the jelly cubes in 280 ml (½ pint) boiled water, then use the strained fruit juice to make this up to 560 ml (1 pint).

Scatter the fruit over the Swiss roll slices and pour the jelly over the top so that it covers the cake. Leave to set for several hours.

Use the custard powder and milk to prepare 560 ml (1 pint) of thick custard in a saucepan and use the caster sugar to sweeten to taste. When the custard becomes thick, immerse the bottom of the pan in cold water to cool the custard, beating the mixture to prevent a skin from forming. When cool, add a little double cream and beat well until the custard has a thick, dropping consistency. Then pour over your trifle base and chill in the fridge until set.

Just before serving, whip about 280 ml (½ pint) double cream until it forms soft peaks. Be careful not to over-whisk. Carefully spoon the cream over the custard and swirl it around to cover in a smooth, circular pattern. Use the glacé cherries, toasted almonds or chocolate curls to decorate.

Remove from the fridge for a while before serving, then enjoy!

PAVLOVA

Recipe by **HUGH FEARNLEY-WHITTINGSTALL**, River Cottage, Devon

SERVINGS: 6–8 | **PREP TIME: 50 MINS** | **COOK TIME: 1½ HOURS** | **SKILL LEVEL: 2 (MODERATE)**

There are few simpler show-stopping puds than the pavlova. The sum really is greater than its parts — simple meringue, whipped cream, ripe fruit. Its key to greatness is in its scale. A great, rough wheel of meringue, with dollops of whipped cream (mixed with some thick yoghurt, for me), piled high with delicious seasonal fruit — what could be better?

INGREDIENTS

For the meringue

4 large egg whites,
  at room temperature

220 g (8 oz) caster sugar

2 tsp cornflour, sifted

2 tsp white wine vinegar
  or cider vinegar

1 tsp vanilla extract
  (optional)

For the topping

300 ml (10½ fl oz) double
  cream or whipping
  cream

200 ml (7 fl oz) natural
  whole-milk yoghurt

400–500 g (14–18 oz)
  ripe, seasonal fruit
  (see variations)

V

METHOD

Pre-heat the oven to 130°C/100°C fan/265°F/gas ½.

Line a baking sheet with baking paper and draw on a circle, about 25 cm (10 in) in diameter. Turn the paper over.

Use either a free-standing mixer or a bowl and electric hand-mixer with a whisk attachment, making sure they are scrupulously clean and free of any grease. Whisk the egg whites to firm peaks, but do not over-beat or they'll turn grainy.

Add the sugar a tablespoonful or two at a time, whisking well between each addition. Keep whisking until the mixture is very stiff and glossy. Using a spatula, gently fold in the cornflour, vinegar and vanilla, if using.

Heap the meringue mixture within the marked circle on the baking paper and swirl it out into a round, gently pushing it up a bit towards the sides. Use a spatula to create some soft peaks in the surface.

Bake for 1¼–1½ hours until the meringue is firm and crisp around the edges but still slightly soft inside. Turn off the heat and leave it to cool and dry out a little in the oven.

Whip the cream until it forms very soft peaks — be careful not to over-beat it until stiff. Fold together with the yoghurt.

Carefully transfer the meringue to a serving plate. Spoon on the cream and yoghurt mixture, spreading it almost to the edges, then pile the fruit on top.

VARIATIONS

Vary the fruit; ring the changes according to the seasons. Try the following:

· Strawberries (larger ones halved or quartered), raspberries, blackcurrants, blackberries — either alone or in combination. About an hour before assembling the pavlova, tip them into a bowl and let them macerate with a sprinkling of icing sugar and/or a small trickle of framboise, kirsch or crème de cassis.

· Ripe peaches or nectarines, peeled and sliced, with a handful of redcurrants if you have some. Leave to macerate for about an hour with a sprinkling of icing sugar and a splash of orange-flower water.

· Slices of ripe mango and passionfruit pulp is a really good mix to heap on top of a pavlova. Finish with a scattering of shredded mint leaves.

INDEX & ACKNOWLEDGEMENTS

INDEX

Jerusalem Artichokes with Olives & Thyme
322, *323*

Marchmont Cake 388, *389*

Minestrone Soup with Orzo Pasta & Mint Pesto
44, *45*

Normandy Tart Made with a Food Processor
360, *361*

Panzanella 280, *281*

Pavlova 406, *407*

Pea & Mint Croquettes 38, *39*

Rhubarb, Apple & Maple Pan Crumble 390, *391*

Roasted Plums with Cardamom Caramel 398,
399

Roquefort & Walnut Soufflés 66, *67*

Roquefort, Pear & Chicory Salad with Walnut
Oil 282, *283*

Shaved Raw Brussels Sprout Salad with
Hazelnuts, Pomegranate & Pumpkin Seeds
300, *301*

Sherry Trifle 404, *405*

Slaw with Pears, Toasted Hazelnuts &
Buttermilk Dressing 288, *289*

Strawberry Jam 28, *29*

Summer Pudding 370, *371*

Tarte Fine au Citron, Lemon Tart 372, *373*

Warm Butternut Squash Salad with Labneh
& Chilli 308, *309*

Warm New Potato Salad with Mint Leaves
& Chives 292, *293*

Yoghurt with Apricots, Honey & Pistachios
18, *19*

CONTRIBUTORS

One of the ways I work is to use lettering graphically and fill the spaces around it with different colours, so it becomes a kind of abstract painting. When I was asked to create the cover art and print for *The Really Quite Good British Cookbook*, I decided that it was perfectly suited to this way of working. The artwork spells out the wording, and each letter and all the spaces around them are a different colour. It is all about working to get the right colours next to each other and eventually it comes together, like making an abstract.

Peter Blake

Today in the UK many thousands of families are struggling to put food on the table. Thirteen million people live below the poverty line and, for those on the lowest incomes, a sudden crisis such as illness, bereavement or an unexpected bill can push finances over the edge, making it impossible to afford even basic necessities like food.

The Trussell Trust helps people in crisis through the provision of emergency food and, by offering a range of extra support and advice, helps people lift themselves out of the cycle of poverty.

With the support of thousands of volunteers across the UK – such as those pictured opposite at Wandsworth and Sparkhill, Birmingham – foodbanks open their doors every day to help people like Sarah, who struggled to afford food for her two young children when her benefits were withheld for several months. She told us, "It's scary as a parent as you don't feel as if you're doing your job properly. You want to be able to support your children in every way and that's not possible when things like this happen."

We are committed to being a lifeline for anyone struggling to afford food; for parents skipping meals so their children can eat, for tenants forced to go hungry just to pay the rent, for the elderly person making the stark choice between heating their home or eating.

Each year more people come to foodbanks for help; often feeling hopeless, scared and full of despair, just like Sarah did. Thank you for helping us make sure we're there to give vital support when it is needed most.

Together, we can stop UK hunger.

To find out more about The Trussell Trust visit trusselltrust.org or phone +44 (0)1722 580 180.

The publisher is grateful for literary permissions to reproduce items subject to copyright.

Every effort has been made to trace the copyright holders and the publisher apologises for any unintentional omission. We would be pleased to hear from any not acknowledged here and undertake to make all reasonable efforts to include the appropriate acknowledgement in any subsequent editions. All recipes not listed below are copyright © the individual contributors.

TOM AIKENS
Braised Lamb Shanks with Pearl Barley & Honey-Roast Garlic adapted from *Cooking* by Tom Aikens, published by Ebury Press. Reproduced by permission of The Random House Group Ltd. Roasted Plums with Cardamom Caramel adapted from *Easy* by Tom Aikens, published by Ebury Press. Reproduced by permission of The Random House Group Ltd.

ANJUM ANAND
Baked Chard Ricotta with a Hot Tomato, Garlic & Pepper Chutney adapted from *Anjum's Quick and Easy Indian: Fast, Effortless Food for Any Time and Place by Anjum Anand*, published by Quadrille Publishing Ltd, 2014.

JASON ATHERTON
Salted Cod with Winter Cabbage, Bacon & Beer Sauce and Yogurt with Apricots, Honey & Pistachios adapted from *Gourmet Food for a Fiver* by Jason Atherton, published by Quadrille Publishing Ltd, 2010.

GERARD BAKER
Bakewell Pudding adapted from *Mrs Beeton's Puddings* by Isabella Beeton and Gerard Baker, The Orion Publishing Group Ltd, text copyright © Weidenfeld & Nicolson 2012.

ANNIE BELL
Annie Bell's Pheasant with Calvados & Apple adapted from *How To Cook: Over 200 Essential Recipes to Feed Yourself, Your Friends and Family* by Annie Bell, published by Kyle Books, 2015.

RICHARD BERTINET
Churros and Duck Pie adapted from *Pastry* by Richard Bertinet, published by Ebury Press. Reproduced by permission of The Random House Group Ltd.

RAYMOND BLANC
Cherry Clafoutis adapted from *Kitchen Secrets* by Raymond Blanc, © Raymond Blanc, 2011, Bloomsbury Publishing Plc.

JORDAN BOURKE & REJINA PYO
Hoogim-Ja Ice Cream (Black Sesame Seed Ice Cream) adapted from *Our Korean Kitchen* by Jordan Bourke and Rejina Pyo, The Orion Publishing Group, London. Text copyright © Jordan Bourke and Reijna Pyo 2015.

ANTONIO CARLUCCIO
Deep-fried Stuffed Olives and Risotto Con Funghi (Risotto with Mushrooms) adapted from *Antonio Carluccio: The Collection* by Antonio Carluccio, published by Quadrille Publishing Ltd, 2012.

SAM & SAM CLARK
Pigeon & Mellow Garlic Purée and Pulpo Gallego (Octopus, Potatoes & Paprika) adapted from *Morito* by Sam & Sam Clark, published by Ebury Press. Reproduced by permission of The Random House Group Ltd.

RICHARD CORRIGAN
Whole Sea Trout with 'Coastal Greens' adapted from *The Clatter of Forks and Spoons: Honest, Happy Food* by Richard Corrigan, published by 4th Estate Ltd, 2008.

ANNA DEL CONTE
Conchiglie Rosse Ripiene Di Spaghettini In Insalata (Radicchio Leaves Filled with Thin Spaghetti) and Rotolo di Spinaci al Burro e Formaggio (Spinach and Pasta Roll with Melted Butter and Parmesan) adapted from *Amaretto, Apple Cake & Artichokes: The Best of Anna Del Conte* by Anna Del Conte, © Anna Del Conte 1989, 1991, 2006.

DAN DOHERTY
Chocolate Bread Pudding with Bacon Custard adapted from *Duck & Waffle: Recipes and Stories* by Daniel Doherty, published by Mitchell Beazley, octopusbooks.co.uk.

GIZZI ERSKINE
Spanish Chicken Stew with Chorizo, Sherry & Garbanzo Beans and Walnut Bagna Cauda adapted from *Gizzi's Healthy Appetite: Food to Nourish the Body and Feed the Soul* by Gizzi Erskine, published by Mitchell Beazley, octopusbooks.co.uk.

HUGH FEARNLEY-WHITTINGSTALL
Pasta & Greens with Goat's Cheese and Pavlova adapted from *Love Your Leftovers: Recipes for the Resourceful Cook*, © Hugh Fearnley-Whittingstall, 2015, Bloomsbury Publishing Plc.

SABRINA GHAYOUR
Eastern Mess adapted from *Persiana: Recipes from the Middle East and Beyond* by Sabrina Ghayour, published by Mitchell Beazley, 2014, octopusbooks.co.uk.

SKYE GYNGELL
Slaw with Pears, Toasted Hazelnuts & Buttermilk Dressing and Summer Pudding adapted from *Spring: The Cookbook* by Skye Gyngell, published by Quadrille Publishing Ltd, 2015.

HENRY HARRIS
Black Pudding & Smoked Haddock Hash adapted from *The Fifth Floor Cookbook* by Henry Harris with Hugo Arnold, published by 4th Estate Ltd, 1998.

ALICE HART
Geranium Leaf Frozen Yoghurt with Berry Ripple and Soba Noodle Soup With Duck Egg & Greens adapted from *The New Vegetarian* by Alice Hart, published by Square Peg, an imprint of Penguin Random House UK, 2016.

ANGELA HARTNETT
Deep-Fried Courgette Flowers and Spaghetti Aglio, Olio e Peperoncino (Spaghetti with Peperoncino & Garlic) adapted from *Cucina: Three Generations of Italian Family Cooking* by Angela Hartnett, published by Ebury Press. Reproduced by permission of The Random House Group Ltd.

JASMINE & MELISSA HEMSLEY
Chia Chai Butternut Breakfast Pudding and Courgetti & Beef Ragù adapted from *The Art of Eating Well* by Jasmine & Melissa Hemsley, published by Ebury Press. Reproduced by permission of The Random House Group Ltd.

DIANA HENRY
Blackberry & Apple Rye Galette adapted from *A Change of Appetite: Where Delicious Meets Healthy* by Diana Henry, published by Mitchell Beazley, 2014. Roast Jerusalem Artichokes & Chicken with Anchovy, Walnut & Parsley Relish adapted from *A Bird in the Hand: Chicken Recipes for Every Day and Every Mood* by Diana Henry, published by Mitchell Beazley, 2015, octopusbooks.co.uk.

OLIA HERCULES
Garlicky White Rabbit adapted from *Mamushka: Recipes from Ukraine and Beyond* by Olia Hercules, published by Mitchell Beazley, octopusbooks.co.uk.

MARK HIX
Cockle, Parsley & Cider Broth adapted from *Hix Oyster and Chop House* by Mark Hix, published by Quadrille Publishing Ltd, 2010. Potted Shrimps on Toast adapted from *Mark Hix: The Collection* by Mark Hix, published by Quadrille Publishing Ltd, 2013.

LUCAS HOLLWEG
Pot-Roasted Chicken with Chicory adapted from *Good Things to Eat* by Lucas Hollweg, published by HarperCollins Publishers, 2011, text © Lucas Hollweg. Reproduced by permission of HarperCollins Publishers.

SIMON HOPKINSON
Poached Chicken with Saffron Sauce & Cucumber and Roquefort, Pear & Chicory Salad with Walnut Oil adapted from *The Good Cook* by Simon Hopkinson, published by BBC Books, 2011. Reproduced by permission of The Random House Group Ltd.

NADIYA HUSSAIN
Burnt Garlic, Chilli & Lemon Squid adapted from *Nadiya's Kitchen* by Nadiya Hussain, published by Michael Joseph. Reproduced by permission of Penguin Random House UK.

ANNA JONES
Farro with Roasted Leeks & Smoky-sweet Romesco adapted from *A Modern Way to Eat: Over 200 Satisfying, Everyday Vegetarian Recipes (That Will Make You Feel Amazing)* by Anna Jones, published by 4th Estate Ltd, 2014. Rhubarb, Apple & Maple Pan Crumble adapted from *A Modern Way to Cook: Over 150 Quick, Smart and Flavour-packed Recipes for Every Day* by Anna Jones, published by 4th Estate Ltd, 2015.

LIZZIE KAMENETZKY
Sticky Bourbon Ribs adapted from *Winter Cabin Cooking: Dumplings, Fondue, Strudel, Glühwein and Other Fireside Feasts* by Lizzie Kamenetzky (Ryland Peters & Small), 2015.

SYBIL KAPOOR
Artichoke Vinaigrette adapted from *Simply Veg: A Modern Guide to Everyday Eating* by Sybil Kapoor, Pavilion Books, 2016.

EDD KIMBER
Blood-orange Marshmallows adapted from *Patisserie Made Simple: From Macaron to Millefeuille and More* by Edd Kimber, published by Kyle Books, 2014.

FLORENCE KNIGHT
Brown Shrimp, Kohlrabi & Apple adapted from *One: A Cook and Her Cupboard* by Florence Knight. Copyright © 2013 Florence Knight. Reproduced by permission of Salt Yard Books, an imprint of Hodder and Stoughton Limited.

NIGELLA LAWSON
Chocolate Guinness Cake adapted from *Feast: Food That Celebrates Life* by Nigella Lawson, published by Chatto & Windus. Reproduced by permission of The Random House Group Ltd. Ham in Coca-Cola adapted from *Nigella Bites* by Nigella Lawson, published by Chatto & Windus. Reproduced by permission of The Random House Group Ltd.

PRUE LEITH
Normandy Tart Made with a Food Processor adapted from *Leith's Cookery Bible* by Prue Leith and Caroline Waldegrave, © Prue Leith and Caroline Waldegrave, 1991 and 2003, Bloomsbury Publishing Plc.

ELISABETH LUARD
Jerusalem Artichokes with Olives & Thyme adapted from *A Cook's Year in a Welsh Farmhouse*, © Elisabeth Luard, 2011, Bloomsbury Publishing Plc.

UYEN LUU
Cà Ri Gà (Chicken Curry) and Gỏi Cuốn Sai Gon (Saigon Fresh Summer Rolls) adapted from *My Vietnamese Kitchen: Recipes and Stories to Bring Vietnamese Food to Life on Your Plate* by Uyen Luu (Ryland Peters & Small), 2013.

JAMES MARTIN
Sausage, Radicchio and Lemon Gnocchi adapted from *Home Comforts* by James Martin, published by Quadrille Publishing Ltd, 2014.

ALLEGRA McEVEDY
Cornish Saffron Cake and Spatchcock Poussins with Sweet Chilli & Yoghurt Marinade adapted from *Big Table, Busy Kitchen: Recipes for Life* by Allegra McEvedy, copyright © Allegra McEvedy 2013. Reproduced by permission of Quercus Editions Limited.

PIPPA MIDDLETON
Traditional Roast Rib of Beef from *Celebrate: A Year of British Festivities for Families and Friends* by Pippa Middleton, published by Michael Joseph. Reproduced by permission of Penguin Random House UK.

THOMASINA MIERS
Dark Chocolate, Chilli Caramel & Macadamia Nut Tart adapted from *Chilli Notes: Recipes to Warm the Heart (Not Burn the Tongue)* by Thomasina Miers, copyright © 2014 Thomasina Miers. Reproduced by permission of Hodder and Stoughton Limited. Pork Pibil adapted from *Wahaca: Mexican Food at Home* by Thomasina Miers, copyright © 2012 Thomasina Miers. Reproduced by permission of Hodder and Stoughton Limited.

ELLA MILLS
Courgette Noodles with Avocado Pesto adapted from *Deliciously Ella: Awesome Ingredients, Incredible Food That You and Your Body Will Love* by Ella Mills (Woodward), copyright © 2013 Ella Woodward. Reproduced by permission of Yellow Kite, an imprint of Hodder and Stoughton Limited.

RUSSELL NORMAN
Burrata with Lentils & Basil Oil adapted from *Polpo: A Venetian Cookbook (Of Sorts)*, © Russell Norman, 2012, Bloomsbury Publishing Plc. Clams, Borlotti Beans & Wild Garlic adapted from *Spuntino: Comfort Food (New York Style)*, © Russell Norman, 2015, Bloomsbury Publishing Plc.

JAMIE OLIVER
Happy Fish Pie adapted from *Jamie's Great Britain: Over 130 Reasons to Love Our Food* by Jamie Oliver, published by Michael Joseph. Reproduced with permission of Penguin Random House UK.

YOTAM OTTOLENGHI
Grilled Banana Bread with Tahini & Honeycomb and Pea & Mint Croquettes adapted from *Plenty More* by Yotam Ottolenghi, published by Ebury Press. Reproduced by permission of The Random House Group Ltd.

Firstly, thanks are due to New Zealand-based publishers Geoff Blackwell and Ruth Hobday for approaching me to edit this wonderful book. Together we conceived a tome that would celebrate the food we cook for the people we love as well as raising funds for the work of The Trussell Trust. So at its heart, this is a book that works to raise the profile of this vital charity and to donate funds for its ongoing projects.

And there would be no book without Rosie Ramsden. As our food editor she has worked tirelessly to coordinate all the contributors' recipes and to help create a perfect balance of dishes, with the invaluable help in the kitchen of Chloe Ride, Clara Grace Paul and Esther Clark. All of this delicious food has been shot by the wonderfully talented and joyful photographer Lizzie Mayson. Lizzie also shot all the portraits with the assistance of Amber Felix. Completing this amazing team was Tabitha Hawkins, surely this country's greatest food photography art director and props stylist.

Thanks also to Chris Wold, of UK publisher Nourish, who, very sensibly, jumped at the chance to bring this book to thousands of UK food lovers.

William Sitwell

Left to right: Chloe Ride (food stylist assistant), Lizzie Mayson (photographer and videographer), Tabitha Hawkins (food photography art director & props stylist) and Rosie Ramsden (food editor and food stylist).

NOURISH
EAT WELL, LIVE WELL

Nourish, an imprint of Watkins Media Limited
19 Cecil Court
London WC2N 4EZ
United Kingdom
enquiries@nourishbooks.com
Twitter: twitter.com/nourishbooks
Facebook: facebook.com/nourishbooks

Produced and originated by PQ Blackwell Limited, Suite 405 IronBank, 150 Karangahape Road, Auckland 1010, New Zealand, pqblackwell.com

PUBLISHER: Geoff Blackwell
EDITOR IN CHIEF: Ruth Hobday
DESIGN: Helene Dehmer
ADDITIONAL EDITORIAL: Rachel Clare, Mary Dobbyn, Benjamin Harris, Leanne McGregor, Teresa McIntyre, Kate Stockman

The publisher is grateful to everyone who contributed to the making of *The Really Quite Good British Cookbook* and would especially like to thank: Todd Antony, Sir Peter Blake, Troy Caltaux, Liam Cooper, Benjamin Cox, Lisette du Plessis, Cameron Gibb, Tim Harper, Stefanie Lim, Edd Pearman, Kate Raven, Murray Thom and Adrian Wolfson, and Sam Lane, Helen Franks and Elana McIntyre at The Trussell Trust.

Inspired by *The Great New Zealand Cookbook* and *The Great Australian Cookbook* created by PQ Blackwell and Thom Productions, and *The Great South African Cookbook* created by PQ Blackwell and Quivertree Publications.

A portion of royalties from sales of *The Really Quite Good British Cookbook* will support The Trussell Trust, which helps people in crisis through the provision of emergency food and, by offering a range of extra support and advice, helps people lift themselves out of the cycle of poverty. The Trussell Trust will receive a minimum of £10,000 from the sales of the book in the UK, Ireland, USA, Canada, Australia, New Zealand and South Africa. The Trussell Trust is a registered charity in England and Wales (1110522) and Scotland (SC044246). Registered Limited Company in England and Wales (5434524).

Find us and follow us on:
reallyquitegoodbritishcookbook.com

ISBN: 978-1-84899-328-0
Printed in China by 1010 Printing Group Limited

10 9 8 7 6 5 4 3 2 1